THE ANTIQUITIES OF WISCONSIN,

AS SURVEYED AND DESCRIBED

This facsimile of the 1855 edition has been published by the
University of Wisconsin Press in partnership with the
University of Wisconsin–Madison Libraries

THE ANTIQUITIES OF WISCONSIN,

AS

SURVEYED AND DESCRIBED

I. A. LAPHAM

THE UNIVERSITY OF WISCONSIN PRESS

The University of Wisconsin Press
2537 Daniels Street
Madison, Wisconsin 53718

3 Henrietta Street
London WC2E 8LU, England

1   3   5   4   2

Printed in Canada

Library of Congress Cataloging-in-Publication Data
Lapham, Increase Allen, 1811–1875.
The antiquities of Wisconsin, as surveyed and described / Increase A. Lapham.
196 pp.   cm.
Originally published: Washington, D.C. : Smithsonian Institution, 1855.
Includes index.
ISBN 0-299-17040-3 (cloth : alk. paper)
1. Indians of North America—Wisconsin—Antiquities.
2. Mounds—Wisconsin. 3. Earthworks (Archaeology)—Wisconsin.
4. Wisconsin—Antiquities. I. Title.
E78.W8 L2   2001
977.5'01—dc21   00-041762

CONTENTS

FOREWORD

Robert A. Birmingham

———————

When Increase A. Lapham published *The Antiquities of Wisconsin, as Surveyed and Described* in 1855, little was known about the pre-Columbian civilizations that had occupied North America. So little, in fact, that a great debate raged in American scholarly circles about the origin of the mysterious earthen mounds and other elaborate earthworks found throughout the eastern part of the United States. Most who considered the matter were unwilling to believe that native North Americans were responsible for the frequently huge and sophisticated monuments. They argued that the mounds were instead the products of some mysterious "lost race," superior to native North Americans, that had disappeared at some point in the distant past. Many different candidates, originating mainly in the Old World or Mexico, were presented as the "lost race." During the nineteenth century, public interest in the North American earthworks and the identity of their makers was so great, in fact, that it precipitated decades-long investigations and major publications by a new government agency, the Smithsonian Institution, and ultimately stimulated the development of the field of North American archaeology.

Some of North America's most spectacular and perplexing earthwork sites, consisting of huge enclosures, mounds, and embankments, are found in Ohio. The pioneering essay "Ancient Monuments of the Mississippi Valley" by Ephraim G. Squier and E. H. Davis, published in 1848 as the first volume of the Smithsonian's *Smithsonian Contributions to Knowledge,* focused heavily on these earthworks. The study emphasized that the mound builders where different from and superior to native North Americans and thus contributed to the persistence of the "lost race" hypothesis. The Smithsonian, however, would eventually embrace the reverse of this position based on its own research and influenced by evidence and ideas such as those provided by Lapham.

The Antiquities of Wisconsin, as Surveyed and Described contributed to the body of knowledge concerning America's ancient past by presenting empirical data on the types of earthworks found in the Midwest and offering evidence to suggest that the people who built the mounds were quite simply the ancestors of native North Americans. It stands today as both a remarkable source of detailed maps of the cultural landscape of Wisconsin prior to major settlement and as an important historical document on the evolution of American science and history.

Lapham's interest in ancient mounds and earthworks was stimulated by those he encountered after moving to Milwaukee in 1836. He was especially struck by Wisconsin's high concentration of effigy mounds—those that had been built in the shape of huge birds and animals and were rarely found elsewhere. Although a mystery to Lapham and others at the time, they are now known to have been built during the Late Woodland stage, circa A.D. 500 to A.D. 1200, and are believed to represent powerful spirit beings in the cosmology of the builders. By the end of his first year in Milwaukee, he had published a newspaper account of one round-bodied, long-tailed animal earthwork in what is now the city of Waukesha, coining the name "Turtle" for this type of effigy mound. Undoubtedly stimulated by Squier and Davis's 1848 work, he traveled throughout southern Wisconsin, between 1849 and 1852, mapping and describing hundreds of mounds, earthworks, and other antiquities and opening a few mounds to learn more about their builders. The results of this research were published by the Smithsonian Institution as *The Antiquities of Wisconsin, as Surveyed and Described.*

Although Lapham intended *The Antiquities of Wisconsin* to be primarily descriptive, he weighed in on the "lost race" debate by drawing links between the mound builders and modern native North Americans in the types of artifacts, such as pipes and pottery, he and others recovered from the mounds. Based on his field observations, he was even able to offer a rough chronology of one site starting with the mound builders and concluding with modern native North Americans, the latter identified by the presence of artifacts of European manufacture. In general his research convinced him that the mound builders of Wisconsin were none other than the ancestors of the present tribes of North American Indians. But Lapham was not convinced that modern tribes of the region—whom he considered "little advanced in civilization"—were mound builders, although he left the door open to that possibility. Perhaps, he suggested, the mound builders had been overrun and driven off or had migrated elsewhere, their territory occupied by others. On the other hand, he anticipated modern ideas of cultural evolution by pointing out that societies throughout the world change dramatically over time without being replaced by new people. Perhaps, he speculated, there had been considerable change between modern native North Americans and their ancestors. At least part of this change, he reasoned, could well have been brought about as a consequence of European contact and encroachment.

The real strength of *The Antiquities of Wisconsin,* however, is its descriptive detail of mounds and mound groups, many of which no longer exist. Since Lapham was a skillful surveyor and cartographer, modern researchers still use his maps and descriptions to locate vestiges of sites that once existed or to help reconstruct Wisconsin's ancient cultural landscape. Lapham's maps characteristically contain topographical details that provide the natural setting for the mounds and other archaeological sites just before wide-scale farming and development transformed the landscape. Further, his maps are quite striking, somehow conveying the power and majesty of the mounds in a way that has not been duplicated. For these reasons, modern articles and books that deal with Wisconsin effigy mounds are frequently illustrated with Lapham's drawings.

One extremely important map is Lapham's rendition of Aztalan, Wisconsin's premier archaeological site and so named in the early nineteenth century because of the mistaken belief that the site was connected with the Aztec. Even Lapham speculated that the site could support a theory of colonists from Mexico. Aztalan is now known to have been built and occupied by the Middle Mississippian culture between A.D. 1000 and A.D. 1250. When Lapham mapped the site in 1850, the ruins of this ancient town could easily be viewed. The ruins included large stepped platform mounds, remnants of the town walls, interior town features, as well as numerous nearby circular mounds (plate 34). The site was subsequently farmed by settlers, who erased or disfigured many of the surface features. Lapham's map, therefore, is a vital key to the location of specific areas of archaeological interest. Indeed, generations of archaeologists, starting with Samuel Barrett of the Milwaukee Public Museum in 1919, have consulted Lapham's Aztalan map and field notes to help guide research. Recent archeological excavations at the site illustrate the usefulness and accuracy of Lapham's map. Huge underground storage pits have been discovered in the northwest corner of the town in the same place where Lapham had mapped large curious depressions in 1850.

Despite public and scholarly interest in the book, *The Antiquities of Wisconsin, as Surveyed and Described* has long been out of print and largely inaccessible. This problem was addressed in 1999, when the University of Wisconsin–Madison Libraries provided computer access to the volume. This facsimile edition, however, will allow historians, mound researchers, and those interested in Wisconsin's ancient past to have Increase A. Lapham's landmark publication in their personal libraries.

INTRODUCTION
THE MAKING OF *THE ANTIQUITIES OF WISCONSIN,*
AS SURVEYED AND DESCRIBED

Robert P. Nurre

"Perhaps with some of our readers it may excite a smile to hear us talk about the *antiquities* of a country so recently brought into notice as this Territory; but nevertheless we can assure them that there are in this vicinity many remains which seem to indicate that this country was once very densely populated, and that too, by a people far advanced in the arts. Our object however in noticing this subject at present is not so much to describe any new or interesting discovery, as to call the attention of those living near them, to the subject; and to make an earnest appeal to the proprietors of the land on which they are found for their preservation. Many of the works of this kind in the United States are now entirely destroyed, or so much injured as to lose all their interest in the eyes of the antiquarian. Let us hope that in Wisconsin, the case will be different— that here at least the future traveler will not have to regret the loss of those records of an ancient people. Now is the time, when the country is yet new, to take the necessary measures for their preservation, which does not require that the land on which they are found should remain useless, for if sown to grass or planted with fruit trees it may be made to yield a rich return without injuring the ancient works. In many places it would be proper to inclose a small field of woodland, and allow the original forest trees to remain.

"These remarks were suggested a few days since when examining that singular mound at Prairie Village, eighteen miles west of Milwaukee, which is supposed to have been intended to represent the form of a turtle. It is of an oval shape, 56 feet long and about 5 or 6 feet high, having four projections or ridges of earth which are supposed to represent the legs—the anterior pair are turned forward at the extremity and the posterior pair, backwards. The tail is composed of a ridge of earth *two hundred and fifty feet long,* and diminishes, gradually to a point at the extremity. Near the end of the tail stands a mound 60 feet in diameter and 6 feet high, from which the present proprietor or *claimant* has *removed the human* bones to make room for his stock of potatoes! Such sacrilege should be made a punishable offence by the law. The dimensions here stated are from actual measurement.

"An Indian grave has been made on the back of the turtle and a trail leading from their village to the waters of the Fox river passes directly over the tail, on which it is worn down to the original surface of the ground. So it appears that both the red and white men have combined to destroy these interesting remains."

With these words, published as a letter to the editor in the *Milwaukee Advertiser* on November

24, 1836, under the title "Antiquities of Wisconsin," Increase A. Lapham recorded some of his earliest observations of the Indian effigy mounds in the vicinity of Milwaukee. He also appealed for the preservation of these artifacts of a past culture that had previously occupied the land that was then so quickly being transformed by the settlers' axes and plows. Lapham had arrived by steamboat at the shore of the rapidly growing new city of Milwaukee, Michigan Territory, on July 1, 1836, just in time to witness the creation of the Wisconsin Territory three days later on Independence Day. At only twenty-five years old, Lapham was already a skilled civil engineer. Although he had little formal schooling, he had learned his trade while working on the canals of New York, Kentucky, and Ohio in the company of his father and an older brother. He came to Milwaukee to work as a surveyor for one of the city's founders, Byron Kilbourn, and soon was in charge of planning a canal intended to connect the Milwaukee and Rock Rivers in southeastern Wisconsin. His attention would not be limited, however, to engineering, for Lapham possessed a seemingly insatiable fascination for the world around him, and, in this new territory, he found ample fodder for his wide-ranging curiosities. Later in life, when asked to describe his field of specialization, he would simply respond, "I am studying Wisconsin."[1] Immediately upon his arrival in Milwaukee, he was intrigued by the landscape he found near the city and began recording his observations. He had these earliest records printed in the autumn of 1836 in a slim volume entitled *A Catalogue of Plants & Shells Found in the Vicinity of Milwaukee: On the West Side of Lake Michigan*.[2] Although simple, this publication is considered to be the first scientific paper to emanate from Wisconsin.

Over the course of the next four decades of his life, Lapham's interests would range widely. Foremost was his passion for the natural sciences. He was an avid recorder of natural phenomena and a collector of natural history objects, eventually compiling a cabinet of specimens that would be sought out by researchers and later acquired by a university. He was a botanist, a conchologist, a meteorologist, and, perhaps before all, a geologist. He would combine his engineering skills and artistic abilities to draw some of the earliest and most beautifully executed maps of Wisconsin. Dedicated to the development of educational and cultural institutions in Milwaukee and in Wisconsin, Lapham would become a member of the Milwaukee School Board, help develop what would become the Milwaukee Public Library, serve as a trustee for both Carroll College and the Milwaukee Female College, hold the presidency of the State Historical Society of Wisconsin for a decade, and assist in founding the Wisconsin Academy of Sciences, Arts and Letters. In the midst of all of these endeavors, he would occasionally return to his interest in the effigy mounds scattered across the Wisconsin landscape. This work was most pronounced during the years 1849 through 1855 as he researched, wrote, illustrated, and edited what would be his most prominent publication, *The Antiquities of Wisconsin, as Surveyed and Described*, which was published by the Smithsonian Institution in 1855.[3]

The story of how Increase A. Lapham's *Antiquities of Wisconsin* came to be written and published includes several themes. At the center is one man's fascination with the natural and cultural landscapes around him and the fervent desire to share that fascination with others. There is also the evolution of the nascent field of archaeology. Not yet an accepted science, it was comprised of a diverse group of individuals trying to puzzle out the mysteries of the people who had previously occupied North America based on the scattered remains they had left behind. Archaeology was a field fraught with speculation, but one that was beginning to gain a respectable status. Finally, there is the development of the Smithsonian Institution. Although now widely known as one of this country's, if not the world's, premier cultural and scientific institutions, at the midpoint of the 1800s it was a small organization just beginning to develop a reputation among the more established learned societies, such as the American Antiquarian Society.

Lapham was most likely well aware of the presence of Indian mounds on the landscape before coming to Wisconsin, having previously lived for several years in Ohio, a region well known for its rich stock of these remains of past civilizations. His extensive travels in that region and the published works of the day would have acquainted him with these land formations. Lapham used the term "antiquities," which, though largely unfamiliar to the modern ear, carried a rather specific meaning in the mid-1800s; that is, the remains left by past human inhabitants of the landscape. These might include pottery, bones, tools, and, most specifically, mounds. Other words are used to describe the mounds including "earthworks," "monuments," "ancient works," "embankments," "enclosures," and "tumuli." Although sometimes intended to describe certain structures, these words were often used synonymously. The types of mounds that Lapham found in abundance in Wisconsin—though rarely found elsewhere—were those representing the shapes of animals, the effigy mounds.

In 1844 Lapham wrote what was, in his own words, "the *first* book published for the trade in Wisconsin."[4] *A Geographical and Topographical Description of Wisconsin* was essentially an immigrants' guide to the territory, though it contained a greater sense of history than is found in most works of this genre.[5] It provided a wide range of information about the territory including its government, history, agriculture, transportation, climate, geology, and topography. Lapham's dual purposes in writing this book are clearly explained in his preface:

> This work is now given to the public with the hope not only of furnishing the thousands of new comers, who are annually flocking to our Territory, and to others, in a cheap and convenient form, a large amount of useful information, which it would be difficult for them to obtain from any other source; but also to preserve for the future historian many interesting facts which might otherwise soon be forgotten and lost.

In a section entitled "Antiquities" Lapham wrote:

> Wisconsin does not fall behind the other portions of the western country in the monuments it affords of the existence of an ancient people who once inhabited North America, but of whom nothing is known except what can be gathered from some of the results of their labors. . . . There is a class of ancient earthworks in Wisconsin, not before found in any other country, being made to represent quadrupeds, birds, reptiles, and even the human form. These representations are rather rude, and it is often difficult to decide for what species of animal they are intended; but the effects of time may have modified their appearance very much since they were originally formed. Some have a resemblance to the buffalo, the eagle, or crane, or to the turtle or lizard. . . . The ancient works are found all over the Territory, but are most abundant at Aztalan, on the Rock river, near the Blue Mounds, along the Wisconsin, the Neenah and the Pishtaka rivers, and near Lake Winnebago.

In this early writing, Lapham demonstrated his interest in the Indian mounds of Wisconsin, his observational skills for recording them, his commitment to their preservation, and the ability to describe them in the written word. He would soon decide to conduct a statewide study of

Wisconsin's Indian mounds but would first need to find a source of financial support for this project.

FINDING A SOURCE OF SUPPORT

Lapham's Wisconsin, as his 1844 book became commonly known, received wide distribution in this country and beyond. Numerous copies found their way to the European countries that were the source of many of Wisconsin's immigrants. Perhaps it was one of these copies, brought to the attention of the Société Royale des Antiquaries du Nord (Royal Society of Northern Antiquarians) in Copenhagen, Denmark, that led to Lapham's election as a corresponding member of that learned society in 1846. At that time, it was common for such societies to elect corresponding members in order to obtain reports and information from distant sources and to encourage the exchange of publications. (Lapham received a large membership certificate, which mistakenly listed his first name as "Ingram" rather than "Increase," an error that he, always attentive to detail, could not overlook and asked to have corrected.[6])

In a letter dated October 16, 1846, to Charles C. Rafn, the Royal Society's secretary, Lapham thanked the society for the honor bestowed upon him and wrote: "I suppose it is the desire of the society to obtain information of all kinds relative to the ancient mounds &c. of Wisconsin, which have attracted some attention on account of their peculiar, imitative forms."[7] Lapham went on to propose a study of Wisconsin's effigy mounds for publication in the *Memoires de la Société Royale des Antiquaires du Nord.* He would be "willing to devote the necessary *time* to it without compensation, provided that the actual expenses attending the investigation can be refunded by the society." Lapham enclosed with his letter four sketches of effigy mounds that he had examined within the city of Milwaukee. The society's next known letter to Lapham arrived in 1852 and contained an apology for the delay in communication, the effect of a recent war involving Denmark, but no specific mention of his proposal.[8] He had, however, long before the arrival of this letter, made other arrangements to support his archaeological research.

In a letter to the American Antiquarian Society (AAS) dated November 26, 1849, Lapham proposed conducting a study of the mounds with the sponsorship of the AAS and under the same terms he had proposed three years earlier to the Royal Society in Denmark:

> Now I propose to visit and survey these mounds, opening occasionally one, provided the actual expense can be defrayed by your society, charging nothing for my time &c. . . . The results of course to be communicated to the Society with the right to a certain number of copies in the case of publication by the Society; and of publishing, in case the society should refuse or neglect to publish. [9]

This society responded quickly. On December 7 Samuel F. Haven, the AAS librarian, replied that Lapham's letter had been received and would be discussed by the Council of the AAS later in the month.[10] Haven believed the AAS would be interested in the project and asked Lapham to provide more information about his proposed study, in particular an estimate of the expenses for his work. Lapham responded in a letter written on Christmas Eve:

It would be best to employ a horse and light wagon, with a boy for an assistant, the daily expense of which, including tavern charges while traveling about the state would be about four dollars. If three months are consumed (say ninety days) and an addition for laborers to open 20 or 30 mounds, and another for the purchase of such articles as have already been dug out, it will be safe to estimate the expense at about five hundred dollars.[11]

Approaching the AAS for funding proved a wise course of action for Lapham. That organization, founded in Worcester, Massachusetts, by printer Isaiah Thomas in 1812, was a leader in the study of mounds, ethnology, and archaeology during the first half of the 1800s. Among its early missions was the collection of evidence of prehistoric life in North America. In 1820 the AAS had published Caleb Atwater's "Description of the Antiquities Discovered in the State of Ohio and Other Western States" in the first issue of *Archaeologia Americana,* the society's transactions.[12] Although just three years earlier the AAS had declined a request for financial support for the research of Ephraim Squier and Edwin Davis that was later published as "Ancient Monuments of the Mississippi Valley," the organization did decide to support Lapham's work.[13] By a letter dated February 20, 1850, Haven informed Lapham that the AAS had accepted his proposal and would provide the sum of five hundred dollars to fund his study of the effigy mounds of Wisconsin.[14] Lapham was to provide to the AAS a written report of his findings for publication, as well as all artifacts that he found. If the AAS chose to publish his findings, Lapham was "entitled to a certain number of copies" of the resulting publication. With funding for his project secured, Lapham set about planning a strategy for his work.

FIELDWORK

On June 27, 1850, Lapham set out from Milwaukee on his first excursion to gather information on the effigy mounds. A young assistant named John accompanied him in a wagon drawn by Billy, Lapham's horse. The next day, he would write to his wife, Ann, from the town of Summit: "For your gratification I have concluded to write my 'pencillings by the way' in the form of letters to you. Please preserve them for future use."[15] At the end of this letter he added: "Now if you do not wish to be bothered with any more letters of this kind just say so in an answer to this directed to *Madison* where I shall probably be after a few days." As there are at least six letters to her over the next several weeks, Ann apparently did not object to her role as keeper of the correspondence. These letters detailed his travels and included occasional sketches of mounds. Lapham spent most of his first week examining the extensive earthworks along the Rock River. These mounds, which had first been brought to notice thirteen years earlier by N. F. Hyer, had been the source of much interest and speculation.[16] Even the name they had been given, Aztalan, which derived from their supposed connection to the Aztec, implied a certain degree of mystery. The remainder of the trip across southern Wisconsin included investigations at Madison, Prairie du Sac, Mineral Point, and Janesville.

In September Haven wrote to Lapham to inquire about the progress of his research and to request that he submit a brief report for the AAS's annual meeting.[17] In his reply, Lapham described his "grand tour" of June and July.[18] He enclosed three pages of drawings of the mounds and noted that "some excavations of a particular character have been found in different parts of the state, of which you will find a drawing enclosed." These are the unique intaglio effigies, one of which, the Panther Intaglio near Fort Atkinson, survives to the present day. Lapham continued: "I fear I shall not be able to complete the survey this season. I find it much better to work in the spring and autumn, than in the summer when the bushes are covered with foliage." Lapham's report, though not his drawings, was published in the *Proceedings of the American Antiquarian Society* for 1850. In an editorial note, Haven described the drawings as being "curious, and very neatly executed," citing drawings of earthworks that Lapham had described as resembling birds, a buffalo, and "a Behemoth." [19] He went on: "Not less curious than these are earthworks, apparently in the form of weapons or implements. Some of them resemble the clubs with knotted heads, which, when armed with pointed stone or metal, are known to have been the original tomahawks." By this, Haven showed his bias for the widely held belief that the mounds were primarily related to warfare among their creators. While many of the earthworks found in Ohio gave the appearance of being fortifications, such formations were less commonly found in Wisconsin. Lapham had interpreted the mounds, which Haven thought represented tomahawks, more benignly as being in the shape of lizards.

Lapham lectured before the Milwaukee Young Men's Association concerning his effigy mound research on January 16, 1851.[20] He described the challenge of his work by saying of the moundbuilders: "Destitute of literature, these people have handed down to us, no account of their history, their manner and customs; their origin; their migrations; nor have we any certain means of ascertaining what has become of them. These are questions for the antiquary to settle, as best he can, from the slight materials left for his examination." He illustrated the talk with his prepared drawings and sketches on a blackboard. Much of the discussion concerned his observations of the mounds at Aztalan, which he had investigated the preceding summer. Lapham noted that the Turtle Mound near Waukesha, for which he had eloquently urged preservation fifteen years earlier, was now compromised as "a private dwelling now stands upon the body of the great turtle and the Catholic Church is built upon the tail."

Lapham's fieldwork during 1851 was rather limited. On November 1 he wrote to Haven:

> For the past season I have not been able to make as much progress as was intended. The excessive rains of the early part of the year made the roads, in much of our new country, almost impassable. . . . I have however added considerably to my stock of surveys by three or four shorter tours—from one of which to the upper part of the Rock river, I have just returned.[21]

He added: "It has been one of my objects to endeavor to interest as many others in this inquiry as possible, and with this view, have offered in some cases to make slight compensation for accurate surveys of such works as were in the vicinity of intelligent surveyors, & not visited by me." Among those who would contribute mound information were William Canfield, who provided descriptions of mounds in the Baraboo area; Erskine Stansbury, who informed Lapham of mounds encountered in his work as a government land surveyor; Professor Stephen Lathrop, who described the mounds on the Beloit College campus; and George Hyer and William Brayton, who shared their knowledge of Aztalan. Even James Duane Doty, then serving as a United States senator, told Lapham of mounds he had seen in his travels throughout the state. None of them accepted compensation for their information. Lapham concluded his November 1 letter to Haven by reporting that he had been engaged in the project for a total of 73½ days and had spent $317.50 of the allotted funds.

During May and June 1852, Lapham conducted his final fieldwork in search of effigy mounds on a tour across the south central portion of Wisconsin including stops in Watertown, Montello, the dells of the Wisconsin River, La Crosse, and Prairie du Chien. His travels on this trip are particularly well documented for, along with his usual letters to his wife, he wrote a series of eleven letters to the editor of the *Milwaukee Sentinel*, under the rubric "Glances at the Interior," detailing his adventures.

THE AMERICAN ANTIQUARIAN SOCIETY, THE SMITHSONIAN INSTITUTION, AND THE PUBLISHING OF *THE ANTIQUITIES OF WISCONSIN*

Soon after Lapham secured funding for his research from the AAS, he wrote to Joseph Henry, the secretary of the Smithsonian Institution, on March 12, 1850, to inform him of the project and to ask the Smithsonian to assist by loaning two barometers, which would be used to determine elevations during the course of the mound explorations.[22] Although the Smithsonian Institution had been founded only four years earlier, Lapham was already a close correspondent, contributing daily meteorological data from Milwaukee. He offered to furnish copies of additional meteorological observations and "a report of the results of my 'Barometrical Survey' if desired" in exchange for the use of the barometers. The Smithsonian agreed to provide Lapham with the instruments, and E. Foreman, Henry's assistant, wrote that two instruments had been ordered.[23] (Unfortunately, the barometers sent to Lapham would be crushed in transit. In a later letter explaining the difficulties of shipping such fragile instruments, Foreman notes, "truly the Express office does a smashing business in more senses than one."[24]) Foreman continued: "We shall be pleased to receive the results of your explorations of the mounds of Wisconsin, and if upon examination they prove to contain interesting additions to knowledge upon that subject, they will be accepted for publication in the Smithsonian Contributions."

That the Smithsonian would be interested in Lapham's work is in keeping with the beginnings of its publishing program. Although Henry himself was a physical scientist, with a particular interest in electricity, he chose to devote much of the Smithsonian's early publishing efforts to the field of archaeology. The first volume of the *Smithsonian Contributions to Knowledge*, which had been published in 1848, consisted entirely of Ephraim Squier and Edwin Davis's "Ancient Monuments of the Mississippi Valley."[25] The second volume would include Squier's article "Aboriginal Monuments of the State of New York," and Charles Whittlesey's "Descriptions of Ancient Works in Ohio" had been accepted for publication in the third volume.[26] Henry and Foreman may have been unaware that the AAS was funding Lapham's study and intended to publish his findings. Their interest in Lapham's work, however, foretold the later agreement that would transfer the publication of Lapham's research from the AAS to the Smithsonian Institution.

In May 1851, before setting out on that year's explorations, Lapham attended the meeting of the American Association for the Advancement of Science held in Cincinnati, Ohio. While there he discussed his mound study with Henry, and the conversation turned to the possibility of the Smithsonian, rather than the AAS, publishing the results of his research. Before the month was out, Henry wrote to Haven and suggested that their two organizations cooperate in supporting and publishing Lapham's work.[27] Specifically, Henry proposed that the AAS publish an abstract of Lapham's results and then transfer the full manuscript, after a thorough examination and edit, to the Smithsonian for publication. Henry's reasoning was that Lapham's work and other similar studies of earthworks being considered for publication by the Smithsonian could then be presented to the public in a uniform style. Henry also felt that the Smithsonian, which had a generous publications budget, could provide wider distribution.

Before the AAS considered the Smithsonian's proposition, Haven wrote to Lapham and asked if it would be acceptable to him.[28] Lapham replied that he was pleased with the new plan for two reasons: he had already planned to take his manuscript to the Smithsonian if the AAS had decided not to publish it, and he believed that the Smithsonian's folio-sized volume would be more appropriate for his illustrations than the AAS's smaller quarto-sized publication.[29] Lapham also introduced an issue that would continue to be a problem—the matter of compensation for his work. Lapham admonished Haven: "If you arrange with him [Henry] please not to forget that a number of copies are to be furnished me, as a sort of a compensation for my *labor*. You only pay for my actual expenses—not for my time & *labor*."

By October 1851 the AAS had finalized the new cooperative arrangement with the Smithsonian.[30] Among the benefits to the AAS would be the welcome availability of funds, previously allocated for publishing Lapham's work, for construction of a planned new building. Haven, Henry, and Lapham all seemed pleased with the new arrangement. The number of copies of the eventual publication that Lapham was to receive, however, had not been stipulated, and this would result in controversy later in the project. With the new plan for publication in place, Lapham continued his research. The only immediate change was that he was now regularly corresponding with both the AAS and the Smithsonian about the details of his project.

THE MANUSCRIPT

Lapham began the compilation of his manuscript as soon as the first season of his fieldwork was completed. In October 1850 he wrote to Haven that he had "accumulated quite a mass of notes, drawings, topographical sketches, &c., which will require some labor to arrange in the form of an essay."[31] There were also the letters sent home during his travels that his wife, Ann, had carefully preserved.

In November 1851 Henry responded to a request from Lapham for suggestions as to what should be included in his manuscript by writing: "Your memoir should be principally a statement of facts and though you may give your hypotheses they should be subordinate to the facts. We are as yet only collecting the bricks of the temple of American Antiquities which are hereafter to be arranged and fashioned into a durable edifice."[32] In preparing Squier and Davis's "Ancient Monuments of the Mississippi Valley" for publication, Henry had endeavored to edit out what he felt was unfounded speculation by the authors as to the origin and meaning of the mounds. Having been trained in the physical sciences, Henry was uneasy with theory that was not founded upon extensive observation. Lapham must have gotten the message for he would later write in his preface to *The Antiquities of Wisconsin*:

> But little effort has been made to construct hypotheses in explanation of the facts observed, or by an extended comparison with results recorded by others, to arrive at

general conclusions. . . . My office has been faithfully to fulfil the duties of the surveyor: to examine and investigate the facts, and to report them as much in detail as may be necessary; leaving it to others with better opportunities, to compare them, and to establish, in connection with other means of information, such general principles as may be legitimately deduced.

In a letter dated July 30, 1852, Lapham informed Haven that he had completed his manuscript.[33] He wrote that he intended to deliver it directly to Henry at the meeting of the American Association for the Advancement of Science in Cleveland, Ohio, the following month, or he could send it to the AAS if Haven should so direct. (Lapham had apparently forgotten that, although the publication of his work had been assigned to the Smithsonian, it remained the responsibility of the AAS to review and approve the manuscript.) He also stated that he had packed a box of artifacts acquired during the course of his investigations for the AAS. Lapham concluded his letter with an accounting of the funds that the society had provided: "The expenditures fall a little short of the $500; and the difference will be refunded if required. I think however, under all circumstances, that I should be allowed to retain this sum." Haven acceded to this request and, at his instruction, Lapham sent the manuscript, secured safely in a tin case, directly to the AAS.

The manuscript, which remains in the collection of the AAS, ran a total of 390 hand-written pages on sheets measuring six by nine inches.[34] It was accompanied, as Lapham described, by "51 plates of the size adopted for the Smithsonian 'Contributions'; 1 of double that size for Aztalan; & 1 of 4 times (in area) the size, being a map of the state showing the localities of all the known works. There are also 97 drawings, intended for wood-cut illustrations."[35] Lapham apologized for the condition of the manuscript: "The ms. is not so *clean* as I could wish, but I cannot find time now, to make another copy." In fact, the manuscript was in somewhat rough condition. Lapham wrote to both Haven and Henry, using similar language, expressing his concern about the quality of his writing in the manuscript: "I must rely upon your proof reader to see that all is right, & to correct any literary defects awkward expressions &c. Not having had the advantage of a classical education, I fear many such defects may be discovered, & hope that they will all be corrected."[36]

The task of examining and editing Lapham's manuscript fell largely to Haven who submitted a lengthy report about it at the AAS's annual meeting on October 23, 1852. Primarily an abstract of Lapham's manuscript, the report was later published in the AAS's *Proceedings*.[37] The actual work of editing the manuscript was still to come, however. Haven wrote to Lapham on November 4, telling him of the report of the Committee of Publication. Regarding the editing of the manuscript, he stated: "We will endeavor to revise it faithfully and avoid injurious meddling with either sense or expression."[38] Specifically, Haven suggested "a change of phraseology now and then to avoid repetition." As witnessed by the surviving manuscript, Haven was quite judicious in the use of his editorial pen. His changes were relatively minor, an occasional simplification of a construction or a substitution of a word. His work did, however, noticeably improve the readability of the text. As Haven completed editing each chapter of the manuscript, he wrote on it in pencil "Examined S. F. H., ready to be copied." By a letter dated December 15, 1852, Haven informed Henry that the manuscript had been reviewed and revised, that it was in the hands of a copyist, and that it soon would be ready to send to the Smithsonian.[39]

Haven wrote to Lapham on February 8, 1853, that the transcription of his memoir had been sent to Henry.[40] If Lapham had hoped that, now that his manuscript was in the hands of the

Smithsonian, it would soon be in print, he was to be disappointed. There would be over two years of editing, proofreading, and revision before the final publication was completed.

A BIBLIOGRAPHY AND CONTROVERSY

On March 26, 1853, Henry wrote a letter to Lapham indicating that his manuscript had been received in Washington and that the drawings intended for woodcuts would soon be placed in the hands of an engraver.[41] Henry also wrote: "I still think a chapter on the Bibliography of American Antiquities would be important and I would advise you to go on with the preparation of an article of this kind." Lapham soon set to work on this bibliography and on May 6 informed Henry that he had "prepared a list of all the works and of all articles in Journals, Proceedings of Societies &c. bearing on N. American Antiquities, so far as I could do it here, and have sent it to Mr. Havens [sic] for additions."[42] Haven agreed to add additional citations to Lapham's draft bibliography but wrote that "to make a complete catalogue of all that has been written on the subject would require a very considerable amount of research and more leisure than I am likely to obtain at present."[43] Haven must have discovered that he had more leisure than he expected, for during the course of the next three years, the bibliography that had initially been intended to be a chapter of Lapham's memoir grew into a full-scale article in its own right. It would be published in 1856 as "Archaeology of the United States, or Sketches, Historical and Bibliographical, of the Progress of Information and Opinion Respecting the Vestiges of Antiquity in the United States" by Samuel F. Haven as the second article of the eighth volume of the *Smithsonian Contributions to Knowledge*.[44]

During the summer of 1854, the lingering issue of how many copies of the completed book Lapham would receive would come up again and was at last resolved, although not without a degree of unease between Haven, Henry, and Lapham. When returning a set of corrected plate proofs to the Smithsonian, Lapham wrote: "It was a part of the arrangement with the Antiquarian Society that I was to be furnished with a number of copies of the memoir, the sale of which in this state &c. would be a sort of return for my services in making the survey &c. I wish to remind you of this so that it may not be forgotten. The number has not been fixed, but I have thought that one hundred would be about right."[45] Henry was no doubt surprised to learn that this issue was still unsettled, believing it had been resolved as part of his correspondence with Haven during the preceding winter. At that time Haven and Henry had agreed to provide Lapham with twenty-five copies; this decision, however, seems not to have been communicated to Lapham. On June 26, Henry wrote to Haven asking again what arrangements had been made with Lapham.[46] Haven's response indicates a certain amount of pique as he pointedly refers to Lapham's request for copies as a "demand" and states that any copies received should be for distribution among his friends and not to be sold as a source of compensation.[47] By the end of July, Henry, ever the conciliator, wrote to Lapham that he would be provided with fifty copies of *The Antiquities of Wisconsin*.[48] This was half of the number that Lapham had requested, but twice as many as Henry felt he had previously agreed to provide. Lapham must have acceded to Henry's offer since no further correspondence on the issue can be found.

Work progressed slowly but steadily on the preparation of the book for publication throughout 1853, 1854, and 1855. A printer in Philadelphia prepared the plates, and the first proofs were routed from there to Washington and then on to Lapham in distant Milwaukee. The process was inordinately time-consuming and was repeated after the corrected text was prepared for printing, Lapham checking each page before printing could commence. In April 1855 Henry finally determined to proceed with printing based on the Smithsonian's best proofreading and issue an errata sheet for any errors that Lapham might find.[49]

FINALLY, *THE ANTIQUITIES OF WISCONSIN*

On November 8, 1855, Spencer F. Baird, the Smithsonian's assistant secretary, wrote to Lapham that *The Antiquities of Wisconsin* had at last been completed as an independent volume—that it bore a publication date of June 1855 seems to have been of little consequence.[50] Baird wrote that "the box containing 48 copies in boards will be sent to you in a day or two." Two others from Lapham's allotment of fifty copies would be sent directly to "Mr. Lea and Dr. Sartwell," two of Lapham's correspondents, as he had directed. Baird also noted that "the work sells at $4.00 per copy." True to form, Baird, always wanting to increase the Smithsonian's natural history collections, added a postscript to his note: "could you get me the skin of an adult woodchuck? with skull, I want to have a Wisconsin specimen very much." Clearly the long efforts of Increase A. Lapham, the American Antiquarian Society, and the Smithsonian Institution to produce *The Antiquities of Wisconsin, as Surveyed and Described* had come to an end, and it was time for all to move on to other projects.

The completed book consists of ninety-two pages of text describing the mounds of Wisconsin and is arranged by the major watersheds of the state. Lapham wrote in the introduction that he had avoided describing locations by counties because these man-made boundaries were still constantly being changed, while the natural ones were immutable. The text is written as if the reader were traveling throughout the state at Lapham's side, encountering the mounds as they journeyed through the country. The mounds are described, sometimes in very general terms, and anecdotes are given concerning their discovery. For the most part, Lapham heeded Henry's advice to concentrate on observations and to avoid speculation. He mentions, but largely dismisses, the commonly held view that the mounds are works of defense. More often he ascribes their purpose as that of observatories. While Lapham described the effigy mounds by the names of the animals that they were supposed to represent, he clearly states that these names are the interpretation of his time and are not necessarily what the mound-builders intended. In a later chapter, Lapham recounts the materials discovered within the mounds that had been excavated. Prominent among these relics are skulls found in mounds that had been used for burial purposes. He even subjects one of these skulls to a phrenological evaluation, a popular mid-1800s pseudo-science in which the size and shape of a person's skull was thought to indicate character and disposition. Fortunately for his later reputation, Lapham expresses some reservations about the validity of this line of investigation. Scattered throughout the text are over sixty wood engravings illustrating mounds, relics, and natural features.

Perhaps the most important element of *The Antiquities of Wisconsin* is the fifty-five pages of plates that are made up of over one hundred individual illustrations at the back of the volume. These drawings are primarily of individual mounds and mound groups, some showing the detailed measurements that Lapham made to determine the exact size of each mound. There are also maps showing the local arrangement of mounds, as well as their statewide distribution. These highly detailed drawings were the result of Lapham's skills both as an engineer and as an artist. The images reveal a perspective that could not easily be seen by a viewer on the ground. Often the mounds were too large to be observed from a single vantage point, or were obscured by vegetation. Lapham's drawings showed views of the mounds that had, perhaps, not been seen since they were envisioned by their creators centuries earlier. Among these drawings is the Turtle Mound near Waukesha, formerly known as Prairie Village, on plate 19. As described in the text: "This turtle was then a very fine specimen of the ancient art of mound-building. . . . The ground occupied by this group of works is now covered with buildings."

The Antiquities of Wisconsin was issued in two forms, both of which appeared in 1855. It was incorporated as the fourth article in volume seven of the Smithsonian Contributions to Knowledge, and it was also issued as a separate volume, the seventieth publication of the Smithsonian Institution.

AFTER THE ANTIQUITIES OF WISCONSIN

Lapham would do little writing about effigy mounds after the publication of The Antiquities of Wisconsin. Perhaps his only published work came in 1859 when he wrote a three-page report for the Collections of the State Historical Society of Wisconsin entitled "On the Man-Shaped Mounds of Wisconsin."[51] This essay detailed a mound in the human form, two hundred feet in length, found near Baraboo by his longtime collaborator William H. Canfield. He also compared this mound to other human-shaped mounds previously discovered in southwestern Wisconsin.

The last two decades of Lapham's life were filled with many adventures and accomplishments. Among these was an extensive treatise written for the Transactions of the Wisconsin State Agricultural Society on the forest trees of Wisconsin, wherein he strongly argued for woodland preservation, and detailed studies of both the grasses and the paleontology of North America, neither of which would be published.[52] He would continue his work as a cartographer, continually updating his maps as more information became available about the state. In 1860 he was awarded an honorary LL.D. from Amherst College in Massachusetts. At the end of the 1860s, Lapham's long-held interest in meteorology and the possibility of predicting storms on the Great Lakes would lead him to write the federal legislation that created the forerunner of the modern U.S. Weather Service. Finally, in 1873, he would be appointed Wisconsin's chief geologist, a position for which he had, in many ways, trained throughout his life. After a change of political party led to his removal from this position in the spring of 1875, Lapham retired to his family's farm on Oconomowoc Lake, west of Milwaukee.

In August 1875 Lapham received a letter from Spencer F. Baird, his old colleague at the Smithsonian Institution.[53] Baird asked if he would be willing to prepare a series of effigy mound models, based on his illustrations in The Antiquities of Wisconsin, now twenty years old. These would be displayed as part of the Smithsonian's exhibit at the 1876 Philadelphia Centennial Exposition. Lapham readily agreed and soon designed an exhibit of fourteen models to fit on a four-by-six-foot table. One of these models portrays the Turtle Mound near Waukesha, which Lapham had first described four decades earlier. Baird requested an additional model of a mound grouping, but Lapham would not live to finish this project. On the afternoon of September 14,

1875, while out in his rowboat on Oconomowoc Lake, Increase A. Lapham passed away. The work on the models was so far advanced, however, that Lapham's son, Seneca, had no difficulty completing them for the exposition. Almost two decades later, Lapham's effigy mound models, by then cast in iron, were displayed by the State Historical Society of Wisconsin in the Anthropology Building at the 1893 World's Columbian Exposition in Chicago. Now, as the twenty-first century begins, these same models can be seen at Wisconsin's State Historical Museum in Madison.

THE ANTIQUITIES OF WISCONSIN AFTER A CENTURY AND A HALF

At least two of Lapham's copies of *The Antiquities of Wisconsin* are known still to exist. One is the copy that he presented to the State Historical Society of Wisconsin, where it is now kept as part of the society's Rare Book Collection. The other is Lapham's personal copy that was kept in his private library. After Lapham's death, his family sold his library, along with his collection of atural history specimens, to the University of Wisconsin. At the time, Lapham's books accounted for nearly 20 percent of the entire university library collection. This copy of *The Antiquities of Wisconsin* remained in the university library for many years until it was inadvertently discarded as a duplicate, most likely during a library reorganization in the 1950s. Fortunately, a professor, Harris A. Palmer from the University of Wisconsin–Platteville, acquired it and eventually gave the book to that school's library. The existence of this book came to light during a recent project to identify, locate, and preserve the extant volumes of Lapham's library.[54] With the cooperation of the University of Wisconsin–Platteville's Karmann Library and the Friends of the University of Wisconsin–Madison Libraries, this book has been returned to the University of Wisconsin–Madison Libraries and now resides in its Department of Special Collections. This particular copy of *The Antiquities of Wisconsin* includes a few marginal notations in Lapham's handwriting. The most prominent notations are on the plates at the end of the volume. On many of these, he has added the page number on which the mounds are described in the text so that he could turn directly to the description without having to refer to the listing of plates at the beginning of the book. Curiously, in his own copy of his book describing the history of the moundbuilders of Wisconsin, Lapham tipped in his own carefully prepared genealogy of the Lapham family dating back seven generations to his first ancestor who arrived in America from England in the mid-1600s.

A century and a half after Increase A. Lapham began his research for *The Antiquities of Wisconsin*, his work remains an important benchmark in the literature of archaeology in North America. Although far from a complete inventory of all of the Indian mounds that would eventually be identified in Wisconsin, Lapham's *Antiquities of Wisconsin* provides a valuable sampling of the mounds known as of the mid-1800s. His work documented many mounds that either had already been or soon would be destroyed and are not known from any other records. During the years since its publication, few papers or books written about the Indian mounds of Wisconsin have failed to cite Increase A. Lapham and his *Antiquities of Wisconsin*.

Approximately 80 percent of the Indian mounds that were once found on Wisconsin's landscape have been destroyed during the past century and a half. Among these is the Turtle Mound near Waukesha for which Lapham urged preservation in his 1836 newspaper article. While his hopes to preserve this particular mound were unrealized, Lapham's efforts preserved, at least on paper, a large amount of information about the Indian mounds of Wisconsin that might otherwise have been "forgotten and lost."[55]

NOTES

The primary source materials for this introduction are the letters exchanged among the three people most involved in the creation of *The Antiquities of Wisconsin:* Increase A. Lapham; Samuel F. Haven, librarian of the American Antiquarian Society; and Joseph Henry, secretary of the Smithsonian Institution. These letters are found in the manuscript collections of the American Antiquarian Society (AAS) in Worcester, Massachusetts, and of the State Historical Society of Wisconsin (SHSW) in Madison, Wisconsin. Generous permission has been granted by the American Antiquarian Society and the State Historical Society of Wisconsin to quote from the letters in their collections.

1. Samuel Sterling Sherman, *Increase A. Lapham, LL.D., a Biographical Sketch Read before the Old Settlers Club, Milwaukee, Wis., December 11, 1875* (Milwaukee: Milwaukee News Company, Printers, 1876), 51.
2. Increase A. Lapham, *A Catalogue of Plants & Shells Found in the Vicinity of Milwaukee: On the West Side of Lake Michigan* (Milwaukee: Advertiser Office, 1836).
3. Increase A. Lapham, *The Antiquities of Wisconsin, as Surveyed and Described* (Washington, D.C.: Smithsonian Institution, 1855); also published as article 4 in volume 7 of the *Smithsonian Contributions to Knowledge.*
4. Inscription in the copy of *A Geographical and Topographical Description of Wisconsin* presented to SHSW by Lapham in 1854, SHSW Library Rare Book Collection.
5. Increase A. Lapham, *A Geographical and Topographical Description of Wisconsin; with Brief Sketches of Its History, Geology, Mineralogy, Natural History, Population, Soil, Productions, Government, Antiquities, &c.&c.* (Milwaukee: P. C. Hale, 1844).
6. Certificate in SHSW Visual Materials Archive.
7. Draft letter, Lapham to Charles C. Rafn, October 16, 1846, Lapham Papers, SHSW.
8. Letter, Charles C. Rafn to Lapham, March 8, 1852, Lapham Papers, SHSW.
9. Letter, Lapham to secretary of AAS, November 26, 1849, AAS Correspondence, AAS.
10. Letter, Haven to Lapham, December 7, 1849, Lapham Papers, SHSW.
11. Letter, Lapham to Haven, December 24, 1849, AAS Correspondence, AAS.
12. Caleb Atwater, "Description of the Antiquities Discovered in the State of Ohio and Other Western States," *Archaeologia Americana: Transactions and Collections of the American Antiquarian Society* 1 (1820): 105–299.
13. David J. Meltzer, "Ephraim Squier, Edwin Davis, and the Making of an American Archaeological Classic," introduction to reprint edition of Ephraim G. Squier and Edwin H. Davis, *Ancient Monuments of the Mississippi Valley* (Washington, D.C.: Smithsonian Institution Press, 1998), 14–17.
14. Letter, Haven to Lapham, February 20, 1850, Lapham Papers, SHSW.
15. Letter, Lapham to Ann M. Lapham, June 28, 1850, Lapham Papers, SHSW.
16. N. F. Hyer, letter to the editor, *Milwaukee Advertiser,* February 25, 1837.
17. Letter, Haven to Lapham, September 11, 1850, Lapham Papers, SHSW.
18. Letter, Lapham to Haven, October 2, 1850, AAS Correspondence, AAS.
19. Samuel F. Haven, "Report of the Librarian," *Proceedings of the American Antiquarian Society* (1850): 17–18.
20. Lapham's lecture manuscript, January 16, 1851, Wisconsin Archaeological Society Papers, SHSW.
21. Letter, Lapham to Haven, November 1, 1851, AAS Correspondence, AAS.
22. Draft letter, Lapham to Henry, March 12, 1850, Lapham Papers, SHSW.
23. Letter, E. Foreman to Lapham, March 29, 1850, Lapham Papers, SHSW.
24. Letter, E. Foreman to Lapham, May 14, 1850, Lapham Papers, SHSW.
25. Ephraim G. Squier and Edwin H. Davis, "Ancient Monuments of the Mississippi Valley, Comprising the Results of Extensive Original Surveys and Explorations," *Smithsonian Contributions to Knowledge* 1 (1848): entire volume.

26. Ephraim G. Squier, "Aboriginal Monuments of the State of New York," *Smithsonian Contributions to Knowledge* 2 (1851): article 9; and Charles Whittlesey, "Descriptions of Ancient Works in Ohio," *Smithsonian Contributions to Knowledge* 3 (1852): article 7.

27. Letter, Henry to Haven, May 29, 1851, AAS Correspondence, AAS.

28. Letter, Haven to Lapham, June 12, 1851, Lapham Papers, SHSW.

29. Draft letter, Lapham to Haven, June 28, 1851, Lapham Papers, SHSW.

30. Letter, Haven to Lapham, October 17, 1851, Lapham Papers, SHSW.

31. Letter, Lapham to Haven, October 2, 1850, AAS Correspondence, AAS.

32. Letter, Henry to Lapham, November 22, 1851, Lapham Papers, SHSW.

33. Letter, Lapham to Haven, July 30, 1852, AAS Correspondence, AAS.

34. Manuscript, "The Antiquities of Wisconsin, as Examined & Surveyed," I. A. Lapham [1852], AAS.

35. Letter, Lapham to Haven, July 30, 1852, AAS Correspondence, AAS.

36. Draft letter, Lapham to Henry, August 14, 1852, Lapham Papers, SHSW.

37. Samuel F. Haven, "Report of the Committee of Publication," *Proceedings of the American Antiquarian Society* (1852): 16–33.

38. Letter, Haven to Lapham, November 4, 1852, Lapham Papers, SHSW.

39. Draft Letter, Haven to Henry, December 15, 1852, AAS Correspondence, AAS.

40. Letter, Haven to Lapham, February 8, 1853, Lapham Papers, SHSW.

41. Letter, Henry to Lapham, March 26, 1853, Lapham Papers, SHSW.

42. Draft letter, Lapham to Henry, May 6, 1853, Lapham Papers, SHSW.

43. Letter, Haven to Lapham, June 8, 1853, Lapham Papers, SHSW.

44. Samuel F. Haven, "Archaeology of the United States, or Sketches, Historical and Bibliographical, of the Progress of Information and Opinion Respecting Vestiges of Antiquity in the United States," *Smithsonian Contributions to Knowledge* 8 (1856): article 2.

45. Quoted in letter, Henry to Haven, June 26, 1854, AAS Correspondence, AAS.

46. Letter, Henry to Haven, June 26, 1854, AAS Correspondence, AAS.

47. Draft letter, Haven to Henry, July 7, 1854, AAS Correspondence, AAS.

48. Letter, Henry to Lapham, July 27, 1854, Lapham Papers, SHSW.

49. Letter, Spencer F. Baird to Lapham, April 7, 1855, Lapham Papers, SHSW.

50. Letter, Spencer F. Baird to Lapham, November 8, 1855, Lapham Papers, SHSW.

51. Increase A. Lapham, "On the Man-Shaped Mounds of Wisconsin," *Collections of the State Historical Society of Wisconsin* 4 (1859): 365–368.

52. Increase A. Lapham, "Forest Trees of Wisconsin," *Transactions of the Wisconsin State Agricultural Society. For the Years 1854–5–6–7* 4 (1857): 195–251.

53. Letter, Spencer F. Baird to Lapham, August 16, 1875, Lapham Papers, SHSW.

54. The Increase A. Lapham Library Project was conceived and conducted by Robert P. Nurre with the support of the University of Wisconsin–Madison Libraries.

55. Increase A. Lapham, *A Geographical and Topographical Description of Wisconsin*, iii.

KEY TO BIBLIOGRAPHIC REFERENCES IN
THE ANTIQUITIES OF WISCONSIN,
AS SURVEYED AND DESCRIBED

———

Approximately thirty references to other published works are included in I. A. Lapham's *Antiquities of Wisconsin*. Some of these are shown explicitly as footnotes, while others appear more casually within the text. As was the custom in scientific papers of Lapham's time, the references were often severely truncated (i.e., "J. Delafield, Jr., Antiquities &c." for John Delafield's *Inquiry into the Origin of the Antiquities of America*) or appeared as short-hand titles (i.e., "Silliman's Am. Journal" for the *American Journal of Science and Arts*). The following list of modern citations of many of Lapham's bibliographic references is provided to assist the reader in locating his sources. Occasionally Lapham's references do not contain enough information to determine exactly which edition of the book is being cited. In these cases the first North American edition is used. Capitalization of titles has been changed to reflect current style.

Lapham had an extensive personal library, which, after his death, was acquired by the University of Wisconsin. This library numbered over twelve hundred volumes and was considered to be one of the finest scientific libraries in the Midwest. Recently a project has been conducted to identify, locate, and preserve the remaining books from Lapham's library that could be found in the University of Wisconsin–Madison's collection. Several of those books are included in his references for *The Antiquities of Wisconsin*. Those volumes in this bibliography that are known to have been in Lapham's library and that have been located are followed by an asterisk (*). Those publications that are known to have been owned by Lapham based on the accession list of his library or from other information but that have not been located are followed by a pound sign (#).

Brunson, Alfred. "Ancient Mounds or Tumuli in Crawford County; Read before the Wisconsin Historical Society, at Its Annual Meeting, January 1850." In *Third Annual Report and Collections of the State Historical Society, of Wisconsin, for the Year 1856.* Madison, Wis.: Calkins & Webb, Printers, 1857.

Buschmann, Johann Karl Eduard. *Uber die aztekischen Ortsnamen.* Berlin: F. Dummler, 1853.

Carver, Jonathan. *Travels in Wisconsin.* New York: Harper & Brothers, 1838.

Catlin, George. *Letters and Notes on the Manners, Customs, and Conditions of the North American Indians/Written during Eight Years' Travel, from 1832 to 1839, amongst the Wildest Tribes of Indians in North America.* New York: Wiley and Putnam, 1841.

Culbertson, Thaddeus A. "Journal of an Expedition to the Mauvaises Terres and the Upper

Missouri." In *Fifth Annual Report of the Board of Regents of the Smithsonian Institution*. Washington, D.C.: Smithsonian Institution, 1851.

Delafield, John. *An Inquiry into the Origin of the Antiquities of America*. New York: Colt, Burgess, 1839.

Drake, Benjamin. *The Life and Adventures of Black Hawk: With Sketches of Keokuk, the Sac and Fox Indians, and the Late Black Hawk War*. Cincinnati: G. Conclin, 1839. *

Eaton, Amos. *Geological Text-Book for Aiding the Study of North American Geology*. 2d ed. Albany, N.Y.: Websters and Skinners, 1832. *

Foster, John Wells and Josiah Dwight Whitney. *Report on the Geology and Topography of a Portion of the Lake Superior Land District in the State of Michigan*. Washington, D.C.: Printed for the House of Representatives, 1850–1851. *

Gallatin, Albert. "A Synopsis of the Indian Tribes of North America." *American Antiquarian Society Transactions and Collections* 2 (1836): 1–422.

Hyer, N. F. Letter to the editor. *Milwaukee Advertiser*, February 25, 1837.

Keating, William Hypolitus. *Narrative of an Expedition to the Source of St. Peter's River, Lake Winnepeek, Lake of the Woods, etc., Performed in the Year 1823, by Order of the Honorable J. C. Calhoun, Secretary of War, under the Command of Major Stephen H. Long, U.S.T.E.; Compiled from the Notes of Major Long, Messrs. Say, Keating, and Calhoun*. Philadelphia: H. Carey and I. Lea, 1824.

Locke, John. "Earthwork Antiquities in Wisconsin Territory." In *Report of a Geological Exploration of Part of Iowa, Wisconsin, and Illinois*, by David Dale Owen. Washington, D.C.: Government Printing Office, 1844.

Martin, Morgan L. *Address Delivered before the State Historical Society of Wisconsin at Madison, January 21, 1851*. Green Bay, Wis.: Robinson & Brother, Printers, 1851.

Morgan, Lewis Henry. *Report to the Regents of the University, upon the Articles Furnished to the Indian Collection*. New York: University of the State of New York, 1850. #

Morton, Samuel George. *Crania Americana; or, A Comparative View of the Skulls of Various Aboriginal Nations of North and South America, to Which Is Prefixed an Essay on the Varieties of the Human Species*. Philadelphia: J. Dobson, 1839. #

Norwood, J. G. "Dr. J. G. Norwood's Report." In *Report of a Geological Survey of Wisconsin, Iowa, and Minnesota; and Incidentally of a Portion of Nebraska Territory*, by David Dale Owen. Philadelphia: Lippincott, Grambo & Co., 1852. *

Parrot, Friedrich. *Journey to Ararat*. New York: Harper & Brothers, 1846.

Pike, Zebulon Montgomery. *An Account of Expeditions to the Sources of the Mississippi, and through the Western Parts of Louisiana, to the Sources of the Arkansaw, Kans, La Platte, and Pierre Jaun, Rivers. . . .* Philadelphia: C. & A. Conrad, 1810.

Richardson, John. *Arctic Searching Expedition: A Journal of a Boat-Voyage through Rupert's Land and the Arctic Sea, in Search of the Discovery Ships under Command of Sir John Franklin*. New York: Harper & Brothers, 1852.

Schoolcraft, Henry Rowe. *Information Respecting the History, Condition, and Prospects of the Indian Tribes of the United States*. Philadelphia: Lippincott, Grambo & Co., 1852.

Shepard, Charles Upham. "Geology of Upper Illinois." *American Journal of Science and Arts* 34 (July 1838): 134–161. #

Spurzheim, Johann Gaspar. *Phrenology, in Connexion with the Study of Physiognomy*. Boston: Marsh, Capen & Lyon, 1833. * (Lapham's library included the 1836 edition of this book.)

Squier, Ephraim George. "Aboriginal Monuments of the State of New York." *Smithsonian Contributions to Knowledge* 2 (1850). #

Squier, Ephraim George. *Nicaragua: Its People, Scenery, Monuments, and the Proposed Interoceanic Canal.* 2 vols. New York: D. Appleton, 1852.

Squier, Ephraim George, and Edwin Hamilton Davis. "Ancient Monuments of the Mississippi Valley, Comprising the Results of Extensive Original Surveys and Explorations." *Smithsonian Contributions to Knowledge* 1 (1848). #

Stephens, John Lloyd. *Incidents of Travel in Central America, Chiapas, and Yucatán.* New York: Harper & Brothers, 1841. *

Taylor, Richard C. "Notes Respecting Certain Indian Mounds and Earthworks, in the Form of Animal Effigies, Chiefly in the Wisconsin Territory." *American Journal of Science and Arts* 34 (July 1838): 88–104. #

Taylor, S. "Description of Ancient Remains, Animal Mounds, and Embankments, Principally in the Counties of Grant, Iowa, and Richmond, in Wisconsin." *American Journal of Science and Arts* 44 (April 1843): 21–40. #

SMITHSONIAN CONTRIBUTIONS TO KNOWLEDGE.

THE

ANTIQUITIES OF WISCONSIN,

AS

SURVEYED AND DESCRIBED.

BY

I. A. LAPHAM,

CIVIL ENGINEER, ETC.,

ON BEHALF OF THE AMERICAN ANTIQUARIAN SOCIETY.

[ACCEPTED FOR PUBLICATION, DECEMBER, 1853.]

PUBLISHED BY THE SMITHSONIAN INSTITUTION,

WASHINGTON, D. C.

JUNE, 1855.

T. K. AND P. G. COLLINS, PRINTERS,
PHILADELPHIA.

NOTICE.

THE systematic exploration of the ancient remains of Wisconsin, of which the present memoir by Mr. Lapham is the result, was undertaken and accomplished by him on behalf of the American Antiquarian Society, from whose funds the necessary expenses were provided. Beyond these expenses Mr. Lapham desired and received no other compensation than the scientific enjoyment which the prosecution of the work itself afforded him.

It happened that, while these explorations were in progress, contributions from other persons relating to the earthworks of the same region were proffered to the Smithsonian Institution, whose publications in that department of American research already embraced the known antiquities of most other sections of the United States. On that account it seemed desirable that the two institutions should co-operate, and that the materials collected should be presented to the world through the same channel, and in the same style of illustration.

The suggestion was therefore made by the Smithsonian Institution to the Antiquarian Society, that, when Mr. Lapham's notes and drawings had been revised and sanctioned by the latter, the care and cost of printing the report should be assumed by the Institution. The proposition was readily acceded to, as better subserving the interests of science, since it would enable the Society to employ its funds in other researches.

In conformity with this understanding, the memoir, after having been carefully examined by a Committee of the Antiquarian Society, was submitted to the Smithsonian Institution, and accepted for publication.

Owing to the great expense attendant upon the issue of a work containing so many illustrations, the publication has been somewhat delayed. This has, however, allowed a number of important additions and corrections to be made—giving to the work still greater value as an accurate and faithful record of the interesting earthworks of Wisconsin, which are so soon to be obliterated by the march of improvement.

JOSEPH HENRY,
Secretary S. I.

Smithsonian Institution, June 1, 1855.

PREFACE.

ALTHOUGH the existence of aboriginal earthworks in the Western country has been known for almost a century, no mounds of imitative design intended to represent animal figures were observed, until a very recent period, when the territory now constituting the State of Wisconsin began to attract the attention of emigrants. This was in the year 1836, and I then made known through the newspapers of the day the fact of the existence of the "turtle-mound" at Prairie Village, now Waukesha, and of other animal effigies at various places. Since that time every opportunity has been embraced to make examinations and surveys of these highly interesting relics of the past, which have been thus not unfrequently saved from oblivion. In some instances, they were destroyed immediately or within a few days after my survey.

The American Antiquarian Society having placed at my disposal the means of paying the actual travelling and other expenses, these investigations were greatly extended; and the results are now presented, in the hope that they may have their use in the settlement of many archæological and ethnological questions of great interest and importance.

But little effort has been made to construct hypotheses in explanation of the facts observed, or by an extended comparison with the results recorded by others, to arrive at general conclusions. The want of extensive collections of books and other facilities at the West may long prevent our inquirers, here, from entering upon such speculations.

My office has been faithfully to fulfil the duties of the surveyor: to examine and investigate the facts, and to report them as much in detail as may be necessary; leaving it to others with better opportunities, to compare them, and to establish, in connection with other means of information, such general principles as may be legitimately deduced.

I. A. LAPHAM.

Milwaukee, Wis.

CONTENTS.

LIST OF PLATES.

B

LIST OF WOOD ENGRAVINGS.

INTRODUCTION.

In the arrangement of my subject, I prefer to make use of the natural features of the State, rather than the political divisions into counties. At almost every annual session of the legislature, the boundaries of old counties are changed, and new ones are established from time to time with the progress of settlement and improvement; while the natural features, the great valleys or basins and their dividing ridges, always remain the same. It is also found that this is a more natural division of the ancient works; for they lie mostly along the valleys of streams, or on the borders of the small clear crystal lakes with which the State abounds. I have also indicated localities by reference to the numbers of the sections, townships, and ranges, as adopted in the government surveys of the public lands, rather than to the names of the towns.

It has been a leading object to ascertain whether any order or system can be detected in the arrangement of the several works. With this view, the exact relative situation of groups of mounds has been carefully observed and delineated; and for the purpose of determining whether there existed any general system of arrangement extending over large districts, the accompanying map (Plate I.) has been constructed, showing the relative position of all the works of which the precise location has been ascertained. This map has been carefully reduced from the public surveys, and exhibits the general features of the State with sufficient minuteness for the purpose intended.

The first narrative in which any notice of the existence of ancient works in this State was made public, is that of Major Long's Expedition in 1823; from which the description of those at and near Prairie du Chien is copied in the following pages. The next is that of the late R. C. Taylor, in Silliman's Journal for 1838, Vol. XXXIV. Dr. John Locke made accurate measurements of several works between the Four Lakes and the Blue Mounds, published in his report on the geology of the Lead Mine District. But the most extended essay is that of Mr. S. Taylor, relating chiefly to the ancient works at and near Muscoda, on the Wisconsin River. The results of these several papers are embodied by Messrs. Squier and Davis in their "Ancient Monuments of the Mississippi Valley," constituting the first volume of the "Smithsonian Contributions to Knowledge."

As the district embraced in these researches has but recently been brought into notice, a short account of its general physical features will not be out of place here, and will aid in understanding the descriptions which follow.

1

The State of Wisconsin lies between the parallels of 42° 30′ and 47° north latitude, and between 87° and 93° of longitude west from Greenwich; or it extends from the State of Illinois on the south to Lake Superior on the north, and from Lake Michigan on the east to the Mississippi and St. Croix rivers on the west. Its area is about 55,000 square miles. About three-fifths of the State lie in the basin of the Mississippi; and the remainder is drained by the streams tributary to the waters of the Great Lakes—Superior and Michigan. The former portion is naturally divided into five great valleys, occupied by as many principal streams—the St. Croix, Chippewa, Black, Wisconsin, and Rock rivers. The latter may be divided into three parts—that drained directly into Lake Michigan, the basin of Green Bay and its tributaries, and that which is drained into Lake Superior.

These several hydrographical basins indicate also the general topography of the State. The dividing grounds between the basins attain usually but a slight elevation above the surrounding country; so that it frequently happens that a lake or marsh is drained in two opposite directions, and the water sent towards the ocean at widely different points. These water-sheds, or "divides," as they are called, attain their greatest elevation about the sources of the Montreal River; where there is found a continuation into Wisconsin of the Porcupine Mountains of the Lake Superior Mining District. At one point near this place, the ridge is about 1,150 feet above Lake Michigan;[1] while at the western boundary of the State it is diminished to about 500 feet. The region around the source of the Wisconsin River is a grand summit, from which the rivers flow in every direction like the radii of a circle. They run into the Mississippi River, Lake Superior, and Green Bay.

The surface of Wisconsin may be characterized as nearly level, or gently rolling, except along the banks of the Mississippi, and the lower portions of some of its principal tributaries, where it is more broken, and where steep rocky cliffs and precipitous hills abound. There are also prominent peaks in this region, which tower above the general surface, so as to form conspicuous objects in the landscape; of these the Blue Mounds are the most elevated, being 1,224 feet above Lake Michigan.

There is a ridge of broken land running from near the peninsula between Lake Michigan and Green Bay, in a southwesterly direction, through the western parts of Manitowoc, Sheboygan, Washington, and Waukesha counties, and thence into Walworth and Rock counties. It is from three to five hundred feet in height, with an occasional peak of even eight hundred feet above Lake Michigan, and consists of irregular elevations and depressions throughout its whole course. At places the depressions are more regular, and from their round form are called "potash kettles." They are doubtless owing to the decay and gradual washing away of the soft and easily decomposed limestone by which the ridge is probably underlaid.

Another prominent feature in the topography of Eastern Wisconsin, is the cliff or escarpment of limestone resembling the "mountain ridge" of Western New

---

[1] U. S. Geological Reports.

York, extending along the eastern shore of Green Bay, and thence, in the same general direction, through Brown, Calumet, Fond-du-Lac, and the eastern part of Dodge counties. It constitutes the cliffs along the east side of Lake Winnebago; and interrupts the flow of the rivers west of it in their course towards Lake Michigan, turning them northward into Green Bay. From its crest another system of rivers originates, which, running in the same general direction, flow into Lake Michigan. Immediately west of this bold escarpment commences a remarkable series of ridges, probably caused by "drift" agencies (whatever they may have been), and of which some notice will be found in the following pages.[1]

The moderate elevations, and the gentle declivities of the several valleys, cause the waters to flow in slow and uniform currents, and to assume, in very numerous instances, the form of lakes of greater or less extent. It is precisely such localities that afford the greatest facilities for Indian population. During the hunting season, the wild man roams over the vast forests and prairies; but his village is always established near some lake or gently flowing river, abounding in fish and wild rice, and affording him a subsistence, either directly or indirectly, by enticing within his reach innumerable animals that seek their food at the same place.

---

[1] See Plate XXXVIII.

CHAPTER I.

ANCIENT WORKS IN THE VICINITY OF LAKE MICHIGAN.

THE most southerly point on the west shore of Lake Michigan where traces of ancient labor can be found, is about four miles south of the "State line" between Wisconsin and Illinois. These works are doubtless burial-places, and consist of a series of round or conical mounds, nine in number, from three to five feet in height, and about thirty feet in diameter, arranged in a serpentine row along the crest of a ridge of sand, an ancient lake beach, which extends for many miles along the lake shore. (See Fig. 1.) We first saw this beach in the road three miles north of Racine, and traced it at intervals into the State of Illinois. It has an elevation estimated at fifty feet above the present level of the lake, and at the mounds affords a good view of the country on both sides. It is here about half a mile

FIG. 1.

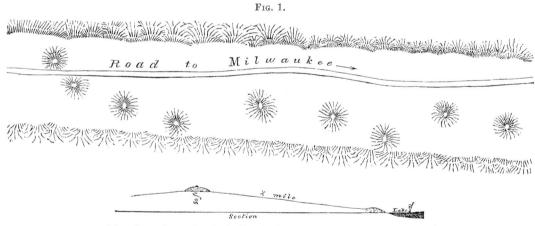

Mounds on the ancient Lake Beach, four miles south of the State line.

distant from the lake. It consists of sand and gravel, and rests upon a bed of hard clay. There is no doubt that this ridge extends south to the end of the lake, and is connected with the remarkable series of ridges described by Prof. Shepard.[1] It is occupied by the main road from Milwaukee to Chicago, and is frequently so broad on the top as to afford room for buildings.

We saw no other mounds, nor could we hear of any in this vicinity. Some surveys, however, made by Professor Lathrop, indicate that the "turtle" form extends down Rock River as far as Rockford, or within six miles of the Kishwaukee. Traces

---

[1] Amer. Journ. of Science and Arts, XXXIV. 134.

were discovered between this place and the State line. We were told that the row
of mounds found here was straight; but examination shows it to be otherwise.
Their serpentine arrangement is not, however, deemed a matter of much importance; for where no efforts were made to secure regularity, some such disposition of
the mounds would be quite natural. A few miles south of this place is the town of
Waukegan, which was formerly called Little Fort, in commemoration of the fact
that something once existed there supposed to be the remains of a small fort; but
whether or not it was the work of the aborigines, is not known.

At the city of Kenosha we found, on the ancient sandy beach upon which the
city is partly built, abundant evidence of a former manufactory of arrow-heads
and other articles of flint. Several entire specimens were collected after a little
search, besides numerous fragments that appear to have been spoiled in the process
of chipping them into form. It is not easy to conceive how such work could be
done at all with the scanty tools of the natives; and we are not surprised to find
that there were many failures. The chips, or small fragments of flint, were very
abundant in numerous places along the sandy ridge, especially near the "Durkee
House," and in the vicinity of the burial-ground immediately south of the city.
Many different kinds of flint, or more properly of chert, appear to have been
wrought at this place, as is shown by the fragments. It is quite probable that
the pebbles or boulders along the lake shore furnished the material employed by
these early manufacturers; for flint of the same kind may be seen there in abundance. These pebbles are from the corniferous rock of Eaton, and here constitute
a portion of the drift, being associated with the tough blue clay that underlies
the sand, and is the basis of the whole country around. The clay is carried away
by the dashing waves, leaving a beach of clean pebbles, kept constantly smooth
and round by attrition. Numerous fragments of pottery, of the usual form and
composition, were also found on the same sandy places.

No ancient works were noticed along the valley of the Des Plaines[1] River, which
here lies between Lake Michigan and the Pishtaka River.

Proceeding northward from Kenosha, along the west shore of Lake Michigan,
the next evidences of ancient labor are found at Racine; showing that, notwith-
standing the great difference between the moral, social, political, and other conditions of the red and white man, they usually fix upon the same points as
favorite places of residence. The map (Plate II.) will convey to the reader a
correct idea of the interesting groups of works at this place. In the examination
of them, and in the preparation of this map, I have been materially assisted by
Dr. P. R. Hoy, of Racine. The works occupy the high ground bordering upon
Root River, from one to two miles from the margin of the lake, and immediately
back of the city limits. They consist mostly of circular burial-mounds, of no great
size or height, with one circular inclosure, and several tapering ridges. There are
also two semicircles opening on the edge of the bluff towards the river. The group
of very numerous and remarkable mounds represented at the lower part of Plate II.

---

[1] Usually called "Aux Plaines."

was surveyed with some minuteness, with a view to detecting the order of arrangement upon which they were constructed. The result shows very clearly that no order or system was adopted. Each person buried was placed where chance might lead the relatives or friends to select the spot. No three mounds could be found on the same straight line; indeed, it seems as if it were the intention of the builders to avoid all appearance of regularity. Large mounds are interspersed with smaller ones, without regard to symmetry or succession.

Dr. Hoy has recently opened one of these mounds, and found in it the skeletons of seven persons, buried in a sitting posture, and facing the east. (See Fig. 2.) The bones were not accompanied by ornaments or articles of any kind that had resisted the destructive effects of time. The teeth of the adult skeletons were much worn,

FIG. 2.

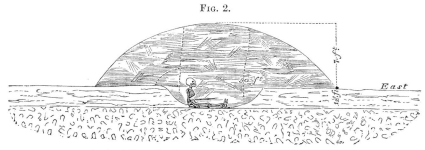

Ancient Mound at Racine, examined by Dr. P. R. Hoy.

but sound and firm. It was observed that the muscles of the jaws must have been unusually large and strong. The bones of the skull, except in one instance (probably that of a female), were found to be remarkably thick and solid. These skeletons were much decayed, and could not be restored. The mound opened was seven feet high and fifty feet in diameter, being the largest of the group. A basin-shaped excavation had been made in the original soil, about eighteen inches deep, reaching to the gravelly subsoil, upon which the skeletons were placed side by side, all facing in the same direction. The legs, which had been laid horizontally, retained their original position; but the skulls and bones of the bodies were huddled together by the settling upon them of the earth in which they were placed. There were no indications of fire.

Another mound of smaller dimensions, opened under my inspection, contained a confused mass of bones, also very much decayed, and resting upon the gravel, which was here two feet below the original surface. Bones of at least three individuals were discovered. Their confused condition might be owing to the custom, still prevalent among the Indians, of placing the bodies of those who die or are killed away from home, in trees, where they remain until the softer parts are decayed and gone, when the bones are collected and buried. No ornaments, or indeed remains of articles of any kind, could be found in this mound; nor was here any charcoal, burnt clay, or other indication of fire.

These mounds were made from the surface soil; and no traces of excavations, or places whence the materials were taken, could be detected. It is not probable that the earth was penetrated more than a few inches to obtain the quantity necessary to form the mounds, some of which are quite small, not more than one or two feet in height above the original surface of the ground. They are of various dimensions, from five to fifty feet in diameter, and from one to seven feet in height. Many of them are now nearly levelled by the plough. They may still, however, be detected in the cultivated fields by a trifling elevation, or by a slight difference in the color of the soil. In one case, at least, the plough had turned up the bones from beneath.

The plank road leading from the city to Rochester and Burlington, on the Pishtaka River,[1] passes near this great group of ancient mounds. Many of them are on the line of another road, and are levelled from time to time by the inhabitants in working out their road tax, without regard to the sacred deposits they contain; and in a few years, all traces of them will be gone for ever. This spot was probably the common cemetery for the neighboring tribes, and not their place of residence. Its situation, on the level ground back from the river and bluff, and at the head of a deep and narrow ravine, may be adduced as an evidence of this. The fact that seven bodies were buried in one mound apparently at the same time, and three or more in another, seems to indicate that many died simultaneously by some calamity.

Subsequently to my visit to this locality, Dr. Hoy informs me that he " had the good fortune to obtain two vases of pottery from one of the mounds. They were in a gravel-pit, two feet and a half below the original surface of the ground, in immediate contact with the fragments of two skeletons much decayed. One is made of cream-colored clay and white sand, quite similar in composition to our pale bricks. It has a nearly uniform thickness of about one-fifth of an inch, and was originally quite smooth and hard. I have so far restored it as to render it a good specimen. It would hold about five quarts, being seven inches in diameter at the mouth, and eleven and a half inches high. The other is of a red, brick color, about half as large, much thicker and coarser, and crumbled a good deal in handling. A considerable portion of gravel was used in connection with the clay in its fabrication."

Dr. Hoy further adds: "Some workmen, in digging a ditch through a peat swamp, near Racine, found a deposit of disks of hornstone, about thirty in number. They were immediately on the clay at the bottom of the peat, about two feet and a half below the surface. Some of the disks were quite regular; they vary from half a pound to a pound in weight."

The following account of the ancient works near Racine, furnished by Dr. Hoy, will be found to contain additional details, with some inferences in regard to their age, and the character of the people who made them.

"The most numerous and extensive group is situated one mile west of the city. It embraces sepulchral mounds, all small, from one to eight feet high, unaccompanied by circles, effigies, or other earth-works. The city cemetery, just located, embraces a part of these mounds, which will be preserved, adding not only beauty but interest to the rural spot.

---

[1] Or Fox River of the Illinois.

"On the point of the high bluff marked A on the map (Plate II.) is a mound six feet high, in connection with an embankment 235 feet long. This embankment is two feet high, and twelve feet wide at the point nearest to the mound, and tapers gradually to a mere point at its western extremity, near a spring. I am informed that there were formerly other works connected with this, which have been obliterated by cultivation and other improvements. (An enlarged plan of this interesting group is shown on Plate II.)

"A little further east, on the same side of the river, is a single low mound, occupying the projecting point of a bluff. Opposite this, on the north bank of the stream, there is a cluster of mounds crowded into a small space, bounded on the east by a long mound, and on the west by a 'lizard mound'[1] eighty feet long.

"The remaining works, situated on the bluff north of those last named, consist of three lizards, one oblong and six conical tumuli, and three inclosures. The two semicircular embankments are situated on an almost inaccessible bluff eighty feet high. The embankments are slight, not over one foot in elevation, and ten or twelve feet broad, but perfectly distinct and well defined. There is some evidence that they formerly constituted graded ways leading to the river. They are tolerably well situated for works of defence, but, without the addition of palisades, could afford no protection. The small circle, from its size and position, could scarcely have been designed for a work of defence. Neither of these has any perceptible ditch on either side; if one formerly existed, it is now obliterated. The 'lizards' are much alike, from two to two and a half feet high, and from twelve to fourteen feet broad at the shoulders, the tail gradually tapering to a point. The longest is 130 feet, and the shortest 80 feet in length.

"In addition to the works represented on Plate II., there is a cluster of eight mounds, situated on a sandy ridge, three-fourths of a mile further south.

"I opened one of the lizards, but found nothing. We excavated fourteen of the mounds, some with the greatest possible care; they are all sepulchral, of a uniform construction, as represented by Fig. 2. Most of them contained more than one skeleton; in one instance, we found no less than seven. We could detect no appearance of stratification, each mound having been built at one time, and not by successive additions. During these investigations, we obtained sufficient evidence to warrant me in forming the following conclusions. The bodies were regularly buried in a sitting or partly kneeling posture, facing the east, with the legs flexed under them. They were covered with a bark or log roofing, over which the mound was built. The apparent confusion in which the skeletons are sometimes found, is owing to their falling over at different angles, at the time, perhaps, of the giving way and caving in of the temporary roofing. It is quite common to find skeletons before reaching the primitive receptacle or pit. These were undoubtedly subsequent interments, made by the modern Indians. They are in a

---

[1] This appellation is given for convenience to a class of mounds having two projections or legs on one side near the larger extremity, without pretending that they were actually intended to represent lizards.

2

different state of preservation, and are mostly found in an extended posture. All the primitive crania were crushed and flattened by the weight of the superincumbent materials. In two instances, however, I succeeded, by great care and labor, in restoring these flattened fragments to their original shape. One of them is represented on Plate LIII. It was found in one of the mounds of the crowded group on the north side of the river. The two are much alike, and quite different in several particulars from the various Indian crania that I have examined. The zygomatic arch has not the same projection, the angle of the cheek-bone is more obtuse, and the orbits are rather less angular than in the modern Indian. The heavy, projecting jaw, and the flattened occiput, are quite characteristic of these ancient mound skulls. Facial angle, 76°. Internal capacity, eighty cubic inches.

"No implements or ornaments were observed in the mounds, excepting in three instances, in which rude pottery was found. The shape of the pots is precisely similar to those said to be used by the Burmese for all culinary operations. They place three stones in a triangle to support the pot in a perpendicular position.

"The disks of hornstone were obtained while digging a ditch through a peat swamp one-fourth of a mile south of the mounds represented on the plate. (Plate II.) About forty were taken out. They were situated immediately on the clay stratum, underneath the peat, which was two feet thick at this point. A number of arrow-heads and stone axes have been found in the vicinity.

"In regard to the antiquity of the works at Racine, it may be stated that, on the mound from which I obtained the pottery, there was a burr-oak stump (*Quercus macrocarpa*), which contained two hundred and fifty rings; and the tree was cut ten years since, when the land was first occupied. Near this I excavated another mound, on the centre of which were the remains of a large stump which must have been much older. Immediately under the centre of this stump I obtained the cranium before mentioned. A stump on the long mound at A (Plate II.) has 310 rings; and near by are the remains of a large tree, and an oak stump five feet in diameter. These facts indicate an antiquity of at least a thousand years.

"In conclusion, I must remark that whatever be the legitimate inference drawn from similar works and remains in other places, concerning the state of civilization attained by the mound-builders, the evidence here goes to prove that they were an extremely barbarous people, in no respect superior to most of the savage tribes of the modern Indians."

Much care has been taken to present an exact figure of the skull discovered by Dr. Hoy, which he proposes to contribute to the museum of the Smithsonian Institution.

Between Racine and Milwaukee we found a single mound, which was six feet high, and the remains of one or two more about half a mile below the place where the main road crosses Oak Creek. This mound was more than usually steep on its sides, and may consequently be supposed to be of recent origin, time not having levelled it down as much as those of greater antiquity. A mound that had been removed several years since, disclosed a number of skeletons of human beings, and an earthen cup said to hold about a pint.[1]

---

[1] During the investigations of which the results are here given, I was often led to examine places supposed to be the work of the aborigines, but which proved to be attributable to other than artificial causes. On the northwest quarter of section fifteen, in the town of Lake, three miles south of Milwaukee, are three elevations, supposed by some to be artificial. They are composed of gravel and small boulders, and fragments of limestone; materials seldom used by the mound-builders. They are larger than any artificial mounds heretofore discovered in this State, though not larger than some in Ohio and other portions of the West. There are numerous other swells similar to these in the vicinity, though not so regularly conical. These undulations of the surface were produced by the same causes that transported to this region from the north the vast superficial deposits known to geologists under the name of drift. One mile north of this place we stopped to examine an embankment extending across the road, which was at first supposed to be artificial, and to represent the "serpent." (See Fig. 3.)

Fig. 3.

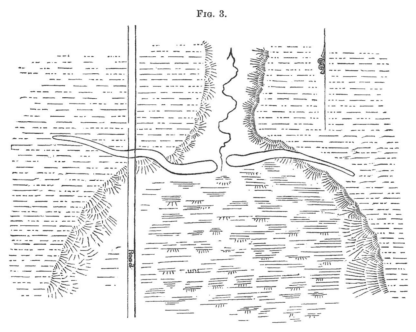

Beaver dam, four miles south from Milwaukee.

It was traced for about 150 feet west of the road, where it gradually disappeared as the sloping ground became more elevated. Towards the east it gradually enlarged. It was irregularly curved, or serpentine, in its shape. At a short distance to the east it had been worn through by a small stream, but continued again, until it gradually disappeared as before, on the gently rising ground beyond the creek. It had evidently once been continuous across the stream, where it was largest and highest. Above the embankment was a marsh covered with flags (*Iris versicolor*) and sedges (a species of *Carex*), where evidently a pond had once existed. This embankment was the work of the beaver, being the remains of a "beaver dam." These industrious animals have left as indelible traces of their former existence here as have the mound-builders. Their works are scattered very extensively over the State, causing, as in this instance, many of the "cat-holes," or marshy places in the woods. The remains of their "washes," left on the sloping banks above the dams, have been mistaken for Indian excavations in search of lead or other ores, &c.

But the most remarkable natural appearances we were led to examine were the ridges in a large natural meadow in the town of Brookfield, Waukesha County, which were supposed to be artificial

The relative position and extent of the earthworks in the vicinity of Milwaukee, will appear on reference to the map, Plate III. They extend from Kinnickinnic Creek, near the place known as the Indian Fields, to a point six miles above the city. It will be observed that they occupy the high grounds along the margin of the river and streams, but not on the immediate shore of the lake. Although the mound-builders often occupied the margin of the smaller lakes in the interior, they seldom or never selected the immediate shore of Lake Michigan for the site of their works.

---

representations of the Massasauga rattle-snake. My attention was first called to them by Mr. M. Spears, who detected them. They vary from a few inches to two feet in height, above the otherwise uniformly level surface of the marshy ground; and in length they vary from ten or fifteen to one hundred and forty feet. Many of them are obtuse at one end, and tapering and acute at the other, as if intended to represent the head and tail of a snake; others are acute at both extremities. (See Fig. 4.) The accompanying figures show their appearance and relative situation. Some are so

FIG. 4.

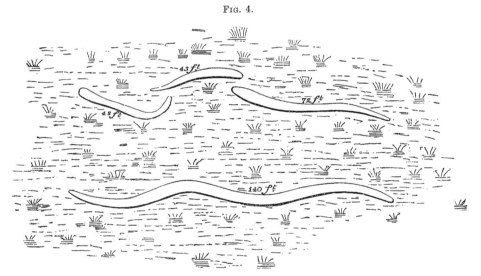

Serpent-form ridges, Brookfield.

arranged that, were they larger and differently situated, we might suppose them portions of a fort, with a guarded entrance. They are composed of the same black mucky earth that constitutes the surface soil of the marsh. They have all the same general direction, being parallel, or nearly so, with that of the marsh. There are great numbers of these ridges, not less, perhaps, than one hundred on this marsh.

To understand how these ridges were probably formed, we must take into account the soft nature of the surface soil; and the fact that, except in the driest portion of the year, it is completely saturated or covered with water. The ice formed on the surface in winter must therefore include a considerable portion of the soil. During very cold weather, this covering of ice contracts, leaving in the middle of the marsh numerous irregular cracks, probably assuming the arrangement and directions of these ridges. As the temperature moderates, the ice expands, closing up the cracks, but moving towards them a portion of the soil, and leaving a slight elevation. The next winter, the same thing is repeated; but the ice being thinner on these slight ridges, it would naturally separate where they occur: and thus the same ridges are enlarged from year to year, until they assume the size and shape now so much resembling serpents. We afterwards saw similar ridges in several other marshes.

The banks of rivers appear to have been their favorite localities; and in this respect they resemble the present Indians, who select sites commanding a view of the country around them (so as to be able to detect the first approach of an enemy), and near hunting and fishing grounds. They appear also to have had an eye for the beautiful as well as the useful, in choosing their places of abode.

From the same hills on which are found these mounds, the workmen, in grading streets, digging foundations for buildings, preparing terraces for gardens, &c., often disinter the skeleton of an Indian, with its accompanying ornaments, and perhaps his brass kettle placed at the head. A number of the skulls thus brought to light were sent to Dr. S. G. Morton, to be used in the preparation of his Crania Americana.[1]

The bluffs along the Milwaukee River, on which these works are mostly situated, have an elevation of from 30 to 100 feet above the water. They are usually quite steep, though not so much so, except in one or two places, as to be precipitous.

There is evidence, drawn from the presence of deposits of fresh-water shells in layers of sand and gravel, that the waters of the lake at this place once stood at a level considerably above their present height; and at that time much of the site of the present city was submerged. The bluffs were then washed by the waters of the bay, and presented steep broken fronts. The banks were gradually undermined, and slides of considerable extent occurred precisely as is now seen on the present margin of the lake. Whether this subsidence was subsequent to the erection of the mounds, is uncertain, their situation being such as to throw no definite light upon the subject. There are no works below that level that can lay claim to great antiquity.

The ancient works about Milwaukee are most numerous at a place near the small creek called the Kinnickinnic, and on lands known as the Indian Fields. They are chiefly in section twelve, township six, and range twenty-one, town of Greenfield. When the country was first settled (in 1836), the place was destitute of trees, and exhibited signs of recent Indian occupancy and cultivation. The creek borders it on the south and west, and an extensive swamp on the north and east, thus separating it from the adjacent country, and rendering it secure from sudden surprise or attack, without the necessity of extensive works of defence. It will be observed, as we proceed, that similar circumstances were often taken advantage of by these careful people.

The fields lie at a considerable elevation above the bottom-lands of the creek, and are much broken and uneven in surface. The soil is loose, sandy, or gravelly, and could be easily worked by the rude instruments of the aborigines; which may have been an inducement for selecting this spot. The subsoil is gravel, to an unknown depth. The Milwaukee and Janesville plank road passes through the fields; and the wood land adjoining has been adopted on account of its gravelly soil, undulating surface, and beautiful forest-trees, as the site of a cemetery for the city, named appropriately the " Forest Home."

---

[1] See that work, p. 179.

About fifty circular mounds, and four or five of the lizard form, have been found here. Some of these can yet be traced, though the plough has made sad havoc with most of them. Two of the latter class were here associated in a manner not observed elsewhere in the State. (See Fig. 5.) One is two hundred

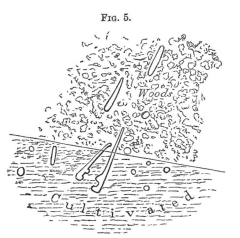

FIG. 5.

and fifty feet in length. It is not asserted that these figures were meant by the builders to represent an animal of the lizard form, or an animal at all. Still their great numbers in the eastern part of the State, and their uniformity of general outline, show that this peculiarity of form was not without design. It has been suggested that they may have been intended to represent a war-club with points set in, as is common among some savage tribes; but the attenuated form of the extremity would seem to oppose this idea.

As is the case with the works of other forms, there are no two precisely alike in their dimensions, or in their direction with reference to the cardinal points. But it has been observed that the larger extremity, or head, is usually directed *towards the south*. They vary in length from one hundred to four hundred feet. The usual height of the body may be stated at four feet; from which there is commonly a gradual diminution both in height and width to the extremity. It is frequently impossible to decide exactly where it terminates. They are almost always associated with mounds of round or oblong form, usually having about the same general direction. When they occupy the edge of elevated ground, the head generally points obliquely towards the low ground; and the projections or "legs" are on the side towards the ridge. (See Plate V.)

On the land of Mr. Geo. O. Tiffany, half a mile south of Forest Home Cemetery, is a sort of inclosure opposite some very large springs. (See Plate IV. No 1.) The walls are about eighteen inches high, and three or four feet wide. It is on a level flat, from which there is a descent of about eight feet to the springs. The wall is double, as shown by the figure, the outer one interrupted by two gateways. There are some irregular excavations within the inclosure. Large trees grow upon and near the works, constituting a dense forest of thrifty growth. The flat on which these works are built terminates in the rear by high hills surmounted by the mounds before described.

There can be no doubt that this wall of earth is the only remaining trace of some building erected here on account of the copious springs opposite the main opening; but the nature of the edifice can only be conjectured. Perhaps it may have consisted of palisades or timbers set in the ground, against which a bank of earth was erected to secure greater strength and permanency. There is no regular ditch accompanying the wall, as is found in similar works in New York and elsewhere. Immediately above these works another was traced, with a ditch very irregular in its form, direction, and dimensions, which proved to have been the work of the beaver. This industrious little animal had here set up a colony, and erected his works; his "nation" has had its rise, and its decline and fall, since the aboriginal structures were abandoned.

Further up the creek, on the west side, north of the plank road, and not far from some very large mounds, are three similar works, except that they are not on the immediate bank of the creek. Two of them are represented in Fig. 6.

FIG. 6.

The inclosure is about one hundred feet long, and thirty wide, in its greatest dimensions. The opening at d appears to have been caused by the washing away of the earth by the rain that fell within the inclosure. The walls were nine feet wide and one foot high. The small size of these inclosures prevents their ranking with the "works of defence" or other extensive embankments described in the first and second volumes of the Smithsonian Contributions; and we can only suppose them to be the remains of ancient buildings, or structures of some kind, needful in the simple condition of those who erected them.

A few rods east of the cemetery, on the land of Mrs. Hull, may be seen a remarkable excavation, surrounded in part by the earth thrown from it. (See Plate IX. Fig. 1.) It has four sloping ways or entrances, one of them very much elongated; and the reader will not fail to discover in its general figure that of a lizard mound reversed. There are other similar excavations to be described hereafter; from some of which, if we could take a cast and reverse it, we should have an exact representation of a lizard mound.

At Walker's Point were several circular mounds and lizard mounds, now dug away in the process of grading streets. One of them, exhibited in section, was

FIG. 7.

Lizard mound, Walker's Point.

examined during the excavation, and found to be composed of whitish clay, of uniform texture and appearance. The blue, yellow, and red clays, found abundantly in the country, all assume a whitish color upon exposure at the surface; and it is, therefore, not difficult to account for the difference in the color of the clay composing this mound, without resorting to the improbable conjecture that it was brought from a great distance. The several layers of soil, brown subsoil, and blue clay, run uninterruptedly under the mound, showing that it was built upon the natural surface. (See Fig. 7.) No excavation had been made, and no relics of any kind were found in it. Indeed, the animal-shaped mounds have never been found productive in ancient relics or works of art. It was probably for purposes other than the burial of the dead, that these structures were made.

Only one locality has been discovered on the east side of the Milwaukee River where the mound-builders erected their mysterious works. This was at the intersection of Johnson and Main streets, where there were formerly two lizard mounds, and some others, as represented on Plate V. On one of these is given the dimensions in feet, showing the method usually adopted in surveying these earthworks. One of the mounds has a slight angle near the extremity of the tail, as represented in the plate; but this is not very common. The other figure is of the more common form. These figures are in their normal position, being on high ground near the edge of a hill or bank, their heads towards the south, legs towards the bank, and their general direction obliquely towards the edge of the bank. A simple oval mound, and one with arms or wings, are seen near the lizards; and a few rods to the north was an oval ring, whose diameters were forty-four and thirty-one feet. The wall was nine feet wide, and only one foot in height.

On the west side of the river, within the limits of the city, were numerous mounds occupying the several promontories overlooking the city and bay. The most remarkable group was near the intersection of Walnut with Sixth Street, as represented on Plate VI. Four different varieties of structures may be seen. The oblong (a), which is simply a ridge of earth; the lizard (b), an elongated ridge terminating in a point at one end, and having two projections or legs at the other; the winged mound (c), being a circular tumulus, with two long, slightly curved arms or wings; and the anomalous mound (d), differing from the ordinary form by having the legs on opposite sides, instead of the same side. These works were, in 1836, covered with a dense forest. The oblong, at a in the plan, appears to have been the "observatory," being in a very conspicuous place, from which may be seen all the works, while in the opposite direction there is presented a magnificent view of the valley of the river, and the bay of Lake Michigan, now called Milwaukee Bay. It is eighty-three feet long, twenty wide, and four in height.

Two of these mounds were opened, but produced nothing beyond the fragment of a bone, and a slight admixture of carbonaceous matter near the original surface. They were composed of the same tough, reddish, sandy clay that constitutes the adjacent soil. There are two large natural elevations or mounds near these works, and upon the summit of one was a small "winged mound." The other, though the largest, was apparently not occupied by the aborigines. In that part of the city known as Sherman's Addition, we first find mounds of undoubted animal forms. One of these (Plate IV. Fig. 2) is on ground covered by the corn hills of the present race of Indians, who occupied the lands in this vicinity down to a very late period. It may be considered as a rude representation of a wolf or fox guarding the sacred deposits in the large though low mound immediately before it. Both of these are of so little elevation as to be scarcely observed by the passer by; but when once attention is arrested, there is no difficulty in tracing their outlines. The body of the animal is forty-four feet, and the tail sixty-three in length. A more graceful animal form was found on block No. 36. (See Plate VII. Fig. 2.) It may be regarded as the representation of an otter. Length of head and neck, twenty-six feet; body, fifty feet; tail, seventy feet. Its direction is a little south of west.

Whatever may be said in regard to the mounds which I have denominated "lizards," there can be no doubt that they do, and were intended to represent the forms of animals. But what shall we say of the next figure (Plate VII. Fig. 3), with its long, slightly curved arms? If, like some others hereafter described, it had a beak, it would be considered a representation of one of the feathered tribe; or, if it had legs as well as a body, it might be deemed a rude imitation of the human form. We may suppose that in the lapse of ages these works have been more or less modified by natural causes, and also that portions were constructed of different and more perishable materials, now entirely gone. This figure points almost directly south. It is thirty-four feet long, the arms being sixty feet. It was surveyed by me a number of years since, and was almost immediately afterwards removed to prepare the foundation of a house. How many more of these interesting structures have been lost to the antiquary, by being destroyed before a plan and record of them were made, it is impossible to determine; but their number must be very great.

Proceeding up the river, we find the next works on the school section, between the plank road from Milwaukee to Humboldt and the river. (See Plate VII. No. 4.) They consist of three lizard mounds, and four of the oblong form, occupying a high level plateau completely covered with the original forest trees.

We next find, on sections twenty-nine and thirty, in township eight, and range twenty-two, on the west side of the river, at a place usually known as the Indian Prairie, about five miles north of the city of Milwaukee, a very interesting system or group of works. They are situated on a beautiful level plain, elevated about thirty feet above the river, which runs along the eastern border. The bank of the river is nearly perpendicular, forming a safe protection against attack from that direction. It may be seen by the map presented (Plate VIII.), that these works are further protected on the north and south by deep ravines. The works are all included within these natural defences. Whether they were ever protected on the west seems doubtful. No traces of embankment or ditch could be found, nor any indication of other modes of defence usually adopted by uncivilized nations. There may have been defences of wood, long since decayed.

There are two principal mounds situated near the middle of this space. They are both fifty-three feet in diameter at the base, where they almost touch each other, and eight feet high. The southern one has a level area of twenty-five feet diameter at the top.

3

It often occurs in a group of works like this, that one mound is erected on the highest position, from the top of which the whole may be seen. These may be called the "Observatories," a name that in this case belongs to the mound with the level area. It may also have been the place of sacrifice or altar-mound; but of this we can only judge from the analogy in form and position to similar works which elsewhere were undoubtedly used for that purpose. Surrounding these are numerous tumuli of a circular form, the exact relative positions of which were ascertained by survey, and represented on the map. No definite system or order of arrangement was observed, as will be evident on inspection.

These tumuli are from two to four feet high, and from ten to fifty-four feet in diameter at the base; many of them being unusually broad in proportion to their height. None are so high and prominent as the two first mentioned. The two mounds in the form of a cross at the southern extremity of this group will at once attract the attention of the reader. An enlarged plan is given of one, with its dimensions. The head of the cross is level on the top and rectangular. This form of mound is frequently found in Wisconsin.

But what marks this locality as one of peculiar interest, is the discovery of five works of excavation, of regular form, being the reverse of the usual works. Instead of an embankment of earth thrown up, we have here a cavity in the ground. Four of the excavations lie in a southwest direction from the two larger central mounds. In approaching the former from the latter, a small trail or path is discovered, which gradually becomes larger and deeper, until it leads into a sunken area surrounded by embankments, composed probably of the earth thrown out of the excavation. Upon looking back, it is perceived that this pathway goes directly to the mounds. These excavations are shown on an enlarged scale on Plate IX. Figures 2 and 3. There are usually three curved entrances to each excavation, as shown in the figures.

The other excavation is similar to these, except that it lacks the long guarded way or approach, leading towards a mound; though the principal openings are towards the "Observatories." (Plate IX. Fig. 4.) It is quite probable that the bottom of these pits was once level, and that the sides were perpendicular, or nearly so; but now they have a gentle slope, and the bottom is concave, as shown by the sections. (Plate IX. Figs. 2 and 4.) With our present limited knowledge of the habits of the people who constructed these works, it would perhaps be idle to attempt to conjecture for what purposes the excavations were made. What structures of wood may have been connected with them is of course unknown. All traces of so perishable a material would long since have entirely disappeared.

The earth thrown from one of these excavations encroaches slightly upon the path leading to another, thus indicating (unless this circumstance has been caused by rains), that they were made at different times. Indeed, it is hardly to be supposed that any extensive system of works was ever planned out by the aborigines, and built up at one time. Those we find were doubtless the results of successive efforts, perhaps by separate and distinct generations, and even in some instances by distinct tribes.

We observed four small circular inclosures, about thirty feet in diameter, the ridge having no great breadth or elevation. One circle surrounded a cavity two feet deep, in which was growing a group of basswood-trees (*Tilia americana*) of large size. There are at this locality two crosses, two oblong and twenty-two circular mounds, and five excavations.

Although this spot has long since ceased to be the residence of an Indian population, yet it is annually visited by a few families, and numerous traces of their presence are still visible. Many of the mounds have been opened for the burial of the remains of Indians recently deceased; and we saw on one mound three graves but lately formed. They were secured from the ravages of the wolves and other animals, by logs of wood held in their places by four stakes, in the manner represented on Plate VIII. Only one kind of wood is used on the same grave, there being no mixture of different trees on any. One grave was covered with logs of iron-wood (*Ostrya virginica*), the other two with those of oak; even the stakes are of the same wood as the logs. These logs were from four to six inches in diameter, and four and a half feet long. The grounds in the neighborhood, and for some distance north and south of the ravines forming the boundaries of the more ancient works, are covered with those common mammillary elevations known as "Indian corn-hills." They are without order of arrangement, being scattered over the surface with the utmost irregularity. That these hillocks were formed in the manner indicated by their name, is inferred from the present custom of the Indians. The corn is planted in the same spot each successive year, and the soil is gradually brought up to the size of a little hill by the annual additions. This is the work of the women.

At the southern extremity of these remains, another evidence of former cultivation occurs, consisting of low, broad, parallel ridges, as if corn had been planted in drills. They average four feet in width, twenty-five of them having been counted in the space of a hundred feet; and the depth of the walk between them is about six inches. These appearances, which are here denominated "ancient garden-beds," indicate an earlier and more perfect system of cultivation than that which now prevails; for the present Indians do not appear to possess the ideas of taste and order necessary to enable them to arrange objects in consecutive rows. Traces of this kind of cultivation, though not very abundant, are found in several other parts of the State.

But, however ancient these garden-beds may be, they were not made until long after the erection of the earthworks; for, as will be seen (Plate VIII.), they extend across them in the same manner as they do the adjoining grounds. Hence it is evident that this cultivation was not until after the mounds had lost their sacred character in the eyes of the occupants of the soil; for it can hardly be supposed that works executed with so much care would be thus desecrated by their builders. The original inhabitants must therefore have been succeeded at an early period by probably another race, and the labors of the white man have consequently not alone tended to obliterate these vestiges of an ancient people.

We have thus traced four probable epochs in the history of this interesting locality. 1st. The period of the mound-builders, who, perhaps, selected it on account of its naturally secure position. 2d. That of the "garden-bed" cultivators.   3d. That of occupancy by the modern race of Indians.   4th. The present period, when their descendants continue to visit it, and to bring hither the remains of their departed friends.

A few circular mounds, but no other works, are found near Saukville, on the Milwaukee River, in Ozaukee County.   At this place was discovered one of the most regular and best finished stone axes that we have obtained.   A little further west, on the road to Newburgh, is a group of oblong embankments, occupying the end and flanks of a ridge, as represented on Plate X.   Here is a mound established, as is usual, on the highest point; and if the forest were removed, it would command a very extensive view of the surrounding country.   Whether the peculiar arrangement of these oblong elevations is the result of design or accident, is not easily determined.   There can be little doubt that the place was a station for a look-out, or post of a sentinel, whose duty it might be to give notice of the approach of an enemy, or perhaps to detect the presence of game in the country. The earthworks are not of such magnitude, nor are they so arranged, as to justify the conclusion that they constituted a work of defence; and they may be only receptacles of the last remains of some distinguished persons.

On the south side of the Milwaukee River, in the town of Trenton, are several groups of works not visited by me.   One of them, surveyed by my friend, Mr. L. L. Sweet, is represented on Plate X., and, as described by him, consists of a turtle, two crosses, two club-shaped, three oblong, and five conical mounds.   They are situated on lots numbered six and seven, of section eighteen, in township eleven, and range twenty.   "I carefully noted," says Mr. Sweet, "the dimensions, &c., of the most important of these mounds, and send you the result.   The largest cruciform figure is one hundred and eighty-five feet in length of trunk; the head, twenty-four feet long; the arms, seventy-two feet each; the height at the head, three feet ten inches; at the centre, four feet six inches.   Uniform width of the head at the base, twenty-eight feet.   The shaft gradually diminished in height and width to a point at the end.   The appearance is that of a cross sunk in light earth, in which the lower extremity is still buried beneath the surface.   I was forcibly struck with the fact that the arms were of exactly equal length, and at right angles to the trunk.   I felt and said, Here is order and design; but what that design is, we probably never shall know.   Is it possible that the people who constructed these works found their way to this continent after the Christian Era?   Perhaps not; yet curiosity will make the inquiry.   Two round mounds near the foot of this cross are each three feet high, and twenty and twenty-two feet in diameter at the base.   The oblong bears N. 22° E., and is sixty-eight feet long, twenty-two wide, and four feet five inches high; the ends are square."

"The smaller cross is one hundred and sixty feet long; the head, twenty-two feet; the arms, each fifty-one feet; the height two feet eight inches.   It terminates in a point, and resembles the large one in every respect.   The body of the "turtle" is twenty-two feet long, and fifteen feet wide; the head, four feet long; the height three feet eight inches.   It has but three legs, one of which seems to have been left unfinished or destroyed.   The head is towards the river.   There are some other small mounds in the vicinity, not represented on the plate.   The ground on which these works are situated has a gentle inclination towards the river, the banks of which are about three and a half feet high; the water has but a moderate current. The soil is composed of a dark sand, with a slight admixture of loam."

I am further indebted to Mr. Sweet for a survey and brief notice of the group of works on section thirty-one, township twelve, range twenty, represented on Plate XI. They consist mostly of ridges of earth from three to four feet high, and from twelve to fifteen feet wide at the base, and are of various lengths. They are supposed to have been originally square at the ends, but now are rounded by the effects of rain, &c. One mound, one hundred and thirty-two feet in length, is shaped like a war-club. "It has been asserted," says Mr. Sweet, "that this was a regular fort, being an inclosure; but on a careful examination, I find it is not so. The long mound (thirty-two rods in length) with another at right angles to it, upon a hasty examination, might suggest that idea; but the full survey shows that the conclusion would be a wrong one. The land here and for some distance around is level, the soil sandy, lightly timbered with iron-wood (*Ostrya virginica*) and sugar maple, with no large trees. There are no streams of water within half a mile of these mounds." The last mentioned circumstance is rather unusual.

There are said to be other localities still further up the Milwaukee River; but their exact situation could not be ascertained, nor could I obtain any reliable account of their character and extent.

Proceeding northward, in the vicinity of the west shore of Lake Michigan, we find the next ancient works on the Sheboygan River.

Plate XII. shows the general character of a very interesting group at the country residence of Dr. J. F. Seely, on a prominent point of land on the north side of the river, three miles above its mouth. They are in the northeast quarter of section twenty-eight, in township fifteen, and range twenty-two. The mounds are mostly of the kind called "lizards," though presenting some remarkable variations from the usual type of the species, as a naturalist would say. In one the tail is crooked, with a double curve of serpentine form; in another it makes a considerable angle with the body; and a third has the front leg or projection extended forward. Two of the mounds are apparently of the same general character, except that they have two gradually tapering extensions or tails, projecting in opposite directions, as will be seen by reference to the plate. At the Doctor's house is a work consisting of three nearly parallel ridges, united at the southern extremity, not far from the edge of the steep hill on which the preceding works are situated. They are about two hundred feet in length, but have only a slight breadth and elevation.

This promontory resembles in its general form the fortified hills so often found in Northern Ohio and in New York; but, after a careful search, no trace could be found of a wall extending across from one hill to the other. The occupants probably relied for defence upon the natural security of the position, as in numerous other instances in Wisconsin.

Other works are known to exist towards the head of this fine stream.

With the exception of a few small mounds near the village of Manitowoc, we have now described all the ancient works in the vicinity of the "Great Lake." The last named are situated on the northeast quarter of township nineteen, half a mile northwest of the village. One of them was penetrated to some depth below the original surface, but not the least trace of any deposit could be detected. Pits had been dug in several other mounds, and, so far as we could learn, uniformly with the same negative results. The soil here is sandy, and the materials of the mounds consist of sand, with spots of darker color or mould, as if portions of the surface soil were mixed with the sand. There are eight mounds, situated on a level plain elevated about sixty feet above the river, to which there is a very steep descent. They are not exactly round, but of an oval form: the longest diameter lying in a north and south direction, or at right angles with the steep bank.

The following notice of the works near Manitowoc[7] is from a letter written by Mr. Charles Musson of that place. " There are some mounds and embankments, or breastworks (or what seem to have been used for that purpose), found about half a mile northwest from the town, on a high, level, and dry piece of ground of considerable extent. These embankments now rise to the height of about four feet; their breadth at the base being from ten to twelve feet. In one place there are two, ranging north and south, parallel to each other; one about thirty rods, the other forty rods long, and seventy rods apart. They present every appearance of having been works of defence for two contending parties. In the vicinity of the breastworks, between and to the south of them, are about twelve mounds, varying in size; some are as large as fifteen feet in diameter at the base, and eight feet in height. Some of these have been opened, and, I think, in one bones were found; but nothing certain can now be known. It seems highly probable that this might have been a battle ground, and these mounds the burial-places of the slain. The suggestion is not the less probable from the fact of there not being anything in them which can be recognized as human remains. For it is certain, from the size of the trees now growing on the apparent fortifications, that they must have been erected centuries ago; some are pine trees four feet in diameter."

These works are supposed to be the northern limit of ancient monuments on or near the lake shore.

---

[1] Represented on Plate XXXII. No. 3.

CHAPTER II.

ANCIENT WORKS IN THE BASIN OF THE PISHTAKA RIVER.

THIS stream is usually called Fox River; but, to distinguish it from the numerous other rivers of the same name, it is necessary to call it the Fox River[1] of the Illinois. It originates in the northeastern part of Waukesha County, and runs in a southerly direction through the western part of Racine and Kenosha counties into Illinois. It thence passes by way of the Illinois River into the Mississippi. Within the State of Wisconsin its basin covers an area of nine hundred and forty-five square miles.

The ancient works in the valley of the Pishtaka extend as far down as to the place where Major Long and his party crossed it, a little north of west from Chicago. "At this point," says the narrator, "the river has a fine gravelly bottom, and was very easily forded. On the west side we reached a beautiful but small prairie, situated on a high bank, which approaches within two hundred and fifty yards of the edge of the water; and upon this prairie we discovered a number of mounds, which appear to have been arranged with a certain degree of regularity. Of these mounds we counted twenty-seven. They vary from one to four feet and a half in height, and from fifteen to twenty-five in length; their breadth is not proportioned to their length, as it seldom exceeds six or eight feet. They are placed at unequal distances, which average about twenty yards, and are chiefly upon the brow of the hill; but some of them stand at a greater distance back. Their form appears to have been originally oval; and the slight depression in the ground observed sometimes on both sides of the mound, seems to indicate that it has been raised by means of the earth collected in its immediate vicinity. Of their artificial nature no doubt could be entertained."[2]

About a dozen localities are known along this stream and its branches, within the limits of Wisconsin, at which mounds have been erected by the ancient occupants of the country. Near the southern boundary of the State are a few works, as on the northwest side of Silver Lake, in the town of Salem (section eight, township one, range twenty), where there are some burial mounds; and a little north of the road (southwest quarter of southeast quarter of section five, township one, range twenty) are two oblong mounds, which, from their position, are supposed to be

---

[1] It is said that the Indians called all rivers with numerous short bends by this name, from the resemblance of their course to that of a fox when pursued.

[2] Narrative of an Expedition to the Source of the St. Peter's River, &c., I. 176. Philadelphia, 1824.

"look-out" stations. They are situated near some quite remarkable bluffs of limestone gravel, and command an extensive view of the valley towards the south,
with its beautiful lake and ancient remains.

Mound Prairie, in the western part of Wheatland (township one, range nineteen),
is a small and beautiful prairie lying between two fine groups of lakes; and is so
named from some artificial works near the centre of the prairie. We found six
or eight circular mounds, and one that appeared to have been a "turtle." They
were nearly destroyed by the plough.

Near the village of Geneva (section thirty-five, township one, range seventeen),
there were two turtle mounds, and several of the ordinary circular or conical form.
They are situated near the lake with their heads towards the water. A road passes
directly over them, and they are now (1850) nearly destroyed. Further search
would probably reveal the localities of other works about these lakes.

Five miles south of Burlington (on the northwest quarter of section twenty-six,
township two, range nineteen), is a solitary animal mound, with curved tail, and
enlarged at the extremity, as shown in the figure. (Plate XIII. No. 1.) It is situated
on a gently sloping hill side, and the road passes directly over it. It is a very
unusual circumstance to find such a mound disconnected from other works; but we
could not learn that any others existed in the vicinity.

On the east bank of the river, opposite the village of Burlington, is a series of
mounds arranged in an irregular row along the margin of the stream. (See Plate
XIII. No. 2.) The largest of the series, near the middle, is ten feet high, and fifty
feet in diameter at the base. It is connected with the next by an embankment, a
circumstance observed in several other cases. At the north or upper end of the
series, are four oblong mounds; one with a divided extremity, or horns, as shown
in the drawing. Eleven conical tumuli may yet be traced; and some others, it is
said, have been removed. Persons of lively imagination might suppose this series
to represent a serpent, with mouth open, in the act of swallowing its prey; the
series forming a sort of serpentine row.

A little west of the village is a small inclosure of oval form, the embankment
having but a slight elevation. It may have been the place of a mud-house, or some
structure the decay of which has left only this evidence of its former existence.
There are said to be others similar to it in the vicinity. A stone axe and a flint
arrow-point were obtained here.

On the west side of Wind Lake (northeast quarter of section eight, township
four, range twenty), we discovered five conical mounds, but no other works in their
vicinity. Also on the west side of Muskego Lake (east half of northeast quarter
of section sixteen, township five, range twenty), is a group of works represented
in Plate XIV. No. 1. They consist of two parallel ridges at the extremity of a
small promontory nearly surrounded by marshy grounds, and a ridge and some
circular mounds on another point of land opposite. There is a remarkable excavation in the bank here, which is doubtless the work of art; but its origin and the
purpose for which it was made can now only be a subject of conjecture.

These parallel ridges have been represented as the remains of a fort or fortified
promontory; but a glance at the plate will show that no such object could have

been the motive of their construction. Instead of extending across the neck of the peninsula, as in the "fortified hills," and thus defending the approach to the position, they occupy a place near the extremity of the high land.

Proceeding up the valley of the river from Burlington, there are no remains for a distance of twelve miles. We then find those represented on Plate XV. By invitation, we took up our quarters at the house of Mr. Isaac Bailey, where it was once proposed to build a village or city, to be called "Crawfordsville." The city was never built, and the name is only remembered by a few of the oldest inhabitants. This is the place mentioned by Mr. R. C. Taylor[1] as stated in the western papers to contain a group of mounds resembling lizards, alligators, and flying dragons.

On Plate XVI., I have endeavored to represent these monsters as they appear upon careful survey and plotting. They occupy ground sloping gently towards the river at the north and northwest, their heads pointing up hill, and their general course southwesterly. The winged mounds or dragons (three in number) appear to lead the flight or march of the other animals, and to be heralded by a host of simple oblong figures, extending nearly half a mile in the same direction. An enlarged view of one of the winged mounds is shown on Plate XVII. No. 1; and the group of oblong mounds, forming the "advance guard," is shown on Plate XIV. No. 2.

The main figure in the general group is shown on an enlarged scale (Plate XVII. No. 2), and is two hundred and eighty-six feet in length. This and the one immediately preceding it are good representatives of the kind called lizards; while the two exterior figures, having four projections or feet, are always called turtles by the most casual observer. One at the right appears to have been intended for a lizard, but is without the tail. These are from two to six feet in height.

A little north of the mounds represented on Plate XVI. is a very large one, ten feet in perpendicular height, and eighty feet in diameter at the base. Its situation is such as to command a view of the valley for two or three miles both above and below. It had been opened prior to our visit, but without important results. It has an appendage consisting of a slight ridge of earth, sixty feet long, extending from its base in a northeasterly direction. Immediately north of it is an excavation from one to two feet in depth. The earth taken from this excavation, however, would make but a small part of the large mound. South of these the ground continues to rise to a high ridge, occupied by the roads, as shown on the map, Plate XV.

As seen by the plate, many of these mounds are in a grove of timber, and have not been disturbed by cultivation. It is very much to be hoped that the good taste of the present intelligent proprietor will induce him to preserve them from destruction. This locality was doubtless one of much importance to the original inhabitants. It is protected on three sides by the marshy grounds along the margin of the river; and on the heights in the rear are several mounds, indicat-

---

[1] Silliman's Amer. Journal of Science and Art, 1st series, XXXIV. 95.

4

ing that outposts may have been guarded, so as to give warning of the first approach of an enemy.

It has been observed that among the figures represented on Plate XVI. is a lizard without a tail; and we found, on the high ground immediately south of the little village of Big Bend, two, which may be considered as turtles, with a similar deficiency. (Plate XVII. No. 3.) They closely resemble the forms described by Mr. S. Taylor.[1]

One of these (on the east side of the river) is apparently a group of two large and four small mounds united into one (Plate XVII. No. 4); or we may suppose the two largest united by a ridge, and the four smaller ones placed adjoining them. In each of these figures one end is larger than the other; thus indicating which was the head of the turtle. One is sixty-five feet long, and sixty-seven feet broad, measured from the extremities of the anterior projections; the other is one hundred and four feet long, and eighty-two feet broad. One, it will be observed, lies nearly north and south, and the other nearly east and west. The most southerly is the largest. May they not have been the depositories of the remains of some distinguished family, consisting of the man, his wife, and four children? We may suppose that each had a mound erected suitable in its dimensions and relative position to the dignity of the person. Thus, the father would occupy the largest, and the children the smallest of the group.

The four mounds on the border of the prairie at the south part of Plate XV. may originally have been of imitative forms, but they are now much obliterated. From these the observer commands a distant view towards the south and southwest. In digging the well near by, sticks, and logs of cedar, or tamarack wood, were found at the depth of nineteen feet below the surface.

Waukesha is the next place which seems to have been occupied by the ancient inhabitants. It was formerly known as Prairie Village or Prairieville; and being on the main road west from Milwaukee, its mounds were early brought into notice. Their general distribution and relative situation, as well as the topographical features of the locality, will be found represented on Plate XVIII. It will be noticed that they occupy three different levels: those in the lower part of the village, mostly conical, are on the lowest ground; while those in the upper part are on what may be called the second bank; and the others are on the highlands east and south of the village.

Plate XIX. represents a group of works surveyed in 1836, with the assistance of Mr. Wm. T. Culley. At that time the log-house near these mounds was the only evidence of civilization in the place; and the works were uninjured by the white man, except that the large mound was made use of for a root-house, or potato-hole. The turtle-mound was then a conspicuous object; and such was its resemblance to that animal, that it was pronounced a good representation by all who saw it. The mere outline of the ground plan, as represented in the plate, fails to convey an adequate idea of this resemblance. But it is better to give the

---

[1] Sill. Journ., XLIV. 28, Plate v. Fig. 6; quoted by Squier and Davis, Smiths. Contrib., I. 130, Plate xliii. Fig. 5.

outline correctly, than to attempt a delineation of what may be supposed to have been intended by the builders.

On this mound was, at that time, a recent grave, protected by pickets driven on opposite sides, so as to cross at the top, as represented on the plate. The Indians had but recently left the place, and the trail leading from the river to their wigwams ran directly over two of the mounds. This turtle was then a very fine specimen of the ancient art of mound-building, with its graceful curves, the feet projecting back and forward, and the tail, with its gradual slope, so acutely pointed that it was impossible to ascertain precisely where it terminated. The body was fifty-six feet in length, and the tail two hundred and fifty; the height six feet.

The ground occupied by this group of works is now covered with buildings. A dwelling-house stands upon the body of the turtle, and a Catholic church is built upon the tail.

Another turtle, represented on the same plate, was found on the college grounds, and differs from the other in being concave on the back, as shown by the section. It is also less symmetrical.

Plate XX. represents a group of structures occupying the very high hill a little east of the town. It consists of two round, four oblong, one turtle, and one bird-shaped mound. Of the last an enlarged view is presented on Plate XXII. No. 1, with its dimensions. Its position is peculiar, on a steep hill-side, with its head downwards. The general outline of the figure, and the shape of the head and beak, leave no doubt that a bird was intended to be represented; but whether an eagle, a hawk, or any particular bird, must be left entirely to conjecture. It will be observed that this bird is but a modification of other forms represented on the same plate (Plate XXII. Nos. 2 and 3); a slight curvature of the wings, and the addition of a beak, being the only difference: and this gradual passage of one kind of mound into another is often noticeable, as we shall have occasion to show elsewhere.

The very fine group, half a mile south of the town (Plate XXI.), fortunately is upon the grounds of Carroll College; and we may, therefore, hope it will be for ever preserved as a record of the past. These mounds form a *quasi* inclosure, and hence, like many other groups of works, have been, by casual observers, called a fort. If we were not well acquainted with works of defence in Ohio and elsewhere, which show that the mound-builders were considerably advanced in military arts, we might suppose this was intended for a rude fortification; but we can only regard it as an accidental arrangement, and not designed for any such purpose.

Much of the ground about Waukesha was, in 1836, covered with " Indian corn-hills," or remains of their recent culture of maize. In this locality, as at numerous others, the mounds occupy the highest ground and the points of hills and other places, whence the most extensive view, both above and below, can be obtained. The town of Waukesha stands on a slightly undulating plain, surrounded by hills, forming a fine amphitheatre, which, in ancient times, was doubtless crowded, as it is now, with a numerous population.

The mound marked *a* on the map (Plate XVIII.) was selected for examination; much of the earth having been removed by the town authorities, so as materially to lessen the labor.   At about two feet above the original surface of the ground, the top of a circular wall or pile of stone, about nine feet in diameter, was discovered.   It was composed of loose fragments of white limestone, which exhibited evidence of long contact with the earth, by their decayed and softened exterior. The wall was interrupted on the west side.   (See Section, Plate XVIII.)

We commenced the exploration by opening a trench three feet wide, beginning on the east side of the original mound, deep enough to reach through the black and mottled earth of which the mound was composed, and to the surface of the yellowish clay subsoil.   Continuing this trench towards the centre, we passed the loose stone wall, and found the black earth suddenly extending down about two feet below the natural surface of the ground, and reaching the gravel below the yellow clay.   Upon this gravel, two feet below the original surface, directly under the centre of the mound, and surrounded by the circular heap of stone, was found a human skeleton, lying on its back, with the head towards the west.   Stones had also been placed at the sides and over the body, forming a rude sort of coffin.   The bones were very much decayed, and only fragments could be obtained.   The plates of the skull were too far gone to be restored.

In the left hand was a pipe of baked clay or pottery, ornamented with holes around the bowl, and also a quantity of red paint.   In the right hand was a smaller pipe, cut from a soft kind of stone.   They are both very small, and appear to have been articles of fancy, rather than use.   At the head were found many fragments of pottery which had been crushed by the weight of the earth; these fragments were originally portions of two vessels, which had the form represented in Fig. 8.   They are of the same coarse and rude materials as the fragments so frequently found on and near the surface in many localities throughout the State.   The earth immediately over the skeleton was hard and black, indicating the action of fire, though no other evidence of this was discovered.   Fragments of fresh-water shells (of the genus *Unio*[1]) were found with the fragments of pottery. No wood was found, nor were any vacant places noticed where it might have decayed.

FIG. 8.

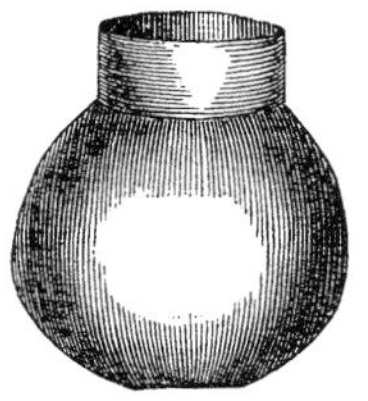

Another mound was opened a short distance west of the first, by sinking a shaft in the centre five feet in diameter.   We soon reached burnt clay, of a yellow or reddish-yellow color, with stones almost calcined into quicklime by the intensity of the heat.   Much charcoal was obtained, showing still the original pores and concentric circles of the wood, which appeared to be oak.   The bones of a portion of the leg of a human being were found; but the remainder of the skeleton had evidently been consumed at the time of the interment.   There had been no excavation below the natural surface of the ground in this case.

The materials composing these mounds were taken from the surface, so that no perceptible excavations are left in their vicinity; and the whole body of the tumulus consists of black mould, with occasional spots of yellowish clay.   The difference between the artificial and natural soil was quite apparent.   No articles

---

[1] Apparently the *Unio siliquoides* of Barnes.

of ornament or use, indicating any commerce with the white race, were discovered; and we are led to the conclusion that the mound was erected before the discovery of the country. The position of the skeleton, and other indications, show conclusively that no disturbance had taken place since the interment, and that the articles obtained were the original deposits. The skeleton was, without doubt, that of the personage for whom the mound was erected.

In one of the vases at the head of the skeleton were the remains of a shell, apparently the *Unio siliquoides*, a very common species in the rivers and lakes of Wisconsin. These shells are often used for spoons; and this vase probably contained a supply of food for the departed while on the journey to the spirit-land.

It is impossible to estimate, with any degree of precision, the length of time that human bones may have remained when placed two feet in the earth, and covered with a mound still retaining an elevation of four feet; but it is certain that all traces of them would be gone in a few centuries, unless they were longer preserved by peculiar circumstances. The skeletons found here were, as before stated, very much decayed; but it is believed that their antiquity could not be very great. Roots of trees had penetrated to the bones, and drawn nourishment from their mouldering remains, thus hastening their decay; and their depth (four and six feet) below the top of the mound, was not so great as to exclude entirely the effects of moisture, especially in wet seasons. It is true, the hard layer of earth and the covering of stone had a preservative influence; but, upon the whole, it is not probable that these mounds have an antiquity of many hundred years.

It is clear, then, that this was one of the latest works of the mound-builders; one that connects them with the present race of Indians; and yet its origin is, without doubt, anterior to the discovery of America. The pipes, the red paint, and the pottery, are so many circumstances connecting this mound with the recent race; while the tumulus itself is a relic of the more ancient one of the mound-builders. The progress of discovery seems constantly to diminish the distinction between the ancient and modern races; and it may not be very wide of the truth to assert that they were the same people.

It is not strange that changes should, from time to time, take place in the character and habits of a people so rude and so little advanced in civilization. Different tribes have different habits; and a stronger one may have overrun and swallowed up a weaker, and thus changed its customs and destroyed its institutions. In this way the mode of burial, and even the religious ceremonies, may be altered; those of the conquerors being substituted for those of the conquered. History records many such events. The inhabitants of Egypt have ceased to build pyramids and sphinxes; the Greeks have ceased to erect temples: and yet, we have reason to believe that their descendants occupy the same countries. Is it more strange that the ancestors of the present Indians should have erected mounds of earth, than that the aboriginals of any country should have had habits different from their posterity? We need not, therefore, look to Mexico, or any other country, for the descendants of the mound-builders. We probably see them in the present red race of the same or adjacent regions.

Since the red men have become known to us, numerous tribes have been extinguished, with all their peculiar customs and institutions; yet, as a whole, the Indian remains.   Many tribes have been overrun by others, and have united with them as one people.   Migrations have taken place; one tribe acquiring sufficient power has taken possession of lands belonging to another, and maintained its possession.   In the course of these revolutions it is not strange that habits and practices, once prevalent in certain places, with certain tribes, should become extinct and forgotten.

Another fact is important in this connection.   The mound-builders occupied the same localities that are now the favorite resort of the present Indians, who still often make use of the mounds for the burial of their dead.   They have a kind of veneration for them, which may be the result of a lingering tradition of their sacred origin.   The implements and utensils of the mound-builders were the same in many cases as those used by the recent inhabitants before their intercourse with the whites; and, as it has been quite clearly shown that the latter have in former times erected mounds of earth over their dead, we may consider such facts as tending to prove the unity of these people.

A mile and a half above Waukesha, on a very high and commanding position, are three round mounds in front of four "lizard-mounds." (Fig. 9.)   They are

FIG. 9.

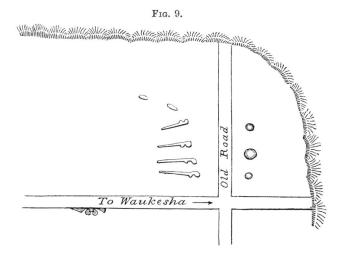

at the crossing of the old "Madison road," in the southwest quarter of section twenty-six.   A sentinel stationed on them could give warning to the inhabitants of the approach of any hostile force, long before they could reach the village.   The "lizards," as in most other cases, have their heads towards the south.

On the northwest quarter of the same section are also some small mounds, and one of the lizard shape.   They are at the foot of the hill that borders the outlet of Pewaukee Lake.   Still further, on the road (S. E. qr. of Sec. 22, T. 7, R. 19), were found the remains of another lizard mound, now nearly destroyed.

But the most remarkable collection of lizards and turtles yet discovered is on the school section, about a mile and a half southeast from the village of Pewaukee. (See Plate XXIII.)   This consists of seven turtles, two lizards, four oblong mounds, and one of those remarkable excavations before alluded to.   One of the turtle mounds, partially obliterated by the road, has a length of four hundred and fifty feet; being nearly double the usual dimensions. Three of them are remarkable for their curved tails, a feature here first observed. (Plate XXIV. Nos. 2, 3, and 4.) One of the smallest has the tail turned back by the side of the body. (Plate XXIV. No. 4.) These curved figures have another peculiarity in the obtuseness of the extremity; the end being round and flat, instead of a sharp point, as in most other similar mounds. While these have a width of about four feet at the end, others so gradually diminish in height and breadth that it is almost impossible, as before observed, to determine the precise point of termination. One has a rectangular bend at the extremity of the tail, and in each there is a change of direction in passing from the body to the tail.

The excavation, Plate IX. Fig. 6, is quite similar to those found on the Milwaukee River, in form and dimensions; except that the extremity is deflected, and it does not appear to be associated with the principal mound by pointing towards it. The oblong structure adjoining the excavation is in the most conspicuous place, and may be styled the "observatory."

This interesting group occupies a secure position, being on a ridge flanked by marshy grounds on either side. At the remote period when these mounds were built, the marshes may have been lakes, since filled up or dried away to their present condition.[1] A diligent search did not reveal any evidence of breastworks, or other means of defence, across this ridge at either end of the mounds. About half a mile off, in a northwest direction, is a very high hill (probably two hundred feet above the level of the marshes), on which are one lizard and three circular mounds. From these there is a fine view, extending over much of the adjacent country.

It will be noticed that there are no round or burial mounds among those represented on Plate XXIII. The cemetery was in some other place, probably on the hill just mentioned. The grounds about the former are covered with scattered oak-trees, commonly called "oak openings," and thickly overgrown with small bushes, rendering it difficult to perform the work of surveying. Such was the density of this undergrowth, that we seldom could see a mound until we were directly upon it; and we are not sure that all were detected. At the time of our visit a fire was raging through the woods about us, consuming the dry leaves and brush, and filling the air with smoke; and our clothes and persons soon became blackened by the charred bushes, nor were we entirely free from danger arising from falling trees. The peculiar noise made by the fire as it entered the marsh, caused by the bursting of the hollow stems of coarse grass and weeds, was very great.

Traces of a few other mounds were noticed at the eastern extremity of Pewaukee Lake, immediately north of the village. They were too much injured in the process of making roads, and by the dam, by which the lake has been raised four feet above its original level, to admit of their precise nature being ascertained.

No other ancient works could be found in the valley of the Pishtaka and its branches; nor could we hear of any more upon inquiry among those familiar with the localities in that part of the country.

---

[1] They are 260 feet above Lake Michigan, as ascertained by levelling.

CHAPTER III.

ANCIENT WORKS IN THE BASIN OF ROCK RIVER AND ITS BRANCHES.

SECTION I.

BELOW AZTALAN.

THE Rock River country is favorably known as among the most fertile and beautiful in the broad West. The early settlers were eager to reach this valley; and it has now become the centre of a numerous, thriving, and intelligent population. It occupies the central portions of the southern and most populous part of the State; having an area of five thousand five hundred and fifty square miles. At Beloit, where the river passes into Illinois, it has an elevation of one hundred and thirty-eight feet; and the rim of the great basin is from three hundred to eight or nine hundred feet above the level of Lake Michigan.

Ancient works exist in this valley below the State line; but of their nature and extent I have been able to obtain no very particular information. It is believed that they are of less importance than those to the north; and, with the exception of some of the turtle form as far south as Rockford, they do not assume those peculiar imitative figures so characteristic of the mounds of Wisconsin. North of the State line, the mounds are profusely scattered over this broad valley (as will be seen by reference to the map), reaching to the very sources of some of the branches.

The following statement is from the "Narrative of an Expedition to the Source of St. Peter's River," &c., under the command of Captain Long, in 1823:

"On both banks of the Kishwaukee, not far from its mouth, there are many mounds in every respect similar to those met with on Fox (Pishtaka) River, but scattered along the bank without any apparent order. Mr. Say counted upwards of thirty of these mounds. It is probable that they were the cemeteries of a large Indian population, which resided along the banks of the Kishwaukee, and which, perhaps, had its principal village at the beautiful confluence of this stream with Rock River."[1]

Only one locality of any importance was found on the Pekatonica, a branch of Rock River that has its rise in the centre of the lead-mine region, where ancient works had been constructed. The necessities of these builders probably did not include lead, for in this region but few works are seen; and we find no indications

---

[1] Narrative, &c., I. 185. See also Chap. II. p. 23, of the present work.

of ancient mining as at the copper mines of Lake Superior. The copper ore associated with the lead was beyond the reach of their metallurgic arts. The works alluded to are sketched on Plate XXV, and consist of several oblong, or circular, and one tapering mound; the last destitute of appendages, or other indications of its relation to the turtle and lizard forms, found further east.

They are situated on the sloping ground, and extend from the top of the hill half way to the river. The soil is here sandy, being in the district of the sand-stone, which is seen cropping out along the road near by. There is nothing to distinguish them from others more within the proper region, as it were, of the mound-builders. One of them had been opened prior to our visit, from which bones were said to have been obtained. Indian graves while exposed along the margin of the river, furnished a few glass beads and some trinkets.

The valley of Sugar river, a considerable stream between the Pekatonica and Rock rivers, appears also to have been avoided by the mound-builders. We could hear of only a few unimportant mounds on sections fourteen and fifteen, township four, range seven; and on thirty-five and thirty-six, township four, range six. None could be heard of about Monroe and Exeter, where lead is dug in considerable quantities. For some unknown reason, they seem not to have occupied this mineral region.

A few mounds of no great interest were seen about Delavan lake, also in and near Beloit, which were not minutely examined by me, but have since been surveyed by Prof. S. P. Lothrop, of Beloit College. (See Plates LIV, LV.) Proceeding up the immediate valley of Rock river, the first works worthy of note are near the junction of the outlet of the four lakes at Fulton.

Plate XXVI represents the works at a place known as Indian Hill, about a mile above the mouth of the outlet. Here is a series of oblong mounds on the steep slope of the hill, converging towards a point where there is a dug-way leading to the river. The hill has an elevation of seventy or eighty feet, and from its summit the valley of the river can be overlooked for several miles above and below. It may be that this was one of the most important posts of observation, and that the peculiar arrangement of the mounds was intended to guard the access to the water from the top of the hill.

The hill is quite steep, and at present covered with trees and an under-growth of hazel-bushes. The graded way has been increased in depth by running water, but it bears evidence of having originally been constructed by art.

At the intersection of Main and State streets, in the village of Fulton, is an irregular oval earth-work, consisting of a flat ridge, and resembling the road-way of a modern turnpike. (See Plate XXV, No. 2.) The breadth varies from thirty to forty feet, and the elevation from two to three feet in the middle. The diameters of the oval are five hundred and three hundred feet. Such a structure might have had its uses in some of the public games or ceremonies of uncivilized life; but it would be idle to attempt to ascertain its particular purpose.

Besides the works already mentioned in this vicinity, there are numerous tumuli of the ordinary circular form, supposed to be sepulchral. They are occasionally

5

arranged in rows, more or less regular, along the margin of a brook or valley, as shown by Fig. 10. Usually two or three mounds near the middle of the row are larger than the others.

Fɪɢ. 10.

Row of Mounds near Fulton.

Three are found on the east side of the outlet, half a mile below Fulton, and a group a mile above the town. Two miles above, on section eleven, is a group of eight (see Fig 10), situated on the edge of a prairie, so as to be seen in profile, as represented in the figure. About a mile below the village, there is a group of fourteen, and another on the side of Rock river. All these are circular mounds, unaccompanied by others of imitative forms, &c. Some have been opened, and are said in most cases to have contained remains of human skeletons, frequently of several persons in the same tumulus.

We visited the mounds noted by the surveyors of the public land near the northeast corner of the town of Dunkirk, in Dane[1] county. When seen from a distance, they might readily be mistaken for a group of large, ancient, artificial mounds: but closer observation shows that they are only abrupt natural swells or elevations, here very numerous, which have been aptly compared to the waves of the sea.

Fɪɢ. 11.

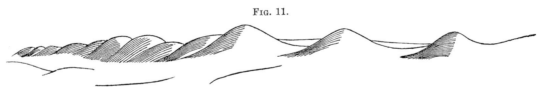

Natural Mounds, northeast corner of the town of Dunkirk, Dane county, Wisconsin.

The sketch (Fig. 11) was taken with the aid of a card, in the centre of which was a square opening crossed by threads, so as to form little squares, as recommended by Mr. Parrot.[2]

A few miles above Fulton, the river expands into a broad and shallow lake, known by its Indian name of Koshkonong, said to mean "the lake we live on." It is eight miles long, with an average breadth of two miles and five eighths; the periphery, measuring all the sinuosities of the shore, is twenty-eight miles and three quarters; the area, twenty-one square miles. According to the report of Capt. T. J. Cram, there is a rapid current, extending about six hundred feet into the lake, with a depth of water of only from two to three feet. In the other portion of the lake, on the usual channel or track for boats and rafts, the water is from four

---

[1] Not *Dade* county, as spelt in Vol. I. of Smithsonian Contributions.
[2] Journey to Ararat, &c.

to twelve feet deep. At the time of our visit (July, 1850), wild rice[1] was growing abundantly over almost its whole surface, giving to it more the appearance of a meadow than a lake. Fish and mollusks also abound in its waters, finding plenty of food in the warm mud beneath, and among the roots and stems of the grass and rushes.[2]

This locality being thus abundantly supplied with the means of subsistence relied upon in a great degree by the American Indians—rice and fish—we were not surprised to find numerous traces of Indians on the banks of the lake, which are known to have been occupied until a very recent period. There are two prominent points projecting into the water from the south shore, which were favorite spots with the natives. At the easterly point, called Bingham's Point, bones of fishes, with shells (various species of *Unio*), are very abundant, enriching the soil by their gradual decay.

On these points were also found remains of pipes, copper kettles, rusty gun-locks, and knives of old fashioned forms, nearly destroyed by rust and decay. From the other, or Thebean Point,[3] we obtained arrow-points, and a triangular ornament of stone, which had probably been brought from Ohio.

On Thebean Point are traces of mounds; and a little further up the lake commences a series of works extending about two miles along the high lands which border upon that portion of it. Some of these works are represented on Plate XXVII.

As in other cases, it will be noticed that the turtles have their heads turned towards the lake, and in a southerly direction. They differ from those heretofore described, in the more eastern portions of Wisconsin, in the diminished length of the tail. It will be observed that there are several mounds of forms varying from those before mentioned in this work. The one at *a*, of which an enlarged plan is given on the plate, with its dimensions, may be deemed a modification of the lizard-mounds of eastern Wisconsin. Near it is one with a slight appendix, which has been compared to a tadpole. Next to this is a tapering mound, with a slight curve at the smaller extremity. The three, connected by a ridge that extends beyond them in both directions, are quite peculiar. Unfortunately, the lateness of the evening prevented our making a triangulation of the three-pronged mound at the top of the plate; a circumstance which we regretted less from having previously surveyed several of the same kind, hereafter to be described.

As happens in many other cases, these mounds are placed on high and commanding situations; evincing a taste for beauty of scenery, or a watchfulness, perhaps, rendered necessary by the proximity of enemies. The ground is very uneven, presenting many prominent swells, occupied by the most important mounds, and numerous depressions in the surface, usually of an oval form, caused, perhaps, by the carrying away of soft materials from below by running water; thus leaving the surface unsupported, and ready to sink into pits or depressions. They are now

---

[1] *Zizania aquatica*, Linn.   [2] *Scirpus lacustris.*
[3] Thebean Point is separated from the main land by a broad marsh, which is not the case with Bingham's Point.

covered with trees, shrubs, and herbage, as are also the other grounds in the vicinity.

Fort Atkinson is the name of a flourishing village on Rock river, a little below the mouth of Bark river. In this vicinity are several groups of mounds, usually in irregular rows, three or four at a place. Some very large burial tumuli, half a mile below the town, on the right bank of the river, have been opened by citizens of the place. One, the largest, is ten feet high and sixty feet in diameter, composed in part of gravel, taken doubtless from the bed of the river, but mixed with the black earth of the surface.

Graves of Indians were passed in penetrating this; and at the bottom was a cavity lined with clay, hardened apparently by water, with an impression, as was supposed, of the rough exterior surface of oak bark, as if a log of this wood had been buried, now entirely decayed and gone; or, perhaps, it was a skeleton enveloped in bark for interment. It will be remarked that, in opening mounds and penetrating to the original deposits, but few implements or ornaments of any kind are found. In this respect, the Wisconsin mound-builders differed from their successors, who are in the habit of burying articles of supposed value and utility with their dead; and from this fact it may perhaps be inferred that they had less material notions of the spirit world, or at least of the necessities of those who were on the journey to that happy land.

Half a mile below the group of circular mounds last referred to, is the remarkable succession of works represented on Plate XXVIII, No. 1. The excavation has been before alluded to. (See pages 15 and 18.) In its general character it is precisely like those near Milwaukee, and the one on the school section at Pewaukee. (See page 31.) In shape it very much resembles some of the figures that have been denominated lizards. (See Plate IX, Fig. 7.)

Are we, then, to consider this as of the same origin, formed in the inverse order, and for similar purposes as the mounds? As at Milwaukee, a large mound stands near the smaller extremity.

These works are situated on the immediate bank of the river, which here has an elevation of ten or fifteen feet. The irregular cross at the west end of the group is quite peculiar, as are also the elongated and tapering mounds at the opposite extremity, which, in shape, may be compared to the tear drop! One cross near the fence is exactly like those of Waukesha and Crawfordsville. (Plates XVII and XXII.) The road runs directly over several of these mounds, and they will soon be destroyed and forgotten. Then, the present record only can be referred to as evidence of their former existence, and of their nature and extent.

A mile west of Jefferson, the county town of the county of the same name, situated at the junction of the two principal branches of Rock river, are the works represented on Plate XXVIII, No. 2. There we find the first lizard-mounds observed on Rock river. They have the same form and relative proportions as those before described, but differ in direction, their heads being a little north of west; all those before observed having had a direction towards points of the compass lying south of east or west. Another circumstance which probably governed their direction is, that they have their heads towards the water or low grounds, either directly or obliquely. In this respect these mounds do not differ from others.

The bird, or cross, is fifty-two feet in length of body, and one hundred and seventeen feet in alar extent, and resembles those before described. The elongated mound crossing the road to Jefferson, is remarkable for its great length; but it does not extend through the country for many miles, as is represented by some casual but positive observers. The exact length, as ascertained by the tape-line, is, as marked on the plate, four hundred and twenty-five feet. This mound is called "the snake," which it resembles in form, though being exactly straight, it does not at once convey the idea of a serpent. If other mounds are termed lizards, frogs, or turtles, surely the mounds of this form are entitled to an equally distinct name.

But what most distinguish these mounds from others, are the two raised or graded ways leading to prominent points on the steep bank of the river. They have, like the ring at Fulton (see page 33, Plate XXV), about the form and dimensions of the road-bed of a modern turnpike. It would be impossible, in the present state of our knowledge of the habits and customs of the authors of these works, to form a reasonable conjecture respecting the purposes of these graded ways. At their upper extremity they are guarded on each side by mounds.

The works under consideration are situated on one of the very remarkable series of diluvial ridges, so common in the upper portions of the Rock river valley, and to which it will be necessary frequently to refer in the following pages. The river has cut away the base of the ridge at this point, so as to present an almost perpendicular cliff of clay and gravel. A little east of the works the ground descends towards the east; but the mounds are either on the summit or on the western slope. The ridge runs a little east of north, and west of south; preserving, in this respect, a general parallelism to the whole system of ridges. There were numerous other ancient works in and about Jefferson, now mostly destroyed. The ridge on which the village is built, as well as the next one towards the east, were formerly covered by a series of them, traces of which are still to be seen in the court-house square. The high bank of the river on the west side above the town, had its group of mounds, serpents, and other effigies. The story of there having formerly been a mound here of the human shape is probably not correct; at least we could not find it, nor learn anything of its whereabouts. Among these mounds there were probably none presenting new forms.

On the banks of a small lake, called Ripley lake, ten miles west from Jefferson, is a group of works represented on Plate XXIX. It will be seen to exhibit some peculiar features, though the mound representing an elephant, said to exist here, could not be found. The two figures near the middle of the group may be considered as in an attitude of defiance or of combat. The elongated embankment to the east is cleft in such a manner as to suggest very readily the idea of a serpent with its mouth slightly opened. These works are on the north bank of the lake; and similar ones extend at intervals along the shore, occupying the higher points, for a distance of half a mile.

The lake is a mile and a half in length; and covers an extent of four hundred and ninety-three acres, with a coast line of four miles and three eighths. It is a fine sheet of pure water, with banks sufficiently elevated to present a picturesque and beautiful scene; and, at the time of our visit (July 4, 1850), the neighboring inhabitants were enjoying a sail upon its smooth surface. It has a prominent cape jutting in from the south, giving variety to the appearance of the shore; and glimpses of farm-houses, seen through the trees on the bank, show that this lovely spot is a favorite place with the modern civilized, as it was with the ancient barbarous people. Nature touches chords in the human heart that vibrate alike in the breasts of all, however different their conditions of life.

Bark river is a considerable tributary of Rock river, entering it at Fort Atkinson. Towards its source are some remains deserving notice. The most extensive group is on the fine level prairie at Summit, represented on Plate XXX. This plain has an elevation of about three hundred feet above Lake Michigan, is very fertile, the soil being two feet deep, and based upon an extensive bed of white limestone, gravel, and sand. It is bordered on all sides by small but very beautiful and picturesque lakes. Some prominent points of the series of hills passing through the State can be seen towards the southeast from this plain.

The mounds are circular and oblong, with occasionally one of imitative form; but nearly all have been ploughed over, so that it is now quite impossible to trace their exact outlines. One appears to have had the bird form. There are one or two resembling lizards, and several of them turtles. Two of the latter were here found with the head in a northerly direction, being on the south side of the lakes; showing that the object was to direct the head towards the water, rather than towards the south. (See Plate XXIX.) Several are simple ridges, gradually diminishing from one end to the other, and may be intended to represent the serpent; they do not differ from the tails of the turtles and lizards. One of unusual length was noticed near the line between sections fourteen and fifteen.

On the southwest quarter of section fourteen, is a natural elevation, formed, probably, by a ledge of limestone beneath, on which is a group of four mounds—two oblongs, one lizard, and one turtle; the feet of the latter appeared to have been curved forward. They were much effaced by cultivation.

Several mounds had been opened, but I could not learn that any discoveries of interest had been made; nor have any articles of importance been thrown up by the plough. In such cases we may suppose that the place was not abandoned, or the people drawn off in haste; but that they had time to gather up and remove all light articles.

A short distance above Hartland, on the east side of Bark river, immediately north of the burying-ground, is a series of oblong mounds, one of which is enlarged at the extremities and in the middle, as shown in the figure. (Plate XXXI, No. 1.) This appears to be a form intermediate between the plain oblong and the more elaborate animal-shaped mounds. The turtle at the northern extremity of this group is nearly destroyed by the road. These works are on the southeast quarter of section twenty-six, township eight, range eighteen.

Two miles and a half further up the river, at the village of Merton (northeast quarter of section twenty-four, township eight, range eighteen), are a number of circular and oblong elevations, and one called "the cross." (See Plate XXXI, Nos. 2 and 3.)   This last is certainly entitled to the name, from its striking resemblance to the cross as emblematically used and represented by the Roman Church in every part of the world; and yet there can be no doubt that this mound was erected long before the first Jesuits visited this country, and spread the doctrines, and presented the emblem of the Christian faith.

The ground here is high, and there are ridges running along the plain, as shown on the map.   An excavation had been made in the cross at the intersection of the arms, and bones found of a large size, probably of some Indian who had been buried there.

Mr. Miller, who resides near here, gave us a stone instrument, called by him a "skinner;" for, said he, "I have seen the Indians use a similar instrument in skinning a deer in the State of New York."   It is a beautiful green stone, well polished towards the sharp end, showing, perhaps, that it had been much used.

The place just above the village, called Fort Hill, has on it two oblong embankments, but bears no resemblance to a work of defence.

FIG. 12.

Lapham's Peak (as seen from the south).

North of Merton we left the main road to ascend a very high, conical, isolated peak (on section fifteen, township eight, range eighteen), in the west part of Washington county.   It is composed of drift materials, no solid rock being observed. Towards the summit gravel only is found, the pebbles being mostly limestone.   In its general appearance this peak resembles the Blue Mounds in the mineral region further west, though on a smaller scale.   (See Fig. 12.)   We found three artificial mounds occupying the whole of the narrow summit of this remarkable peak, as shown in the figure.   (Fig. 13.)   The middle and largest of these was

FIG. 13.

Enlarged view of the Summit (as seen from the west).

opened, and proved to be composed of black vegetable mould, covering a base of stone; but nothing could be found to show for what purposes they were erected. Whatever these purposes may have been, they were clearly of much importance to those who built the mounds; for the labor of transporting the stone and soil from the plain below up so steep an ascent, must have been very considerable, and not likely to be undertaken for any trivial object.   The central mound was six feet in height; the others, four.

A mean of seven good observations with the barometer, gave for the elevation of this peak above Lake Michigan   .   .   .   .   824 feet.

Add height of that lake .   .   .   .   578 "

Total height above the ocean   .   .   .   1402 "

The height above the surrounding grounds is about 275 feet.[1]

In the vicinity of the Four Lakes, where Madison, the capital of the State, is situated, the mound-builders have left unusually numerous traces of their former occupancy and industry. The lakes are united by a stream called the Catfish, through which the waters are conveyed to Rock river at Fulton. The mounds situated six and twelve miles west of the Four Lakes were among the first of the animal-shaped mounds of which an account was published;[2] and as I have no additional facts to communicate in regard to them, a reference to the places where they are noticed and very fully described, is all that is now required.

A figure on the third lake, within the limits of the town, was fortunately rescued from oblivion by Mr. F. Hudson, whose very accurate drawing I was permitted to copy from the papers belonging to the Wisconsin State Historical Society. (See Plate XXXII, No. 1.) It will be seen that it differs from any mound heretofore described, in having a neck and a proportionately smaller body. Like most mounds of this general character, it has its head directed towards the water. It occupies high ground, having a gentle slope towards the lake, and is very near the steep broken cliff.[3]

Along the road to Munroe (on section twenty-two, township seven, range nine), north of the small lake called Lake Wingra, is one of the rows of mounds so often alluded to, and which is represented on Plate XXXII, No. 2. The difference in their relative size may indicate the different degrees of dignity of the persons in whose honor they were erected. The row is irregular, being accommodated to the shape of the ground. It occupies one of the highest places about the lakes. Two quadrupeds, one bird, one mound with lateral projections, five oblong, aud twenty-seven circular tumuli, make up this group.

Plate XXXIII represents what still remain of the works near the south angle

---

[1] In consideration of the interest manifested by Mr. Lapham in this prominent feature of this part of the State, by measuring its altitude, and opening its artificial mounds, it has been proposed to name it Lapham's Peak.—*Secretary S. I.*

[2] R. C. Taylor, Silliman's Am. Journal, XXXIV, 92, Plate i, Fig. 1, Plate ii, Figs. 2, 3, and 4. John Locke's Report, pp. 136, 139–42, Plate, iii, iv. Squier and Davis, Smithsonian Contributions, p. 125, Plates xl, xli, and xlii.

[3] The following are the dimensions as given by Mr. Hudson :

Total length	318 feet.
Length of head	33 "
Length to first pair of legs	63 "
Length to second pair of legs	105 "
Breadth of head	27 "
Breadth of neck	21 "
Breadth of body	40 "
Diameter of the mounds	42 "

of the third lake. Here the rows present more the appearance of order and system than those of any other locality surveyed. The rows of smaller mounds parallel with the principal range, may have been for persons of inferior grades belonging to the families buried in the larger ones. The parallel ridges are upon ground sloping considerably towards the lake; and rise one above another, like the seats of an amphitheatre, to which they have been compared. The work in the rear of these ridges is quite regular, and intermediate in its character between a true cross and a bird-shaped mound.

At the foot of this slope commences a flat, extending around the east end of the lake, from which it is separated by a low, sandy ridge. Along this ridge is a very remarkable series of irregular elevations, twenty-four in number; a part of them are represented on the plate. They are largest and most abrupt towards the water, and are covered with soil and a forest of scattered trees. On several are artificial mounds, one of them a turtle; but whether they are themselves artificial seems doubtful, though it is difficult to understand how they could have been formed by any natural process. A recent Indian grave occupies the summit of one; and we noticed, near by, the poles of a wigwam but recently abandoned by the red men, though we were in sight of the capital of the State.

A ridge of sand or gravel is often formed around the margin of the small lakes in Wisconsin, by the expansive force of ice in winter; the materials near the shore being gradually moved year by year a little towards the land. But this cause is hardly adequate to the production of a series of mounds.

There are traces of other mounds south and west of those represented on Plate XXXIII, but they were too much reduced by the plough to enable us to trace them and ascertain their original forms.

On the north shore of the fourth lake, also on the first and second lakes, are said to be numerous works, which we did not visit. Eight miles northeast of Madison, the surveyors of the public lands have reported the existence of mounds (sections thirteen, twenty-three, and twenty-four, township eight, range ten), which we also were obliged to omit in our survey.

SECTION II.

ANCIENT WORKS AT AND IN THE VICINITY OF AZTALAN.

These important works are represented on Plates XXXIV and XXXV, and give evidence of greater labor than those at any other locality in the State. They are important also on account of their resemblance or analogy to works in other parts of the United States. It is the only ancient inclosure, properly so called, in Wisconsin; and although it is usually termed a fort or citadel, it will be shown hereafter that it falls more properly into the class denominated "sacred inclosures." Without this we might be led to suppose that the ancient mound-builders of Wisconsin were a distinct people from those of Ohio, so different is the general character of their monuments.

6

The "ancient city of Aztalan" has long been known, and often referred to, as one of the wonders of the western world. Many exaggerated statements respecting the "brick walls" supported by buttresses, the "stone arch," &c., have been made; for all of which there is little foundation in truth. The remains were discovered in October, 1836, and hastily surveyed in January, 1837, by N. F. Hyer, Esq., who soon afterwards published a brief description of them, with a rude wood-cut, in the Milwaukie Advertiser, the first, and then the only newspaper, in this part of the country. This survey was made before there were settlements in the neighborhood, and was done in a cursory manner. The brief account, however, as published, gave a very good general idea of the works; and has been the foundation of all subsequent plans and descriptions up to the present time.

Mr. Taylor's description[1] was furnished by a friend, who only made a brief visit to the works, accompanied by Mr. Hyer, and added but little to our knowledge of these ruins; though it was published in a more permanent and accessible form, and hence is more generally known and referred to. Messrs. Squier and Davis have condensed this description, and copied the plan in their work, in the first volume of the Smithsonian Contributions (page 131, Plate xliv, Fig. 1), with a number of judicious suggestions as to the nature of the walls, the object of the "bastions," &c. By comparing the plan and description thus given with what follows, the curious reader may trace the differences, and discover wherein the first fell short of presenting the whole truth.

The name Aztalan was given to this place by Mr. Hyer, because, according to Humboldt, the Aztecs, or ancient inhabitants of Mexico, had a tradition that their ancestors came from a country at the north, which they called Aztalan; and the possibility that these may have been remains of their occupancy, suggested the idea of restoring the name. It is made up of two Mexican words, *atl*, water, and *an*, near; and the country was probably so named from its proximity to large bodies of water.[2] Hence the natural inference that the country about these great lakes was the ancient residence of the Aztecs.[3]

Reference to Plate XXXIV will show that the main feature of these remains is the inclosure or ridge of *earth* (not *brick*, as has been erroneously stated), extending around three sides of an irregular parallelogram; the west branch of Rock river forming the fourth side on the east. The space thus inclosed is seventeen acres and two thirds. The corners are not rectangular; and the embankment or ridge is not straight. The earth of which the ridge is made was evidently taken from the nearest ground, where there are numerous excavations of very irregular form and depth; precisely such as may be seen along our modern railroad and canal embankments. These excavations are not to be confounded with the hiding-places (*caches*) of the Indians, being larger and more irregular in outline. Much of the material of the embankment was doubtless taken from the surface without penetrating a sufficient

---

[1] Silliman's Am. Journal, XLIV, 35.

[2] J. Delafield, Jr., Antiquities, &c., p. 107.

[3] Buschmann (Ueber d. Aztek. Ortsnamen, p. 6) says the name *Aztlan* is composed of the lost word *aztli* and the local termination *tlan.*—*Secretary S. I.*

depth to leave a trace at the present time. If we allow for difference of exposure of earth thrown up into a ridge and that lying on the original flat surface, we can perceive no difference between the soil composing the ridge and that found along its sides. Both consist of a light yellowish sandy loam.

The ridge forming the inclosure is 631 feet long at the north end, 1,419 feet long on the west side, and 700 feet on the south side; making a total length of wall of 2,750 feet. The ridge or wall is about 22 feet wide, and from one foot to five in height.

The wall of earth is enlarged on the outside, at nearly regular distances, by mounds of the same material. They are called buttresses or bastions; but it is quite clear that they were never designed for either of the purposes indicated by these names. The distance from one to another varies from sixty-one to ninety-five feet, scarcely any two of them being alike. Their mean distance apart is eighty-two feet. They are about forty feet in diameter, and from two to five feet high. On the north wall, and on most of the west wall, they have the same height as the connecting ridge; but on the south wall, and the southern portion of the west wall, they are higher than the ridge, and at a little distance resemble a simple row of mounds.

On the inner side of the wall, opposite many of these mounds, is a slight depression or sinus; possibly the remains of a sloping way by which the wall was ascended from within the inclosure.

The two outworks, near the southwest angle of the great inclosure, are constructed in the same manner; but both these mounds and the connecting ridge are of smaller dimensions. The ridge or way connecting the mounds at *a* and *c*, has something of the same general character, though still more obscure. When viewed from the road, a short distance west, these outworks would be supposed to be nothing more than a few circular mounds. The connecting ridge, at least, is too insignificant to be mistaken for the walls of a fort, or other work of defence. Whether these walls are only a series of ordinary mounds, such as are found all over the western country, differing only in being united one to another, it may perhaps be difficult to decide. They may possibly have been designed for the same and for other purposes.

On opening the walls near the top, it is occasionally found that the earth has been burned. Irregular masses of hard reddish clay, full of cavities, bear distinct impressions of straw, or rather wild hay, with which they had been mixed before burning. These places are of no very considerable extent, nor are they more than six inches in depth. Fragments of the same kind are found scattered about; and they have been observed in other localities at a great distance from these ancient ruins.

This is the only foundation for calling these "*brick* walls." The "bricks" were never made into any regular form, and it is even doubtful whether the burning did not take place in the wall after it was built. The impression of the grass is sometimes so distinct as to show its minute structure, and also that it was of the angular stems and leaves of the species of carex still growing abundantly along the margin of the river. As indicating the probable origin of this burned clay, it is important to state, that it is usually mixed with pieces of charcoal, partially burned bones, &c. Fragments of pottery are also found in the same connection. The walls and mounds are composed of a light colored clay, which becomes red on being slightly burned.

From all the facts observed, it is likely that clay was mixed with the straw, and made into some coarse kind of envelope or covering, for sacrifices about to be consumed. The whole was probably then placed on the wall of earth, mixed with the requisite fuel, and burned. The promiscuous mixture of charcoal, burned clay, charred bones, blackened pottery, &c., can only in this way be satisfactorily accounted for. The pottery was broken before it was buried, for the fragments were scattered about in a manner that clearly shows that the vessels were not entire.

A shaft was sunk by us in the sixth mound from the northwest angle on the west wall. A fragment of galena (sulphuret of lead), and another of iron ore used as red paint, and worn smooth, perhaps by long use in adorning the faces of the red men, were near the surface, and were the only articles found. No burned clay was on this mound, and we soon discovered that it is only in a few places that this substance exists. The earth was here a yellowish sandy loam, entirely free from spots of black mould; thus showing that it was built exclusively from the *subsoil* of the adjacent grounds. The builders had carefully removed the black soil before they commenced the erection of this mound. Our shaft was sunk some distance below the original surface. Two of the smaller mounds in the interior were also opened, but without results of any interest.

The mound, or projection, or buttress (whichever it may be termed), at the northwest angle of the inclosure, proved to be one of some interest. (See Fig. 14.) After

Fig. 14.

Section of the northwest corner mound, Aztalan.

removing the sods with which it was covered, we came upon fragments of pottery, charcoal, half-burned human bones, and numerous amorphous masses of burned clay scattered loosely and promiscuously about in the earthy materials of the mound. This continued to the depth of one foot only; below, the earth was quite uniform in appearance, though still showing incontestable proofs of art. Occasional fragments of clay, charcoal, and fresh-water shells almost entirely decayed, were observed as we proceeded. Still deeper we found a cavity which was nearly filled with *loose* earth, in which were indications of bones very much decayed and charcoal. This was divided below into two other cylindrical cavities, extending beneath the original surface of the ground, and filled with the same loose materials.

Two bodies had doubtless been buried here in the sitting posture, near each other, enveloped and covered, perhaps, by some perishable substances, which had decayed and left the cavity above; and this shows that the mounds at Aztalan, though constituting an inclosure, were used for burial purposes, as were other ordinary circular mounds.

Within this inclosure the ground descends towards the river more abruptly near the western wall, forming a kind of second bank, and then with a smooth even surface. This slope is interrupted only by a natural swell or eminence, shown at *c*, Plate XXXIV. The highest point in the interior is at the southwest corner, and is occupied by a square truncated mound, that, when seen from the high ground at *c*, presents the appearance of a pyramid, rising by successive steps like the gigantic structures of Mexico. (See section on Plate XXXIV.) This was doubtless the most sacred spot, as well as the highest. It will be observed that the inclosing walls curve around this pyramid, as if constructed afterwards, and made to conform to the shape of the ground. It is also further guarded by the two outer walls before described.

The level area on the top was fifty-three feet wide on the west side, where, in consequence of the slope of the ground, it has the least elevation; and it was originally, in all probability, a square of this size. On other parts of the mound the sides are high and steep; and the abrading effects of time have acted most upon the summits. There appears to have been a sloping way leading from the top of this mound towards the east; but if so, it has now dwindled to a slight elevation or swell on that side. This road-way was connected with a ridge before alluded to, extending towards the prominent point *c*. From this last point there is a gradual and easy descent to the river. These level-topped mounds may have been the foundation only of some structure of more perishable materials. From the summit of the two high places, and especially from that at *a*, the whole works, and quite an extent of surrounding country, can be seen.

At the northwest angle of the inclosure (*b*) is another rectangular, truncated, pyramidal elevation, of sixty by sixty-five feet level area on the top, with remains of its graded way, or sloping ascent, at the southeast corner, leading also towards a ridge that extends in the direction of the river. This mound occupies the summit of the ridge or bank before spoken of, though it rises but little, if any, above the top of the adjacent walls. It has been partially destroyed by persons curious in antiquarian research, and by one who, it is said, had been *supernaturally* convinced that a large amount of money was deposited in it!

There is another square structure (at *d*), which is level on the top; but as it stands on sloping ground, and has but little elevation, it runs to a grade even with the surface on the upper side. Just at this point a small mound has been erected, perhaps at a subsequent time, and by a different tribe or nation of people.

The analogy between these elevations and the "temple-mounds" of Ohio and the Southern States, will at once strike the reader who has seen the plans and descriptions. They have the same square or regular form, sloping or graded ascent, the terraced or step-like structure, and the same position in the interior of the inclosure. This kind of formation is known to increase in numbers and importance as we proceed to the south and southwest, until they are represented by the great structures of the same general character on the plains of Mexico.

In this inclosure are ridges usually about two feet high, as represented on the plan. The rings or circles connected with them constitute a very peculiar feature, and are supposed to be the remains of mud houses; the materials of the walls having fallen, leaving only a circular mound of earth to mark their original site.[1] No ridge exists along the river bank, as represented on Mr. Hyer's plan; the steepness of the bank probably rendering artificial works unnecessary for the purposes of the builders. Some of the interior ridges, it will be observed, are enlarged at intervals; thus showing an analogy with the main walls and outworks.

There are two excavations (*e* and *f*), the first triangular, and the last circular, which, from their greater depth and regular shape, as well as distance from the walls, were probably not made in the process of obtaining materials for the structures. The excavation at *e* is so deep, and the soil so tenacious, that water stands in the bottom much of the time, affording a place for the growth of flags[2] and other aquatic plants. Perhaps the bottom may have been rendered water-tight by artificial means. Undoubtedly it was once much deeper than at present; the tendency of rains and the accumulation of vegetable matter being to fill it up. The circular excavation (at *f*) is surrounded by a ridge consisting, doubtless, of the materials thrown out in the digging.

Near this point are some springs in a small ravine cut into the bank by the passage of water to the river. This ravine serves also as the outlet of the surface water from within this part of the inclosure. A few stones left along the sides and bottom of this ravine (the force of the water not being sufficient to remove them with the lighter particles of the earth), is all the evidence that could be found of an ancient sewer "arched with stone." It is quite clear that no such arch existed; nor is there any indication that the aboriginal inhabitants of the American continent were acquainted with the nature of the arch.[3] If they were, they certainly did not apply such knowledge in the construction of any works at Aztalan.

---

[1] We are told by Catlin that "the village of the Mandans has a most novel appearance to the eye of a stranger; their lodges are closely grouped together, leaving just room enough for walking and riding between them, and appear from without to be built entirely of dirt. They all have a circular form, and are from forty to sixty feet in diameter. Their foundations are prepared by digging some two feet in the ground, and forming the floor of earth by levelling the requisite space for the lodge. The superstructure is then produced by arranging inside of this circular excavation, firmly fixed in the ground and resting against the bank, a barrier, or wall of timbers, about six feet high, placed on end, and resting against each other, and supported by a formidable embankment of earth raised against them outside. Resting on the tops of these timbers are others of equal size, rising, at an angle of 45°, to the apex or sky-light, which is about three or four feet in diameter, answering also as a chimney. On the top of or over these poles or timbers, is placed a complete mat of willow boughs, of half a foot or more in thickness, that protects the timbers from the dampness of the earth with which the lodge is covered from bottom to top, to the depth of two or three feet, having above all a hard or tough clay which is impervious to water."—N. Am. Indians, I, 81.

[2] *Iris versicolor*.

FIG. 15.

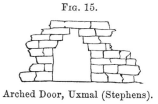

Arched Door, Uxmal (Stephens).

[3] Even in Yucatan and Central America, where the aboriginal buildings display the greatest advance in architecture, the arch was not used; its substitute being stones laid horizontally, and made to overlap, as represented in Fig. 15.—Stephens's Yucatan, I, 429.

Nearly the whole interior of the inclosure appears to have been either excavated or thrown up into mounds and ridges; the pits and irregular excavations being quite numerous over much of the space not occupied by mounds. This want of regularity is opposed to the opinion that these excavations were for the *cellars* of buildings, as suggested by some.

In a letter from Mr. J. C. Brayton, of Aztalan, he says : " Several feet below the surface of the large square mound near the northwest corner of the inclosure was found, a number of years ago, what appeared to be the remains of cloth, apparently enveloping a portion of a human skeleton. Its texture was open, like the coarsest linen fabric; but the threads were so entirely rotten, as to make it quite uncertain of what material they were made.[1]

" Numerous fragments of earthenware have been taken from the mounds at different times : portions of broken vessels, varying in size (judging by the curve of the fragments), from a few inches to three feet across the rim.

" A number of rusty gun-locks, in scattered fragments, have been discovered at or near the surface of the ground; and pieces of iron, copper, and brass, have been found in the neighborhood. But all these, being relics of the recent Indian population, fail to throw any light upon the great questions of who made these works, and for what purpose were they constructed. The Winnebagos, the last occupants of this interesting locality, always answer in the negative by a significant shake of the head, when asked if they can tell who erected the mounds."

Mr. Brayton, who has resided in the vicinity of these works since their discovery, is of the opinion that none of the mounds have sensibly changed from natural causes since the first settlement of the country in 1836.

Our examination of the tumuli exterior to the inclosure led to no very important results. The third from the north end of the long row, seen on the plate (about four feet high and thirty feet in diameter), was penetrated to the bottom, and the opening enlarged below in every direction. A post (apparently tamarack) had been inserted, and was now all decayed, except a portion near the bottom.[2] This may have been set in since the building of the mound, which was composed of black and yellow soil intermixed, having beneath gravel composed mostly of limestone pebbles. If these smaller tumuli ever covered any deposits, they are now so completely decayed that not the least trace of them can be discovered.

While at Aztalan we were informed that upon opening one of the larger mounds some years ago, the remains of a skeleton were found, inclosed by a rude stone

---

[1] This is probably the same that was forwarded by Dr. King to the National Institute of Washington.—See Silliman's Journal, XLIV, 38.

[2] This post may have been the remains of a medicine pole, such as was erected by the Mandans. According to Mr. Catlin, the Mandans were in the habit of erecting mounds of earth near their villages about three feet high, around which were arranged in circles the skulls of the dead, after their bodies had decayed on the scaffolds. On each mound was erected a pole, hung with articles of mysterious and superstitious import. Something of this kind may be the origin of the numerous smaller mounds in Wisconsin, in which no traces of artificial or human deposits could be found.—See N. Am. Indians, I, 190.

wall, plastered with clay, and covered with a sort of inverted vase of the same materials.

A number of these mounds have been opened at different times, and their contents, having been carried away to various parts of the world, cannot now be recovered.

With the view of ascertaining the contents of the larger elevations for ourselves, we selected one in Mound Street, ten feet in height, and sixty feet in diameter at the base, into which a trench four feet wide was dug, extending from the south side to beyond the centre, and down to the subsoil or stratum of gravel that underlies the superficial covering of vegetable mould.

The earth was quite uniform throughout; consisting of dark-colored mould and yellowish sandy loam, mixed in small quantities. Ashes, mingled with charcoal, were observed as we went down, and occasionally fragments of human bones. No skeleton was found; no stonework or earthenware—no stone or metallic implements of any kind could be discovered. Bones of some burrowing animals, and the remains of a fish were taken out. Fragments of rotten wood, apparently oak, were found at all depths. They were not charred, nor did they appear to have had any definite arrangement, but were confusedly placed, as if carelessly thrown upon the mound during the progress of its construction.

From the oft-repeated indications of fire at various depths, we could draw no other conclusion than that this was a "mound of sacrifice," and that at each repetition of the ceremony an addition was made to the height of the mound.

The gopher[1] often burrows in the artificial tumuli to find a dry place for its nest; and roots of trees penetrate to their lowest depths.

The question naturally arises in the mind of the observer, For what purpose was this great inclosure made? Mr. Hyer called it a citadel, and it is usually termed "the fort," and supposed to be a work of defence—a place to which the mound-builders resorted for safety when hard pressed by an enemy. Various reasons have been assigned for this supposition. Its connection with the river, affording a means of supply to the besieged—its buttresses or bastions—its outworks—its watch-towers—might all seem to convey the idea of a military work or a fortification.

Although when we attempt to describe these remains, the technical terms of military men are found convenient, and sometimes applicable; yet the "fort," the "buttresses," the "bastions," &c., have but remote resemblance to such constructions. Expressions like these often lead the superficial observer and reader astray, and may have done so in this case.

Messrs. Squier and Davis show very conclusively that the circular projections on the exterior of the walls could not have been intended for bastions.[2] It is equally clear that a ridge of earth twenty-two feet wide and five feet high, does not need the support of buttresses.

---

[1] The name here universally applied to the thirteen-lined marmot (*Spermophilus tridecemlineatus*).

[2] Smithsonian Contributions, I, 132.

But this fort is entirely commanded from the summit of a ridge extending along the west side, nearly parallel with (see Plate XXXIV), and much higher than the west walls themselves, and within a fair arrow-shot; so that an enemy posted on it would have a decided advantage over those within the defences. This ridge would also constitute an excellent breastwork to protect an enemy from the arrows or other weapons shot from the supposed fort. As if purposely to assist an approaching enemy, a number of mounds have been erected along the ridge, affording secure hiding-places and look-out stations, very convenient to the attacking party. These may, however, have been erected at a more recent date.

Again, the large mounds of the remarkable row northwest of the inclosure are not in connection with it, but are excellent points from which to reconnoitre and annoy the occupants of the supposed fortress.

From the summit of the ridge before alluded to, as will be seen by the sections on Plate XXXV, the ground descends towards the river; so that the inclosure is on a declivity, and is thus commanded from the opposite side of the river. Here, again, as if purposely to render aid and comfort to an enemy, a breastwork is erected, extending along the margin of the stream, from behind which arrows or other weapons could be thrown directly into the fort by persons lying in perfect security.

From the skill exhibited by the mound-builders in their works of defence in other portions of the West, we cannot imagine that they would construct such a fort as this; we might at least expect that the walls would be extended so as to include the ridge parallel to it. There is no guarded opening, or gateway, into the inclosure. It can only be entered by water, or by climbing over the walls.

The only ancient work resembling this in its general features heretofore described, is that of Tuloom, in Yucatan, of which an account is given by Mr. Stephens, and quoted by Mr. Squier.[1] This is an inclosure of about the same dimensions, and bounded on the east by the sea; it consists of a loose stone wall, with watch-towers at the two west corners, corresponding with the two large pyramidal mounds at Aztalan, except that they are placed on the walls.

Mr. Stephens represents this as a walled city; but it must be admitted that only a very small city can be included in a space fifteen hundred by six hundred and fifty feet, or twenty-two and a half acres. Mr. Squier thinks that this structure was erected for some sacred object, though used, probably, as a place of defence in a last resort; and, in view of all the facts before stated, it may be inferred that the inclosure at Aztalan was intended for similar purposes, and not primarily occupied as a place of defence.

We may suppose it to have been a place of worship; the pyramidal mounds being the places of sacrifice, like the teocalli of Mexico. From its isolated situation —there being no other similar structure for a great distance in any direction—we may conjecture that this was a kind of Mecca, to which a periodical pilgrimage was

---

[1] Yucatan, II, 396; Aboriginal Monuments of New York, p. 98, in Smithsonian Contributions, Vol. II. In the accompanying figure the arrow, indicating the cardinal points, is reversed.

7

prescribed by their religion.   Here may have been the great annual feasts and
sacrifices of a whole nation.   Thousands of persons from remote locations may
have engaged in midnight ceremonies conducted by the priests.   The temple,
lighted by fires kindled on the great pyramids and at every projection on the
walls, on such occasions would have presented an imposing spectacle, well calculated to impress the minds of the people with awe and solemnity.   That these
works were designed for some such uses, seems quite probable.

Plate XXXV represents the same structures on a smaller scale, and shows their
relation to the neighboring country.   It will be seen that, excepting a few mounds,
no other artificial works are connected with the great inclosure; nor do these present that variety of imitative forms so common in other localities.   Half a mile
off, in a southwesterly direction, is a square pyramidal mound, similar to those
within the inclosure.

Do not these facts warrant the suggestion that the people of Aztalan, in Wisconsin, were a different people, in many respects, from those who erected the
animal-shaped mounds?   This location may possibly have been occupied by a
colony of Mexicans; since we know that colonies were sometimes sent out by that
singular people.[1]

It is much to be regretted that the efforts heretofore made to preserve these very
interesting remains of the labors of an extinct race are likely to fail.   At the time
of our survey, a crop of wheat was growing on the south part of the great inclosure; and, in a few years, but slight traces of this part of the works will be left.
The north part is still in its original condition, except where excavations have
been made by persons curious in such matters, or by the *money-diggers!*

Would it not be well to select some of the more important monuments, and, by
purchase of the ground, or other means, secure their permanent preservation?
Unless something of this kind is done, and speedily, all knowledge of them will be
confined to the scanty records of those who have attempted to describe them.

SECTION III.

ANCIENT WORKS OF THE VALLEY OF ROCK RIVER, ABOVE THOSE AT AZTALAN.

In the valley of Rock river we find no traces of ancient works for some distance
above Aztalan; the first being in the town of Ixonia (section nineteen, township
eight, range sixteen).   Here are seven or eight mounds along the right bank of the
river, on an elevated position, as usual, commanding a fine view of the river above
and below.   There are said to be others in the vicinity.

One of them has been opened for the purpose of making a place in which to
bury potatoes, to secure them from the frosts of winter.   Numbers of human bones
are said to have been thrown out from near the bottom, where the earth had been
hardened by some artificial process.   No implements or ornaments were noticed.

---

[1] Squier's Nicaragua, Vol. II.

At Wolf Point (section twenty-seven, township ten, range sixteen), in the lower part of the town of Hustisford, we observed traces of a recently abandoned Indian village, but no ancient works. Here, it is said, a great Indian battle was fought, in times long gone by; and here Black Hawk made a stand against his white pursuers in 1832.

At Hustisford a stone was shown us, which, by the aid of a little imagination, may be supposed to represent the head of a bird; and which was held in great veneration by the Winnebago Indians, who have but very recently been removed from this part of the State. It is a boulder of gneissoid granite, of accidental form, caused by the unequal decay and disintegration of the different layers of which it is composed. (See Fig. 16.)

FIG. 16.

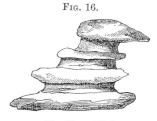

The Stone Bird.

At this place (Hustisford), there are the remains of a number of lizard mounds by the mill race, and also on the point opposite, on the east side of the river. There is a mound only two feet high, but having a considerable level area on the top, near the mill, which is said to be the place where prisoners of war were tortured and sacrificed by the Indian inhabitants. An examination disclosed partially calcined stones, ashes, charcoal, &c., in the centre.

The river here has a rapid current, caused by a ledge of limestone of the same kind as that in the lead districts of the western part of the State; the whole fall being about seven feet.

The country around is made up of a series of ridges like those before referred to, with intervening valleys, having a general direction nearly north and south. They are usually from twenty to fifty feet, and occasionally even one hundred feet in height, and frequently several miles in length. One of these ridges of great height, on the east side of the river, seems to have been selected as the principal cemetery, as we find it occupied by a series of round mounds, forming a nearly straight row along the summit. (Fig. 17.) They are so situated, that if the forest-trees were

FIG. 17.

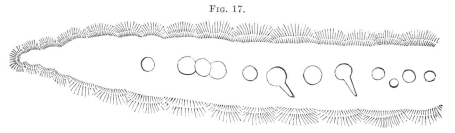

removed, a very extended prospect could be obtained, embracing the site of the village below, and the course of the river in either direction. Three of these are partially blended at the base, and two had a slight ridge extending towards the northeast, or in a direction *from* the village; or the tadpole (the significant name of this variety of mound) was headed towards the principal works and probably main residence of the ancient population.

The lizards are here, as in most localities of a similar kind, placed with the head or largest part towards the water.   Among them are a number with only one projection or leg, as shown in Fig. 18.

FIG. 18.

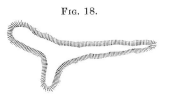

About five miles northwest of Hustisford, on the road to Juneau, the county seat (section twenty-six, township eleven, range fifteen), is an animal-formed mound, headed southward, and a ridge about one thousand feet in length, being much longer than any heretofore noticed.   The direction is a little north of east.   They do not appear to be connected with other works in the vicinity.

In the northwest part of this town are a number of mounds, but presenting no varieties different from those before described; excepting one cross, which, from the uniformity and great length of the arms, appears to differ from others. (See Fig. 19.)

FIG. 19.

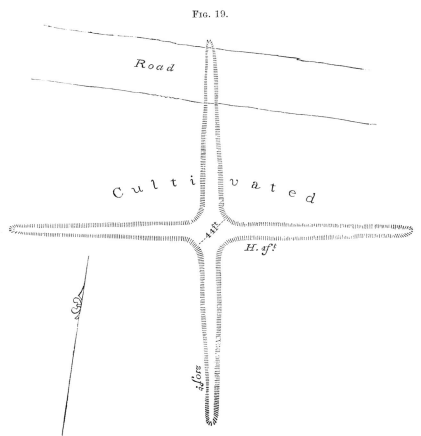

The Cross on section six, township eleven, range fifteen.   Surveyed, 1851, by I. A. Lapham.

It is situated near the road, on the north line of section six, township eleven, range fifteen, one of the arms being crossed by it.   The middle is on a gentle eminence, so that the arms descend in each direction.   Being on an open prairie, there is an extended view from this point.   Each arm appears to be of about the same size and length.   The plough having already commenced its work of destruction, we could not determine the proportions exactly.   The compass indicated that the arms were constructed almost precisely at right angles.

These remains are on the borders of a prairie, which, from the unevenness of its surface, is denominated " Rolling Prairie."   One prominent elevation has been supposed to be artificial (Fig. 20); but a little examination satisfied us that it was natural.

FIG. 20.

Natural Mound on Rolling Prairie.

Towards the source of the Beaver Dam river, we found numerous mounds; especially near the northwest corner of the town of Juneau (township eleven, range fifteen).   On section seven are some "oblongs," one which was probably a "cross," and two others, broad and flat, with tails.   These are much injured by cultivation. They occupy a broad, gently undulating plain, the margin of the Rolling Prairie.

At the village of Beaver Dam, the stream is interrupted by a dam, so as to form a pond ten miles in length, similar, in many respects, to the one at Horicon, on Rock river.   On the border of this pond, a little west of the village, was a series of mounds, now quite destroyed by the road that runs directly over them.   Their forms could not be made out with any degree of accuracy.

Fig. 21 represents two mounds, with a connection probably accidental, situated

FIG. 21.

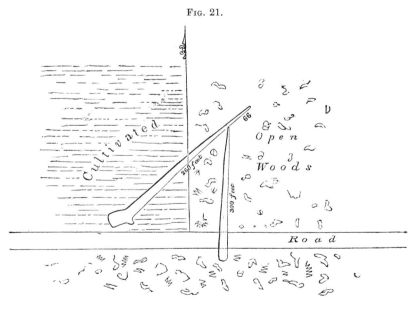

on section one, township eleven, range fourteen.   The effigy could not be made out in the cultivated field; but it was, apparently, of the kind called the lizard.

A few miles N. W. of this locality, on section twenty-seven, township twelve, range fourteen, is a group of various forms, mostly injured or destroyed. Their original number is estimated to have been between thirty and fifty. They were mostly of the turtle form, though some are said to have resembled the lizard, the buffalo, &c.

The works at Waushara, near the outlet of Fox lake, were on both sides of the river; but those on the east side were destroyed by the growth of the village. One circular tumulus was beautifully decorated with flowers, and will be preserved as an ornament in the flower garden of one of the citizens; a commendable instance of good taste.

On the west side of the stream is an extensive group containing a cross, oblongs, circular mounds, one of the bird form, and two that were perhaps intended to represent the elk (see Fig. 22). These are on the ridge, and along the slopes of the ridge, running parallel with the river, and but a short distance from it. Among the figures was a cross, the arms of which were oblique (Fig. 23), and one

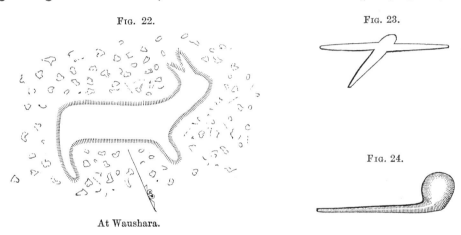

FIG. 22.

At Waushara.

FIG. 23.

FIG. 24.

with the tail forming a tangent to the mound (Fig. 24), its outline resembling some forms of the war-club, or the modern tobacco-pipe.

The next point visited was a high bank at the northeast angle of the lake (sections eleven and fourteen, township thirteen, range thirteen), and near the mouth of a small stream. At this place are several crosses, one structure of the bird form, and numerous ridges, but not arranged with any apparent order or system. In the same locality are numerous corn-hills and "caches" of the present tribes, who still make their annual visits to the spot. We saw a flattish boulder which had been used as a sort of anvil for pounding or pulverizing corn and perhaps other substances.

Near the source of a small branch of Rock river, called the Rubicon, is a fine little sheet of water called Pike lake. The banks are low, except on the east side; and on the north side there is a group of works as sketched on Plate XXXVI, presenting some characteristics not before observed. Here is another mound with a level area on the top, being the frustrum of a cone, similar to the temple mounds, supposed to be places of sacrifice. There are three others of the ordinary form, two of the imitative forms, and a semicircular ridge embracing a circular excavation at one extremity, and partially inclosing another. The figure at the east has but one projection or leg, and a forked tail; the other figure differs from most of the lizard-mounds in the fact that the body and tail are not in the same straight line.

The bank of the lake is more elevated at this point than on either side, where are some low grounds with springs and marshy places. A little east of this lake is a high peak or hill, which we ascended, but found no traces of ancient works on its summit.

But the most extended and varied groups of ancient works, and the most complicated and intricate, are at Horicon. Plate XXXVII represents the principal groups immediately below the town, but does not include all in this vicinity. They occupy the high bank of the river on both sides.

It will be seen that most of the forms heretofore described are represented at this place, and some are combined in a very curious manner. There are about two hundred ordinary round mounds in this neighborhood, and all, with two exceptions, quite small. The two large ones, on the west side of the river, have an elevation of twelve feet, and are sixty-five feet in diameter at the base. The others are from one to four or five feet high. In several of them we noticed very recent Indian graves, covered with slabs or stakes, in the usual method of modern Indian burial. They belong to the Potawattomies. One is protected by slabs driven in a sloping manner, so as to meet at the top like the roof of a house. Another has a kind of pen made of sticks about six inches in diameter. These graves show the peculiarity of having but one kind of wood on one grave; the slabs being made of oak, and the pen made of elm. The larger and more conspicuous mounds are generally selected by the Indians for the burial of their dead.

There are sixteen mounds of the cruciform variety. (See Plate XXXVI, Nos. 1 and 2.) They are not placed in any uniform direction—some having the head towards the north, some towards the south; nor do they appear to be turned towards the river. The form seen, Plate XXXVI, No. 1, is exactly like that of the mounds on the Milwaukee river; but that represented on No. 2 of the same plate was first observed at this place.

There is one mound, of which only a small portion appears on the plate, regularly tapering for a length of five hundred and seventy feet. At the smaller extremity it is slightly curved to the east. At its larger extremity is a large cross, and one of the largest mounds.

The animal form, Plate XXXVI, No. 3, is repeated, with slight modifications, seven times. It may be supposed to represent the otter.

If the two composite figures, one on each side of the river, near the centre of the group, are animals, performing some action, it is quite difficult to decide what the animal or the action may be that is intended to be represented. Yet it can hardly be supposed that these works were erected without design. They doubtless have some meaning which it is now impossible to ascertain.

Several of the mounds had been opened; but we could not learn of any results, excepting the discovery of human bones, and, in one case, the bones of a quadruped. We opened one of the smaller ones, and, after a careful search, could trace no indications that anything had ever been deposited beneath it. If a human body or anything else had been buried there, all traces of it had disappeared. It is difficult to comprehend for what purpose the very numerous small tumuli were made, if not for burial; and yet it is hardly probable that all evidence of such use would have disappeared. They are here commonly made of the black vegetable mould, but slightly mixed with the subsoil, which has a lighter color.

On the other hand, one of the crosses was composed of whitish earth, evidently taken from beneath the surface-soil. The animal mounds and crosses, being composed of whitish earth, can sometimes be traced in a cultivated field, even after it is ploughed down to a level with the general surface. One of the crosses immediately south of the two large mounds seen on the plate, has the arms extended quite athwart the top of the ridge, which is here flanked on one side by the river, and on the other by an extensive marsh, or natural wet meadow.

Immediately above, the river expands into a broad and shallow lake, extending twelve miles, with a mean breadth of five miles. Until recently this lake was four feet lower than at present, and was mostly covered with a floating morass. Immense numbers of fish and water-fowls are found there, and afford subsistence to the inhabitants. These advantages have probably, from the remotest antiquity, given this situation a prominence in the estimation of the various tribes or nations who have successively occupied the country. It is a fact of some importance, in deciding upon the general characteristics of the mound-builders, that they have selected the same localities as their successors, and probably for the same reasons, to wit: the greater facility of subsistence.

The beaver and otter, in former times, doubtless occupied the shores of this lake, as the muskrat still continues to do. The several sources of the Rock river run into the lake at various points, and their united waters are discharged at Horicon. It has an elevation above Lake Michigan of two hundred and ninety feet. The celebrated Sauk chief, Black Hawk, formerly had his residence at this point.

There are various interesting localities of ancient works in the vicinity of Mayville, as will be seen on Plate XXXVIII. The most extended of these is on the northwest quarter of section eighteen, township twelve, range seventeen, two miles northeast of the village. This group is shown on Plate XXXIX. It comprises thirty-five mounds of various forms, and occupies a nearly level strip between the base of a large ridge[1] and brook.

We found here one of the largest and most regular turtle-mounds we had yet seen, and three or four of the quadruped form, one of which is represented on an enlarged scale on Plate XXXIX. The two crosses are directed towards the northeast, while most of the other forms have an opposite direction. Their arms are seldom at right angles with the body, nor are the two parts of the body or trunk in the same line. The head is always largest, highest, and nearly rectangular in

---

[1] On Plate XXXVIII, I have endeavored to represent these diluvial ridges, and to show how they give direction to the water-courses. It would be a matter of much interest to the geologist to determine their extent and exact nature, with the view of ascertaining, if possible, their origin. But such an investigation would be out of place in this memoir.

form. Their height corresponds with that of the other figures, it being usually from two to four feet. If these crosses are to be deemed evidence of the former existence of Christianity on this continent (as some have inferred), we may, with almost equal propriety, assert that Mohammedanism was associated with it, and, as proof, refer to the mound or ridge here represented in the form of a crescent.

Three mounds, near the north end of the group, are cleft at the extremity, like that noticed at Burlington (Plate XIII, Fig. 2). One of them might be supposed to represent a fish, and, as the finny tribe must have afforded a principal source of subsistence to the builders, it would not be surprising if they should include them in the list of animals to be thus depicted. In that case the cleft extremity should be considered as a forked tail, rather than an open mouth. The general direction of the other figures would naturally suggest the same thing, at least in this locality.

In a cultivated field, near these works, were traces of other mounds, whose nature we could not determine; they were too far gone to be restored.

Half a mile east of this extensive group is a smaller cluster, consisting of two animals and two oblong mounds. They were discovered by the engineer party in the survey of the Valley Railroad, who reported the animals as resembling the horse. Mr. Logan Crawford, Deputy Surveyor of Dodge county, made a survey and drawing of one, given on Plate XXXVIII, which, as will be seen, has but little resemblance to a horse. It was, without doubt, constructed by men who had never seen or heard of such an animal, being long before its introduction upon the American continent.

The two figures at this place are almost exactly alike, and Mr. Crawford's outline may be relied upon as correct. The dimensions were ascertained by running a line over the mound lengthwise, and then measuring at right angles from this line to thirty-six of the most prominent points in the outline. The height on the shoulders and fore-part of the body is about two and a half feet. The legs, tail, head, and neck, are not more than one foot high. Its whole length is one hundred and twenty-four feet.

Directly north of Mayville (on the northeast quarter of section fourteen, township twelve, range sixteen), on the eastern declivity, and near the base of a ridge, I saw some traces of ancient cultivation, in the form of garden-beds, with intermediate paths. In one place, where the beds were examined, they are one hundred feet long, and had a uniform breadth of six feet, with a direction nearly east and west. The depressions or walks between the beds were about eight inches deep and fifteen inches wide.

The next group of mounds noticed was at the northern extremity of a ridge near the lower dam and mills (northwest quarter of section fourteen). There were five elevations of the circular form, three of them with a projecting ridge, gradually tapering to the extremity, being of the kind called "tadpoles."[1] There are also two of the lizard form, the tail of one being in contact with the head of the other.

---

[1] This form (see Fig. 18, p. 51), may possibly have been intended to represent the gourd, an ancient American plant, doubtless much used by the mound-builders.

8

On the adjoining tract (northeast quarter of section fifteen), are some round mounds; among them two of larger dimensions than usual, being from twelve to fourteen feet in height, and from sixty-five to seventy feet in diameter.

These several groups form a regular row, from east to west, a little north of Mayville. There is a similar arrangement at about the same distance south of the village, commencing at a group of three mounds near the centre of section twenty-six, which were very accurately surveyed and delineated by Mr. Crawford (see Plate XL)—the cross, as usual, with a direction opposite to that of the other figures, of which the central one is doubtless intended to represent the trunk and arms of the human body. The trunk is two feet high, the arms and shoulders one foot. The animal-shaped figure is brought too near this man on the plate (being ninety feet distant). It differs from most others of similar configuration in its slender form, rounded head, and recurved caudal extremity. The body is for most of its length two and a half feet high; the legs, head, and tail are one foot and a half high; but the tail gradually slopes down to about six inches at the extremity.

On the northeast quarter of section twenty-seven is a group of four mounds, of which one has the unusual form represented on Plate XXXIX. What it was designed to represent, it is difficult to conjecture.

The next group is three miles southwest of Mayville, being on the northwest quarter of the same section, and occupying the southern extremity of one of the remarkable ridges so often mentioned. The road from Mayville to Horicon passes directly by it. The general character of the figures will be understood by inspection of Plate XL. A portion were in a cultivated field, and the breaking-up plough had just been at work upon the remainder. Another year, and it would have been for ever too late to delineate them. It will be observed that all the figures of this group have their heads in one general southwesterly direction, except the cross, which, as is almost always the case, has a course directly opposite. From the extremity of the longest mound, which is on the highest ground, a general view of the whole is obtained; and this may, perhaps, be regarded as the watch-tower or look-out station. It is four hundred feet long.

On section thirty-three, near Horicon lake, are also some mounds, not shown on the plate, lying west of those represented. They consist of two ridges, one of considerable length, on the side of a ridge sloping towards the lake.

On the very high ledge of limestone, at the southwest corner of section twenty-seven, which overlooks Lake Horicon, I was disappointed in not finding artificial works.

On section twenty-five, township eleven, range sixteen, about seven miles south of Mayville, is a cross examined by Mr. S. E. Lefferts, of that place. We did not visit this locality, though we learned that the cross is associated with other mounds.

At the town of Theresa, on the elevated ground on the south side of the river, near the residence of Solomon Juneau, Esq., is a group of figures mostly of the lizard or oblong forms, and among them an excavation similar to those observed at Fort Atkinson and near Milwaukee (see Plate IX, Fig. 5). Most of the lizard mounds here are directed towards the south, but two are in an opposite direction; this being the first case of the kind observed.

A few Indians (Menomonees and Winnebagos) still reside here, and their wigwams are associated with the more substantial buildings of the white man. One of the oblong elevations was entirely covered with graves recently made by them.

I have heard of other works twelve miles east of Theresa, and at Mound Prairie, eight miles north; also about a mile and a half below Waupun, north of Horicon lake.

CHAPTER IV.

ANCIENT WORKS IN THE BASIN OF THE NEENAH, OR FOX RIVER OF GREEN BAY.

THIS important river rises in Columbia and Adams counties, in two small streams that unite a few miles north of Fort Winnebago. Thence it has a sluggish current and crooked course, expanding into broad shallow lakes, or winding through rice marshes, until it enters Lake Winnebago. At a place known as Butte des Morts (or Mound of the Dead), it receives the waters of Wolf river, which is larger than the Neenah itself. Between Lake Winnebago and Green bay the river has a descent, over numerous rapids, of one hundred and seventy feet.

The public surveys not having all been completed, the area drained by this river cannot be exactly stated; but it is estimated at about 6,700 square miles.

At a place on the east side of Green bay, called the Red Banks (township twenty-five, range twenty-two), as we are informed by Hon. Morgan L. Martin, in his annual discourse before the State Historical Society of Wisconsin, delivered in 1851, there are traces of ancient cultivation, still distinct, over a tract of several hundred acres, now overgrown with forest-trees of a large size; the product, according to computation, of five centuries. The remains of an embankment inclosing an acre or two of ground, occupy an elevated position in the immediate vicinity.

No other aboriginal works about Green bay have come to my knowledge, though they may have existed and been long since destroyed; for settlements have existed there since a period nearly or quite as far back as the year 1665.

FIG. 25.

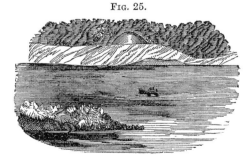

Little Butte des Morts, as seen across the Lake. June 14, 1851.

Nor do we find such traces along the rapids below Lake Winnebago. The advantages of water power had no attraction for the natives. The gently flowing stream and placid lake were more favorite places of resort. Hence, we perceive no indications of ancient mounds till near Lake Winnebago; the first one in ascending the river being on the west side of Little Lake Butte des Morts, a name indicating the existence of the mound, and the purpose for which it was erected.   (See Fig. 25.)

This tumulus is about eight feet high, and fifty feet in diameter.   It is to be hoped that a monument so conspicuous, and so beautifully situated, may be for ever preserved as a memento of the past.   It is a picturesque and striking object in passing along this fine lake, and may have been the cause of serious reflections and high resolves to many a passing savage.   It is well calculated to affect not less the bosoms of more enlightened men.   There is neither necessity nor excuse for its destruction; and we cannot but again express the hope that it will be preserved for the benefit of all who may pass along that celebrated stream.

The summit of the mound is about fifty feet above the lake, affording a very pleasing view embracing the lake and the entrance to the north channel of the river.

Among the articles discovered in the field near by, was some burnt clay in irregular fragments, with impressions of the leaves and stems of grass, precisely like those found at Aztalan.

This had been a place of burial, and, perhaps, of well contested battles; for the plough constantly turns up fragments of human bones and teeth, much broken and decayed.   Arrow-points of flint, and pipes of the red pipestone and other materials, have also been brought to light.

Two miles further east, and half a mile from Menasha, is a group of eight mounds about four feet high, and from forty to fifty feet in diameter.   They are on the southeast quarter of section fourteen, township twenty, range seventeen, not far from the shore of Lake Winnebago.   This ground has been selected for a cemetery by the present inhabitants, who do not scruple to dig up the Indian skeletons to make room for the bodies of a more civilized race.

The ground here, as in numerous other places, exhibits marks of former culture in rows or beds, very different from that of the modern Indians.   These are covered with a dense forest of young and thrifty trees, the largest not more, perhaps, than one hundred and fifty years old; so that the whole have grown up since the time of Marquette, or within one hundred and eighty years.

In the village of Menasha is an elongated mound, quite high at the end towards the river, and terminating at a point at the other.   A similar one exists on Doty's island,[1] forming a sort of counterpart to the first.   They are not exactly opposite, but are both directed towards the river.

The eastern extremity of Doty's island has long been occupied by Indians, as is evinced by the regular cornhills covering nearly the whole surface, as well as by a new feature, not before observed, or supposed to be within the pale of Indian customs.   The ground was originally covered with loose stones, fragments of the solid limestone rock that exists everywhere not far beneath the surface.   These stones had been carefully collected into little heaps and ridges, to make room for the culture of the native crops.   The stone heaps are six or eight feet in diameter, and from one to two feet in height.   The interstices are now filled with soil, and partially covered with grass and weeds.

The country about Lake Winnebago was first inhabited by the Kickapoo tribe;

---

[1] The residence of Hon. James D. Doty, M. C.

though it is stated that the Mascontins (*Gens des Prairies*) were there at one time.[1] The former were driven away by the wandering and warlike tribes of Sauks and Foxes, who very early united, and, penetrating to the west, first established themselves here. They were in turn compelled to move further west by the Chippewas, aided by the French.[2] How long the Chippewas maintained possession is not known. In 1766, Carver found on Doty's island, " a great town of the Winnebagoes ;"[3] and more recently this region has been occupied by the Menomonees.

Which of these tribes, if either, performed the labor of gathering up the stones, it would be difficult to decide; nor are we able to say whether the heaps are of the same age as the mounds or of later origin.

From Menasha we went in a sail-boat across the north end of Lake Winnebago, to examine and survey the mounds on the top of a high limestone cliff or ledge.

On the northwest quarter of section thirty-six is a small clearing on the bank of the lake, not far from the foot of the bluff, in which were traces of three long mounds; and in the adjacent forest are three small embankments, extending across a small ridge from the bank of the lake to a valley back of it. We had much difficulty in climbing the ledge, which has quite a formidable aspect, and is probably two hundred feet high above the water; the last forty or fifty being perpendicular, or nearly so. From the top commences an almost level plateau, extending towards the east; and here we were fully paid for our labor, by the magnificent view of the lake and surrounding country. Those who have examined the banks of the Niagara below the great falls, or the mountain ridge as is seen in western New York and Canada, will have a correct idea of this ledge of limestone; and being composed of a rock of the same geological age, the resemblance is not to be wondered at.

Passing along the ridge, we came upon the series of ancient works represented upon Plate XLI, No. 1,[4] extending for some distance near the edge of the rocky escarpment. It will be observed that they are of the same forms as those heretofore described further south and southwest, and, with one or two exceptions, are arranged with the heads towards the south.

The fact that the first figure is placed transversely, preceded by two mounds or advanced posts, may have a particular significance; but, if so, its meaning is now lost. The cross, near the centre of the group, is usually called " the man" by the few persons who have seen this locality; but it wants the legs and the contraction for the neck, seen in the mounds of human form at the West.

These are the most northern of any animal-shaped mounds in the eastern part of Wisconsin. They terminate near the south line of section thirty-six, township twenty, range eighteen.

Although tormented by mosquitos, and oppressed by the close, hot, and damp atmosphere of the dense forest, we followed the ledge five miles to another series of similar remains, represented on the same plate, No. 2.

---

[1] Drake's Life of Black Hawk, p. 16.

[2] Supposed to have been in 1706.

[3] Carver's Travels, &c., N. Y. ed. 1838, p. 41.

[4] On this plate the figures are brought nearer together than the scale requires; but the distances thus encroached upon are given on the plate.

They are situated on the extremity of a ridge, at a place where the main ledge is further back from the lake, and is much less steep.

Here was found a turtle-mound, but differing from the usual form in several particulars, as will be seen by the figure.

The land along the east shore of Lake Winnebago is among the finest in the State. The growth of trees and shrubs is so dense that it is difficult to penetrate it without the aid of an axeman. It is just such land as would be selected by an agricultural people.

These are, doubtless, the structures alluded to by Mr. R. C. Taylor, from information communicated to him by Dr. Lyman Foote, of the United States Army.[1]

There are mounds of ordinary circular form in the vicinity of the southern extremity of Lake Winnebago; some of them have been opened and found to contain human bones.

We have heard of others of imitative forms on the west side of the lake, between Oshkosh and Fond du Lac, which we did not visit, nor could we obtain very definite information in regard to them.

Just before the Neenah enters Lake Winnebago, it expands into a broad sheet of water called the Great Butte des Morts lake. Near the head of this lake is the mound from which its name is derived, on the north or left bank of the river. This is the site of the conflict between the Chippewas and French against the Sauk and Fox bands;[2] but I can find no authority for the popular belief that the tumulus was raised at that time as a covering for the bodies of the slain.

Near this Butte the Wolf branch of the Neenah enters, being properly the main stream. Col. Charles Whittlesey, of the United States Geological Corps, explored this stream, and he informs me that he found no remains of ancient works on its banks.

At the Falls of the Waupacca (a tributary of the Wolf) mounds are said to exist, and also at some other localities in the vicinity.

Near a small stream, called Eight-mile creek, in the town of Utica, on the land of Mr. E. B. Fiske (northwest quarter of section fourteen, township seventeen, range fifteen), is a mound called the Spread Eagle (see Plate XLI, No. 3). It is of small dimensions, the whole length being only forty-six feet.

There are two oblong embankments in the vicinity; and the house is built upon another called the Alligator, but its form could not be distinctly traced at the time of our visit.

There is a group of conical tumuli, forming an irregular row, half a mile below Ceresco (section seventeen, township sixteen, range fourteen), and others of a similar character formerly existed at and near the village.

At several points along the Neenah, between the Portage at Fort Winnebago and the Butte des Morts, are localities of mounds.

Mr. R. C. Taylor informs us that " on the shores of Buffalo and Apuchwa lakes, wherever the land is dry and sufficiently elevated, one may observe, even from the

---

[1] Silliman's Journal, XXXIV, 95.
[2] Pike's Expedition, Appendix to Part I, p. 45.

water, a vast number of tumuli. Upon the summit of some of these may, from time to time, be recognized the modern grave of some Winnebago or Menomonee chief, strongly protected by pickets. The margins of the Neenah river are remarkable for numerous Indian remains of this description. Colonel Petitval, of the United States Topographical Department, who was engaged during the summer of 1837 in a survey of this river, had the kindness, at my request, to give some attention to these mounds. He describes an immense assemblage of them at a point on the river called the Red Bank, extending far into the interior, both north and south, for an undetermined distance. Twelve of them at this place were opened under his direction, and among them was an animal mound one hundred and fifty feet long. All contained human bones in a very decomposed state."[1]

The mounds examined by me along the Apuchwa and Buffalo lakes, were entirely of the conical form, or burial-mounds. They were observed at the villages of Marquette, Montello, Roxo, and Packwaukee; the same places that formerly were the seats of aboriginal population being now selected as the sites of embryo towns and villages by men of a different race.

There is a fine group on section twelve, township fourteen, range ten, occupying prairie ground near a branch of Grand river. Further up this river (on section eleven, township fourteen, range eleven) is a collection of about one hundred mounds, mostly of the same form. Only one was sufficiently perfect to admit of being surveyed and delineated. It is called the "Man," and is remarkable for the unequal length of the arms. (Fig. 26.) It had been opened before our visit. The

Fig. 26.

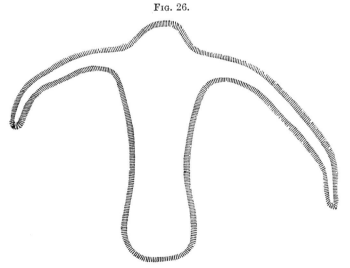

The Man, near Mt. Moriah.

head points to the south, and towards a high hill called Mount Moriah. The soil is sandy, and the mounds do not, therefore, preserve their original shape as distinctly as in other localities. The round mounds are worn down and spread out, so as to form

---

[1] Silliman's Journal, XXXIV, 95.

a very flat cone. In one was found the skeleton of a man, with fragments of pottery, &c.

There are also a few mounds near Lake Maria, at the source of Grand river (sections twenty-five and thirty-six, township fourteen, range twelve).

The Neenah river is in some places bordered by a high sandy bank, frequently higher near the water than further back. Along the margin of this bank, small indistinct mounds are of frequent occurrence, placed as if intended to guard or watch the passage of the river. They are often of a subtriangular form, the shortest side and highest point being towards the river. They are unusually small, and have but little elevation.

At a place known as Moundville, are some structures quite perfect in their shape and outline. They are in the oak-openings, on the west side of the river, in township fourteen, range nine; and consist of several raccoons and bears, with oblong and round mounds, and one animal form (Fig. 27), whose genus and species could not well be made out.

FIG. 27.

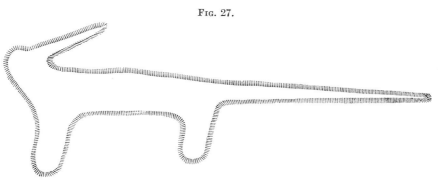

At Moundville.　Forty feet to an inch.

CHAPTER V.

ANCIENT WORKS IN THE BASIN OF THE WISCONSIN RIVER.

THE Wisconsin river is the largest stream within the State, having its source on the boundary line between Wisconsin and Michigan, in a small sheet of water known as "Lac Vieux Désert," and running into the Mississippi at Prairie du Chien. Its general course is nearly south as far as the Winnebago portage, where it almost unites with the Neenah. At this point it is suddenly deflected towards the southwest and west. Its length cannot be less than four hundred miles, and it has an aggregate descent of about nine hundred feet, or two and a quarter feet per mile. It drains an area of about eleven hundred square miles.

The valley of this fine stream, from the Winnebago Portage to its junction with the Mississippi, may be deemed the great central seat of population at the time of the erection of the animal-shaped earthworks; at least we must so infer from their comparative abundance and importance along that valley.

The first published notice of the mounds in the valley of the Wisconsin, is in the narrative of Long's Second Expedition, in 1823. It is there stated that "one of the block-houses of the fort (at Prairie du Chien) is situated on a large mound, which appears to be artificial. It was excavated; but we have not heard that any bones or other remains were found in it."

Mr. Alfred Bronson, in a paper on the ancient mounds of Crawford county, Wisconsin, read before the State Historical Society, remarks that another similar one formerly existed on the prairie, now removed; but no evidences of the design of their erection were found—nothing was observed but bones, rifles, &c., of recent interment.

"One mound, standing in a group at the southwest angle of this prairie, has a base of some fifty feet, and is about ten feet high, on an eminence of about the same elevation. From its top can be seen to advantage the extensive low bottom-lands which lie between the Wisconsin and Mississippi rivers; and were it not for the timber on the margin of the two rivers, their flowing currents could also be seen for some distance. This circumstance induces the belief that it was built for a kind of watch-tower, or look-out place, to watch the approach of enemies."

Traces of mounds were discovered by me (in 1852) along the whole extent of the prairie, apparently similar to others found in the vicinity; but from cultivation, and the light sandy nature of the materials, they are now almost entirely obliterated. The large round tumuli, situated along the island between the "slough" and the main channel of the Mississippi, are so near the level of the river that their bases are often washed by the floods. In 1826, at the highest known floods, (it being eight feet higher than the high water of 1832, and about twenty-six feet above the lowest stage,) the mounds were all that could be seen of this island above the water. These were doubtless for burial, and of less age than the more elaborate works in the interior of the country.

Below the town and fort, towards the mouth of the Wisconsin, are similar tumuli, equally subject to overflow; and on the high bluffs south of that river are some look-out stations or mounds.

Advantage is taken of these elevations for the foundations of the better class of dwelling-houses, above the reach of high water; being, perhaps, the only instance in which the ancient works are rendered useful to the present inhabitants. In general it is deemed necessary to remove them as incumbrances, rather than to preserve them as matters of convenience.

Some traces of a ditch and embankment observed on the island, evidently of a military character, proved, on inquiry, to be the remains of the original American fort, that was taken by the British in the war of 1812.

It is quite clear that this interesting place has been a favorite one with all the different tribes or races of inhabitants, from the days of the first mound-builders to the present time; and the construction of a railroad (soon to be completed) connecting this point with Lake Michigan at Milwaukee, will doubtless render it one of the greatest importance.

Proceeding up the Wisconsin, the first locality requiring notice is called by the French the *Petit Cap au Grés*; which was visited by Messrs. Keating, Say, and Seymour, of Long's exploring party, and of which the following account is given: "They found the bluff which borders on the Wisconsin, about four miles above its mouth, covered with mounds, parapets, &c.; but no plan or system could be observed among them, neither could they trace any such thing as a regular inclosure. Among these works, they saw an embankment about eighty-five yards long, divided towards its middle by a sort of gateway about four yards wide. This parapet was elevated from three to four feet; it stood very near to the edge of the bluff, as did also almost all the other embankments which they saw. No connection whatever was observed between the parapets and the mounds, except in one case, where a parapet was cut off by a sort of gateway, and a mound placed in front of it. In one instance the works, or parapet, seemed to form a cross, of which three parts could be distinctly traced; but these were short: this was upon a projecting point of the highland. The mounds which the party observed, were scattered without any apparent symmetry over the whole of the ridge of highland which borders upon the river. They were very numerous, and generally from six to eight feet high, and from eight to twelve in diameter. In one case a number of them, amounting perhaps to twelve or fifteen, were seen all arranged in one line, parallel to the edge of the bluff, but at some distance from it."

The very numerous and highly interesting remains found on the banks of the Wisconsin at Muscoda, and in its vicinity, are very fully described and delineated by Mr. Stephen Taylor, to whose paper in Silliman's Journal (XLIV, 22), and in the abstract of it in the Smithsonian Contributions (I, 128–133, Plates xlii, xliii, xliv), the reader is referred. Not having visited this locality, I have nothing to add to the ample details given by Mr. Taylor.

It can hardly admit of a doubt that this animal is intended, if we judge from the general form of the image.

One of these figures had apparently been cut in two by some cause since it was completed. Several excavations made in building the dam have injured or destroyed some of these works. We noticed here that the reddish earth excavated from the pits very soon lost its redness on exposure to the air, and assumed the light color of the earth found in the animal mounds. This will explain the difference in hue without resorting to the improbable suggestion that the soil has been brought from a distance. The birds and bear are on the margin of the beautiful level plain, here mostly covered with trees; a part of the great plain or prairie before alluded to.

It is to be observed, that the difference between the mounds evidently birds (Plate XLVI, No. 3) and those resembling the human form (Plate XLII, Nos. 3 and 4), is but slight; so that, strange as it may appear, it is sometimes not easy to decide which was meant by the ancient artist.

The prairie along the river, above Honey creek, gives evidence of recent Indian occupancy in the numerous irregular corn-hills, such as are now made by them. In 1766,[1] and probably for a long time afterwards, it was the site of a village of the united Sauk and Fox tribes—hence, the name of the prairie. But few remains of the labors of the "ancient people," however, were observed on this plain, until we approached its upper margin. Here we found, near the residence of Mr. Charles Durr, several parallel ridges, and a few imitative forms. One of these, with the anterior foot remarkably enlarged, is represented on Plate XLVI, No. 1. These works are near the line between sections seven and eight, township ten, range seven east.

We here found a number of ridges with an angular deflection near the smaller extremity. (See Plate XLVI, No. 2.) They have about the usual height of oblong parapets and ridges, from two to four feet, and vary in length from two hundred to several hundred feet. They differ from the crooked ridge (Plate XLIII), on Honey creek, in having the deflected portion straight.

We noticed here a mound with a horn, apparently intended to represent the elk or deer; which, as night overtook us, we did not survey.

A short distance above commences a series of works surveyed by Mr. William H. Canfield, of Baraboo. and represented on Plate XLVI, No. 4, and on Plates XLVII and XLVIII. They are located on the slope extending from the bluffs to the river, here about two miles apart. The ground is not level or even, but gently rolling, and the principal mounds are handsomely situated on the knolls. The little brook on Plate XLVII is usually dry, and runs in a valley but slightly depressed below the general surface. Towards its source the ground is more level and a little marshy. The bed of the stream is a little gravelly.

The sharp-pointed ridges, some straight, and others with an angle near the extremity, and the animal with several humps on its back, are peculiar features in this group.

The works represented on Plate XLVIII are about a mile north of the last, and

---

[1] Carver's Travels (Harper's N. Y. Ed., 1838), p. 49.

about midway between the bluffs and the river. The pond contains pure water, and now supplies the inhabitants of a very different race with this indispensable element.

About two miles further up the river (on section three, township ten, range seven east), is another group, of which only one figure was surveyed by Mr. Canfield (Plate XLVI, No. 4). The form of the head and wings leaves no doubt that the object intended was a bird.

As this bird is represented in the act of flying, the remark of Mr. Canfield that it may be a messenger-bird carrying something, indicated by the little mound placed below the wing, as if suspended from its beak, seems quite probable. This mound is small (seven feet in diameter), a very true circle at the base, and now less than a foot in height. Perhaps the purpose is to represent the bird as bearing to the spirit-land some person whose remains were deposited in the mound.

Mr. Canfield writes that " the valley of the Wisconsin river above Prairie du Sac, for three or four miles, is completely filled with these works. It is here two miles wide, timbered mostly with black and burr oak, generally of a light sandy soil, and quite undulating, in some places hilly. There are no mounds on the prairie."

There are scattered tumuli of various forms in and about the village of Baraboo, on the river of the same name.

A little east of that remarkable gorge in the sandstone, known as " the Dells of the Wisconsin river," is a small inclosure (Fig. 28), of double walls, which may

FIG. 28.

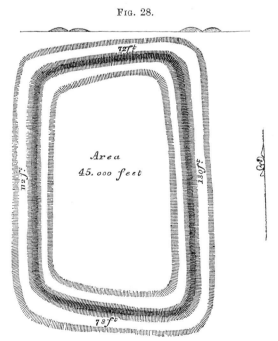

Ancient inclosure, Dells of Wisconsin river.

have been surmounted by palisades, and have formed a sort of fort or stronghold. The breadth occupied by the two embankments is eighteen feet, and the area of the inclosure is about 45,000 square feet, affording room for about 2,000 persons.

There are also some other slight works in this vicinity, mostly oblong mounds, called breastworks by gentlemen of military associations; and there are extensive tracts of ground worked into garden-beds, or low flat ridges, as before described.

There are also some mounds at the foot of the Big Dells, six miles further up the river.

Following up the valley of the Lemonwier river, a branch of the Wisconsin from the west, the first group of works observed was near One Mile creek (section twenty, township fifteen, range four, delineated on Plate XLIX). There are six embankments of different lengths, three bird-shaped mounds with large bodies, and two small oval tumuli, all arranged on or between two sandy ridges that very much resemble ancient lake beaches. The works are arranged in a direction parallel to these two ridges; and the wings of two of the birds extend entirely across the low ground between them. On both sides of the ridges the ground descends into low marshy places of considerable extent.

The two oblong embankments situated upon the sand ridge might be supposed to be works of defence, or breastworks; but as they are of precisely the same character as the others whose position between the ridges precludes such an inference, we must, as in other cases, conclude that they were constructed for a different purpose. The ground is here occupied by the oak-openings, or a scattered growth of trees. The marshes on each side may formerly have been ponds, now filled by the accumulation for ages of vegetable matter.

At Mors creek (section seven, township fifteen, range four, east), there is a series of mounds, as delineated on Plate L. They extend along the river at intervals for two miles. The group near the mill (Plate L, No. 1), is much injured by a removal of the earth to form the dam across the Lemonwier river. It consists, as will be seen, of bird-shaped and oblong earthworks. No. 2 of the same plate is an enlarged plan of the two most perfect of these images. Upon excavating one of them, the remains of a human skeleton were found, which had been deposited in the head of the figure. These mounds are here supposed to represent men. They are upon a gentle slope or nearly level space between the river and the foot of a ridge, or second bank, which is but slightly elevated above the water of the river. Several round tumuli are found on the ridge a few rods further west.

On Plate L, No. 3, is represented a very long-armed figure, situated near Two Mile creek (about two miles above Moss's Mill), where are others quite similar to those exhibited on the same plate, No. 2. These long arms extend quite across from the abrupt bank of the river to some marshy grounds.

In the same neighborhood is said to be a small circular inclosure (southwest quarter of section twenty-one, township sixteen, range three), and also (on the northwest quarter of section twelve, township fifteen, range three) a series of garden-beds.

Leaving the main Lemonwier river, we passed between two isolated sandstone cliffs, known as the Little Bluffs (section twelve, township sixteen, range two, east), and observed two oblong embankments, or breastworks; but they did not appear to be arranged with any purpose of defending the narrow pass between the bluffs.

On section nine, township sixteen, range two, east, we found an oblong embankment; and also one called a man, with the legs expanded, but having no contraction for the neck. (See Plate L, No. 4.)

Several earthworks (one of the man shape) are found on section five, township sixteen, range two, east; and a row of five oblong elevations, with but slight intervals, occupy a swell in the prairie on section four, township sixteen, range one, east.

Above these we discovered no more mounds on the Little Lemonwier. The country becomes more hilly; the valley is narrow, and the stream small; affording no suitable position for an aboriginal population.

Above the mouth of the Lemonwier, on the Wisconsin, I have no information of ancient works, except a few mounds at Du Bays, at Plover Portage, and an inclosure recently discovered and described to me by Mr. Erskine Stanbury. It is spoken of as "a fort" in township twenty-one, and range seven, east, on the line between sections nineteen and twenty, seven hundred and thirty chains from the south corner of those sections. It is on the bold bluff bank of what we call Iron creek. It consists of an oblong or parallelogram, its longer axis with the direction of the stream. The walls are about the usual height, with a

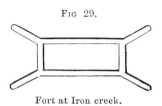

Fig 29.

Fort at Iron creek.

regular ditch or fosse all round them; and in the ditch and fort, trees from six to ten inches in diameter are now growing. From each corner a straight mound is thrown up, running off to some distance, as in the figure. The ground was covered with snow, or we would have taken a survey and measurement.

ANCIENT WORKS AT LAKE VIEUX DESERT.

In the second volume of the History of the Indian Tribes (p. 91, Plate lii), just published by authority of Congress, is a plate representing the ancient works situated on one of the three islands in Lake Vieux Désert, the head of the Wisconsin river, accompanied by the following brief notice:

"The remote position of Lake Vieux Désert, its giving rise to the Wisconsin river, and its having a large island in its centre which fits it for the cultivation practised by the Indians, appear to have early pointed it out as a retreat and stronghold of the interior Indians. No enemy could approach it except by water, and its natural capacities for defence were strengthened by an elliptical embankment in its centre, which appears to have served as the basis of pickets. There were small mounds or barrows within the inclosure, together with some cross embankments, and two large excavations without the embankment, all which are shown in the plate. It appears to have been the most northwesterly point fortified, east of the Mississippi river. The boundary which separates Wisconsin from Michigan cuts the island into nearly equal parts."

It is not stated when or by whom these works were surveyed. The general parallelism of the embankments with the shore of the island, and the occurrence of large pebbles in their materials, lead to the suspicion that they may be natural ridges, caused by the expansive force of ice. Such ridges are quite numerous along the banks of the smaller lakes in this climate.

CHAPTER VI.

ANCIENT WORKS AND ANCIENT MINING, AT LAKE SUPERIOR AND MISCELLANEOUS LOCALITIES.

In the geological report of Messrs. Foster and Whitney, made to Congress in 1850, we have some details of discoveries of traces of ancient mining in the copper district south of Lake Superior, and also on Isle Royale. They "consist of numerous excavations in the solid rock; heaps of rubble and earth along the courses of the veins; the remains of copper utensils, fashioned into the form of knives and chisels; stone hammers, some of which are of immense size and weight; wooden bowls for bailing water from the mines; and numerous levers of wood used in raising the masses of copper to the surface."

Traces of mounds, constructed in the form of mathematical figures, were observed. One on the northeast quarter of section sixteen, township fifty, range thirty-nine, near a small stream, is about ten feet high, in the form of a square, flat on the top, the sides of which are fifteen feet in length. The slopes are regular from the top to the base.

From this description, and the drawing accompanying it (Fig. 30), this tumulus appears to be a regular pyramidal structure, like those within the walls of Aztalan, the temple-mounds so often found in the Southern States, and the teocalli of Mexico. We might draw the conclusion that people having the same form of worship were spread over this whole extent of country, and that those who had gone to the remote regions of Lake Superior had so much respect for their religion as to erect a small altar or temple-mound, to answer their temporary purposes while engaged in the duty of supplying the nation with copper.

The stone hammers (Fig. 31), observed in great abundance about these mines,

Temple Mound, L. Superior.   Stone Hammer of Ancient Miners.   Stone Axe, L. Superior.

show that the process of cutting the masses of native copper was practised then as it is now, only with tools of different materials. These seem to have been manufactured on the ground, and differ from the articles of stone obtained from the mounds further south.

Among them, however, are stone axes (Fig. 32), quite similar (if we may judge from the delineation of Messrs. Foster and Whitney) to those common to the whole country; and they form another connecting link between the mound-builders and the ancient workers of the Lake Superior copper mines.

Dr. C. T. Jackson attributes these operations to the Chippewas; implying that the ancestors of the present race of Indians made the excavations, stone hammers, axes, &c.

If we assume the age of the tree found growing upon the rubbish thrown out of an ancient mine (three hundred and ninety-five years) as indicative of the epoch, or near it, when the mines were worked, it is only about double the time that the Chippewas have been known to occupy this region. The discovery of wooden levers and wooden bowls, forbid us to assign a much greater antiquity to these works. If these Indians have remained unchanged in their general habits for a period of two hundred years, it requires no aid from the imagination to suppose that they had then occupied the same country for one or more terms of equal duration; and there is, therefore, nothing improbable in the supposition that Wisconsin was occupied by the present race of Indians (if not of the same nations or tribes), five or eight hundred years ago.

The existence of wood buried in mounds at Aztalan, and other places, not entirely decayed, and the condition of the bones and other articles accompanying it, show conclusively that they could not have been deposited for a much longer period than that mentioned.

When the country about Lake Superior was first visited by French missionaries, about the middle of the seventeenth century, or two hundred years ago, copper was used by the Chippewas.

Allouer writes (in 1666), "It frequently happens that pieces of copper are found weighing from ten to twenty pounds. I have seen several such pieces in the hands of savages; and since they are superstitious, they esteem them as divinities, or as presents given to them to promote their happiness by the gods who dwell beneath the water. For this reason they preserve these pieces of copper wrapped up with their most precious articles. In some families they have been kept for more than fifty years; in others they have descended from time out of mind, being cherished as domestic gods."[1]

Father Dublon (1669–70) says, in relation to the copper, that the Indians were shy of disclosing their knowledge of it, "so that we were obliged to use some artifice."[2]

If, then, these fragments of copper were held so sacred as to be kept and handed down as household gods, we may certainly allow some lapse of time for such superstitions to originate and become incorporated into the religious system of the

---

[1] Quoted by Foster and Whitney, page 7.
[2] Same, p. 10.

Chippewas; and a comparatively slight draft upon the past, anterior to that period, will carry them back to the age of the ancient mining and mound-building.

Upon a general consideration of these investigations, we are led to the inference that the men who built the earthworks of Wisconsin, and those who first opened the Lake Superior copper mines, were one and the same people, and that they were none other than the ancestors of the present race of Indians. Differences there may have been, as we now see in tribes residing within a few hundred miles of each other; but these differences were perhaps no greater at that remote period than at present.

But to account for the presence of copper among the mound-builders, we need not resort to Lake Superior. Fragments of this metal in its pure or native condition, are very often found associated with the "drift," which has doubtless been transported from the same region of country. Such fragments are frequently washed from the banks by rains, or by the action of the waves on the margin of the lakes. Since the settlement of the country they have often been turned up by the plough. They vary in size from the smallest fragment to twenty pounds or more in weight; and from this source probably all the copper used by the natives, other than that from mines, was derived. The chemical tests applied would not, of course, decide this question.

With regard to the ancient mines at Lake Superior, it might be questioned whether the old French missionaries and traders did not succeed in extorting from the Indians, by artifice, the secret of their locality, and then make abortive attempts to remove some of the large masses there found. In the report of Messrs. Foster and Whitney, before referred to, it is stated that Mr. Samuel O. Knapp (who first laid before the public an account of the nature and extent of the primitive mining) discovered "a mass of native copper ten feet long, three feet wide, and nearly two feet thick, and weighing over six tons. On digging around it, the mass was found to rest on billets of oak, supported by sleepers of the same material. This wood, by its long exposure to moisture, is dark colored, and has lost all its consistency. A knife-blade may be thrust into it as easily as into a peat bog. The earth was so packed around the copper as to give it a firm support. The ancient miners had evidently raised it about five feet, and then abandoned the work as too laborious. They had taken off every projecting point which was accessible, so that the exposed surface was smooth."

Again, "in cleaning out one of these pits, at the depth of ten feet, the workmen came across a fragment of a wooden bowl, which, from the splintery pieces of rock and gravel imbedded in its rim, must have been employed in bailing water."

Now, unless there is some mistake as to these facts, we are not disposed to attribute this work to the aboriginal inhabitants. The sleepers, levers, wooden bowls, &c., are rather indicative of Caucasian ingenuity and art. Nor do the copper knives of Lake Superior have the appearance of great antiquity. Their form indicates quite plainly the knife of the white man; although the method of attaching the handle by turning up the edges, may be of aboriginal origin. See Fig. 33, which is a half-size drawing of a copper knife from Lake Superior, presented to me by Mr.

O. Vandyke. Arrow-points were attached in the same way (see Fig. 34), as shown by one found at Menasha, on Lake Winnebago, and received from Mr. Curtis Reed.

FIG. 33.

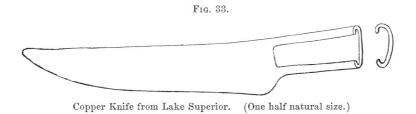

Copper Knife from Lake Superior. (One half natural size.)

In the immediate valley of the Mississippi the animal forms do not appear to be as numerous as on the Wisconsin and in some other localities. So far as I can learn, they extend down only as far as Apple river, in Illinois, a few miles south of the State line of Wisconsin.

FIG. 34.

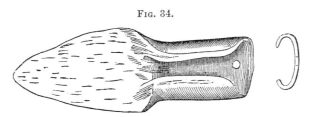

Indian Arrow-head, of copper. Natural size.

There are occasional localities south of the Wisconsin river, where traces of ancient works can be seen; but the immediate bank of the Mississippi is so broken that it could not be explored without much labor and difficulty.

The works at Prairie du Chien, heretofore described (page 66), are the most extensive of any on the river; but these are too much injured to exhibit with distinctness their original forms.

Along the great dividing ridge between the Mississippi and the Kickapoo rivers, there are mounds in great numbers. Their general character is the same as that of those near the residence of Mr. Miller (Plate LI), and they may, without much effort of imagination, be classed among the birds and buffaloes, accompanied by oblong and circular mounds. This ridge may be aptly compared to the back-bone of some gigantic animal, the numerous lateral spurs, extending towards the Mississippi or the Kickapoo, representing the ribs.

The animal effigies along the ridge are usually headed towards the south or southeast. The elevation is from four hundred to seven hundred feet above the adjoining rivers. The arrangement of the strata of rock (as exhibited in the section, Plate LI) is such as to cause numerous springs to gush out on either side, not far below the summit; and that circumstance may have led to the occupancy of the ridge by so large a population, as is indicated by their works still remaining. It is now inducing settlements in the same locality by a different race of men; the prime necessities of man being alike under all circumstances.

Isolated tumuli exist near the waters of the Mississippi along this part of its course; and at the place where the road turns off towards Springville, at Bartlett's Landing, is a very considerable assemblage, mostly of circular and oblong mounds, occupying the summit and sides of a narrow ridge. (Plate LII.)   The river is here divided into several distinct channels, called "sloughs."

At La Crosse there is a prairie between the river and the bluffs, which has always been a favorite place of resort for the Indian.   The conical tumuli forming a row parallel with the river, manifest also the residence of the mound-builders.   The materials of these works being sand, they are now much reduced, and can be discovered only upon close inspection.   I could find none that appeared to have had any animal or other imitative forms.

On the immediate brink of the river are excavations bordered by embankments. Some are circular, and resemble the remains of the Indian caches; while others are of a different form, as represented in Fig. 35.   Several were observed in the shape

FIG. 35.

Mississippi river.

Ancient Works on the bank of the Mississippi, at La Crosse.   Forty feet to an inch.

of a crescent, the excavation gradually deepening from the horns towards the centre. All have the elevated ridge on the side furthest from the river; so that if these works were intended for defence, it was against an enemy from the land.   They are of no great extent; many of them would not protect more than two or three persons.

Perhaps it was to excavations of this kind that Lieutenant Pike alludes in his journal (page 19), where he says: "The Sioux have a mode of defence or secretion by digging holes in the prairie, and throwing up a bank around it, into which they put their women and children, and then crawl in themselves."   The soft sandy nature of the ground here would easily admit of the employment of that kind of protection.

On the eastern border of this prairie are some very high bluffs, presenting towards the top perpendicular cliffs of limestone.   On one of these, known as Gale's Bluff, we found a large crevice or cave, in which, among some loose stones and sand, were several human bones; and a skull has been taken from the same place.   No bones of animals could be found.   The rock above the cave is perpendicular for a great height.

On the south side of the entrance are some markings (Fig. 36), doubtless of aboriginal origin, and possibly intended to record the virtues of the person or per-

FIG. 36.

Indian Hieroglyphics, Gale's Bluff, near La Crosse.

sons whose remains are there deposited. The marks are on a soft, yellow, granular limestone ; often mistaken by casual observers for sandstone. They are not deeply impressed, and have evidently been affected by the crumbling of the surface.

Only an occasional mound was observed along the valley of La Crosse river; and it is believed that no works of any considerable extent exist above this point on the Mississippi.

CHAPTER VII.

CONTENTS OF THE MOUNDS; REMAINS OF ANCIENT WORKMANSHIP.

WE have already stated, in their proper connection, the results of the examinations of the mounds at various places; but some general facts remain to be mentioned.

It is important to determine with certainty whether the relics found buried are the work of the original mound-builders, and placed there at the time of the erection of the mounds, or have been deposited subsequently. This can usually be done with a reasonable degree of certainty by one accustomed to such investigations.

So far as I have had opportunity to observe, there are no original remains in the mounds of imitative form, beyond a few scattered fragments that may have gained a place there by accident. Many of the mounds have been entirely removed, including the earth beneath for a considerable depth, in the process of grading streets in Milwaukee; and it is usually found that the natural surface had not been disturbed at the time of the erection, but that the several layers or strata of mould, clay, gravel, &c., are continuous below the structure as on the contiguous grounds.

Great numbers of the smaller conical tumuli are also destitute of any remains; and if human bodies were ever buried under them, they are now so entirely "returned to dust" that no apparent traces of them are left. If we assume that each mound was a place of burial, we must infer from the absence of utensils that the common practice of depositing with the dead the implements to be used in the other

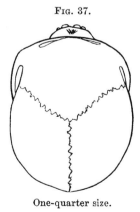

FIG. 37.

One-quarter size.

FIG. 38.

One-quarter size.

world, is of comparatively recent origin; since some of these, at least, would have resisted decay. The middle-sized conical mounds, and those of larger dimension, almost always contain evidence of the deposit of one or more human bodies. These are always very much decayed; only one skull having been found sufficiently entire to enable Dr. Hoy, with much skill and labor, to restore it sufficiently to make out its general characteristics. A fortunate combination of circumstances had caused this preservation. The skull and some other bones were enveloped in a peculiar kind of clay, which seems to have possessed a preservative quality beyond that of ordinary earth, of which most of the accumulation was composed; and on the very top of the mound was a large tree, which had shed off the rains for several centuries. Many peculiarities of this cranium are pointed out by Dr. Hoy. (Chapter I, page 9.)

On Plate LIII, there is a drawing of the natural size; and figures 37 and 38 represent the top and back views of the same skull reduced to one quarter of the natural size.

The following are its dimensions:

	Inches.
Longitudinal diameter	6.8
Parietal diameter	5.3
Occipito-frontal arch	13.8
Length of head and face	8.2
Zygomatic diameter	4.9
Facial angle	76

To give the reader more particular information respecting the supposed characteristics of this interesting relic of an extinct people, I have, with the assistance of a phrenological friend, prepared the following "chart." For the localities of the "organs," &c., reference was had to Spurzheim,[1] whose works have become a portion of the literature of the country, and are to be found in all important libraries. Although the principles of this professed *science* may not be true in all their details, yet its nomenclature affords the means of presenting the conformation of the skull in a definite manner. The figure following the name of each organ indicates its relative development; 0 signifying deficiency, and 6 very full or unusual prominence.

AFFECTIVE ORGANS.

I. PROPENSITIES.
Destructiveness	$4\frac{1}{2}$
Amativeness	6
Philoprogenitiveness	6
Adhesiveness	5
Inhabitiveness	5
Combativeness	$4\frac{1}{2}$
Secretiveness	5
Acquisitiveness	$4\frac{1}{2}$
Constructiveness	$2\frac{1}{2}$

II. SENTIMENTS.
Cautiousness (very full)	6
Approbativeness	5
Self-esteem	4
Benevolence	3

[1] Phrenology, Boston, 1833.

Reverence	. . . .	3
Firmness	. . . .	4
Conscientiousness	. . . .	$4\frac{1}{2}$
Hope	. . . .	$4\frac{1}{2}$
Marvellousness	. . . .	3
Ideality	. . . .	4
Mirthfulness	. . . .	$3\frac{1}{2}$
Imitation	. . . .	$2\frac{1}{2}$

INTELLECTUAL ORGANS.

III. PERCEPTIVE.

Individuality (large)	. . . .	6
Configuration	. . . .	2
Size	. . . .	6
Weight and resistance	. . . . . .	$3\frac{1}{2}$
Coloring	. . . .	3
Locality	. . . .	5
Order	. . . .	$2\frac{1}{2}$
Calculation	. . . .	2
Eventuality	. . . .	$5\frac{1}{2}$
Time	. . . .	$2\frac{1}{2}$
Tune	. . . .	$2\frac{1}{2}$
Language (uncertain)	. . . . . .	5 ?

IV. REFLECTIVE.

Comparison	. . . .	$4\frac{1}{2}$
Causality	. . . .	5

This chart shows that the affective, or feeling faculties, prevail over the intellectual, in the proportion of 4.3 to 3.9; and the several groups of organs are developed in the following order:

Propensities	. . . .	4.8
Reflective	. . . .	4.7
Sentiments	. . . .	3.9
Perceptive	. . . .	3.8

Whether these figures can be relied upon as indicating the character and disposition of the individual to whom the skull belonged, may be doubted; though it will be perceived that their indications correspond with the general character of the aborigines, in the large cautiousness, individuality, &c., and the deficient constructiveness, calculation, &c.

But few implements, ornaments, or works of art of any kind, have been discovered in the mounds of Wisconsin, that could not be traced to recent Indian burials; and yet it is certain that had they been originally deposited, they would still be found there. The stone axes, flint arrow-heads, and articles of pottery, are of a durable character, and could not have decayed since the erection of the mounds. Hence, we conclude that the more ancient mound-builders of Wisconsin were not in the habit of making such deposits.

The tumulus opened by me at Waukesha (See Chapter II, page 28) contained a stone pipe, another of burned clay, and fragments of two vases. These were of the same general kind and composition as the pipes and pottery of the Indians so frequently turned up by the plough.

Fig. 39 represents the pipe found in or near the left hand of the skeleton. It consists of pottery made of the same materials as the ordinary vases or pots.

Fig. 40 was taken from the right hand of the same skeleton, and is made from

FIG. 39.

Two thirds natural size.

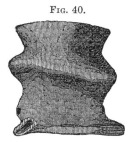

FIG. 40.

Natural size.

a kind of soft argillite of a purplish color. This pipe differs from all others that I have seen, by having the horizontal opening on both sides.

Fig. 41 is made of steatite, green variegated with white.

Fig. 42 is a large calumet, or pipe of peace, made of a fine-grained gray sandstone.

FIG. 41.

One half natural size.

FIG. 42.

One half natural size.

Having been broken, it was mended with plates of lead. The small round punctures are supposed to represent the number of treaties which had been solemnized by this emblem. The drawing reduces the size one half.

Fig. 43 is of the same material as the last, but of finer texture.

Fig. 44 was found on the surface of the ground, on Lake Koshokenong. It has

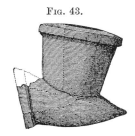

FIG. 43.

Two thirds natural size.

FIG. 44.

One half natural size.

been burned and broken into fragments. It was apparently made of a like soft argillaceous sandstone.

Fig. 45 is a fragment of a pipe made of a reddish argillaceous stone.

Fig. 46 is of gray fine-grained sandstone, so soft that it was apparently cut and reduced to the proper form with a knife.

Fig. 47 is of the same material, in which was found a small nodule of iron pyrites;

FIG. 45.   FIG. 46.   FIG. 47.

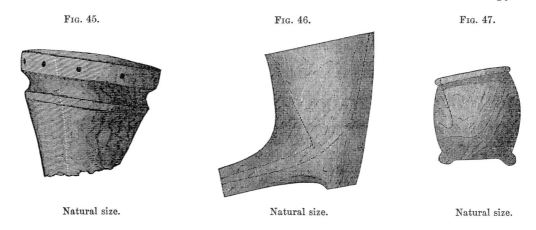

Natural size.   Natural size.   Natural size.

and the artist has taken advantage of this to ornament his work, and to leave a corresponding protuberance on the opposite side for symmetry.   It was presented to me by Miss Amelia E. Higgins.

Fig. 48 is made of the beautiful red pipe-stone from the "Coteau des Prairies," and is probably also a calumet, or pipe of state.

Fig. 49 was made and used by the Menomonee Indians of the Neenah river, from a whitish stone, now injured by accidental fire.

FIG. 48.   FIG. 49.

One half natural size.   One half natural size.

The pipe, Figs. 50 and 51, is of a dark-colored stone or clay slate, with traces of organic remains surrounded by iron pyrites.   The end may be supposed to repre-

FIG. 50.   FIG. 51.

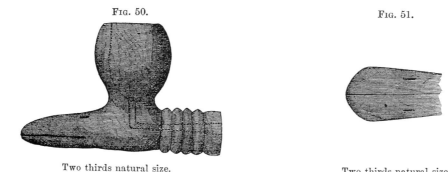

Two thirds natural size.   Two thirds natural size.

sent the head of a snake, or perhaps the bill of a duck.   It belongs to Dr. P. R. Hoy, of Racine.

Fig. 39 is of artificial pottery.   Figs. 40 and 50 are of argillite or clay slate rock. Fig. 41 is of steatite.   Figs. 42, 43, 44, 46, and 47, are of gray sandstone, of a fine grain, and with argillaceous admixture.   Fig. 45 is of reddish sandstone.   Fig. 48 is of the red pipe-stone.   Fig. 49 is of a whitish, or chalk-like stone.

In no one article was so much ingenuity displayed by aboriginal natives as in pipe making.   Many of the pipes are formed with much taste, and are designed to be representations of animals with which they were familiar.

Arrow-points and spear-heads have occasionally been found in the mounds; but they mostly occur on, or not far beneath, the surface of the ground.   They generally consist of schist or hornstone, usually denominated flint.

Fig. 52 represents an interesting form of arrow-point, narrower than usual, lozenge-shaped, and enlarged at the posterior extremity.

Remains of broken pottery are found in the mounds, and also in great abundance wherever there has been an Indian settlement. The pots were formed by hand, of clay and sand, or fine gravel, occasionally mixed with broken shells and other substances, and then slightly burned.   The potter's wheel, that most ancient of all machines, was evidently not in use among the aboriginal inhabitants of America.

Fig. 52.

One half natural size.

The pots, or vases, found in the mounds at Waukesha and Racine, were in connection with the original deposit, and must, therefore, have been the work of the mound-builders.   They agree in every respect with the fragments found about the old Indian villages; and probably with the same articles as now manufactured by the females of tribes residing on the Missouri.[1]

The vessels were variously ornamented by lines and dots stamped upon them, when in a soft state, by hand.   Occasionally the whole surface is so marked, but usually the rim only is ornamented.

The vases obtained at Waukesha, and also at Aztalan, must have been broken before they were deposited in the mounds; for only portions of different vases could be found.

Fig. 53 represents the vase found in a mound at Racine, and restored by Dr. P. R. Hoy, described in Chapter I.[2]

---

[1] Mr. Catlin informs us that "earthen dishes are made by the Mandan women in great quantities, and modelled in a thousand forms and tastes.   They are made from a tough black clay, and baked in kilns which are made for the purpose, and are nearly equal in hardness to our own manufactured pottery, though they have not yet got the art of glazing.   They make them so strong and serviceable, however, that they hang them over the fire as we do our iron kettles, and boil their meat in them with perfect success.   Here women can be seen handling them by hundreds, moulding them in fanciful forms, and passing them through the kilns."—Catlin's North American Indians, I, 116 ; quoted in Squier's Antiquities of New York, page 132.

[2] That the state of the potter's art among the southern nations was not much more advanced than in Wisconsin, appears from the following extract : " The ancient pottery of Nicaragua is always well

Fig. 54 represents a stone axe. These axes are worked to a sharp edge at one end, and have a depression around the head for the handle. Although they all have the same general form, there are no two exactly alike. The one figured must have been used in the manner of a carpenter's adze. These are made of the hardest

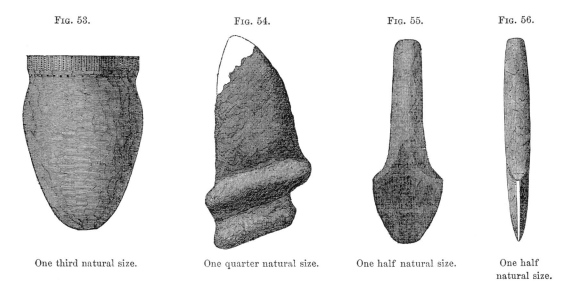

FIG. 53.	FIG. 54.	FIG. 55.	FIG. 56.
One third natural size.	One quarter natural size.	One half natural size.	One half natural size.

stone, selected from boulders very nearly of the right shape, so as to require the least labor. Some of them retain a portion of the natural polish of the boulder on the head and edges.

Figs. 55 and 56 represent a chisel-shaped instrument, which may have been employed in taking off the skins of large quadrupeds.

These stone chisels were perhaps made use of instead of the bone, in dressing skins of the bison as is now practised by the wild Indians of the West. The last process, termed *graining*, is performed by the squaws, who use a sharpened bone, the shoulder-blade or other large bone of the animal, sharpened at the edge, somewhat like an adze; with the edges of which they scrape the fleshy side of the skin, bearing on with the weight of their bodies, thereby drying and softening, and fitting it for service. (Catlin's North American Indians, I, 45.)

An image made of wood (Fig. 57) was discovered at Prairie village (Waukesha), soon after its first settlement by the whites, and presented to me by Mr. C. F. Warren. It is evident that it could have no very great antiquity; though it may have been preserved and handed down for several generations. It is quite rudely carved, the head very much flattened, and the general expression more that of a monkey than of a man.

---

burned, and often elaborately painted in brilliant and durable colors. The forms are generally very regular, but there is no evidence of the use of the potter's wheel; on the contrary, there is reason to believe that the ancient processes have undergone little or no modification since the Conquest. The pottery now generally in use among all classes in Central America, is of the Indian manufacture, and is fashioned entirely by hand."—Squier's Nicaragua, 1852, II, 337–8.

Such images were formerly common with the Indians, and are still to be found among the remote tribes, which retain many of their ancient customs. "Most of the Crees carry with them one or more small wooden figures rudely carved, some of which they state to be representations of a malicious or at least a capricious being named Kepuchikan (or Gepuchikan), to whom they make offerings." (J. Richardson's Arctic Searching Expedition, 1852, page 268.)

Fig. 58 represents a circular stone composed of variegated quartz, of a light gray

FIG. 57.   FIG. 58.

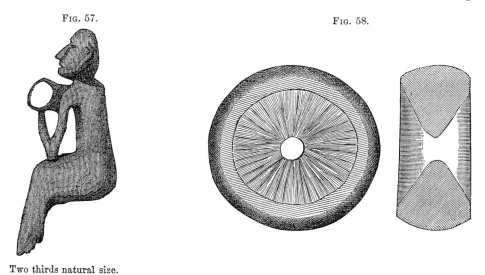

Two thirds natural size.

color, perforated; doubtless intended to be used in the Indian game of tchung-kee, as described by Catlin.[1]

---

[1] The Mandans have a game "which may be said to be their favorite amusement, and unknown to the other tribes about them. The game is tchung-kee (see Fig. 59), a beautiful athletic exercise which they

FIG. 59.

seem to be almost unceasingly practising whilst the weather is fair, and they have nothing else of moment to demand their attention. This game is decidedly their favorite amusement, and is played near to the village on a pavement of clay which has been used for that purpose until it has become as smooth and hard as a floor. For this game two champions form their respective parties, by choosing

This stone was found at Milwaukee, where it had doubtless been lost at some remote time. Its form is precisely such as to enable it to roll the greatest distance without falling.

Similar stones are found in Ohio, and are described by Messrs. Squier and Davis,[1] which were without doubt used for a like purpose.

Fig. 60 represents a chisel or implement of native copper, found at Stephen's

FIG. 60.

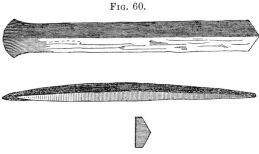

One half natural size.

Point on the upper Wisconsin river, in 1850, and deposited in the cabinet of the University of Wisconsin by Mr. James W. Wright. It appears to have originally had a sort of finish on the upper or convex side, and on the edges; but in many places it is decayed and gone. There are also indications of grinding or rubbing, on the surface. The under, or flat side, is full of irregular cavities, and was probably never smoothed. It is supposed to have been brought to its present shape by hammering, probably with a stone hammer.

---

alternately the most famous players, until their requisite numbers are made up. Their bettings are then made, and their stakes are held by some of the chiefs, or others present. The play commences with two (one from each party), who start off upon a trot abreast of each other, and one of them rolls, in advance of them on the pavement, a little ring of two or three inches in diameter, cut out of a stone; and each one follows it up with his tchung-kee (a stick six feet in length, with little bits of leather projecting from its sides, of an inch or more in length), which he throws before him as he runs, sliding it along upon the ground after the ring, endeavoring to place it in such a position when it stops, that the ring may fall upon it, and receive one of the little projections of leather through it, which counts for game one, or two, or four, according to the position of the leather on which the ring is lodged. The last winner always has the rolling of the ring, and both start the tchung-kee together; if either fails to receive the ring, or to lie in a certain position, it is a forfeiture of the amount of the number he was nearest to, and he loses his throw; when another steps into his place. The game is a difficult one to describe so as to give an exact idea of it, unless one can see it played; it is a game of great beauty and fine bodily exercise, and these people become excessively fond of it."—Catlin's North American Indians, I, 132.

A similar game was practised by the Senecas; as described by Lewis H. Morgan, in the Third Annual Report of the Regents of the University of New York, 1850, p. 79. [And likewise by the Upper Creeks. See Smithsonian Contributions, II, 135–140; Trans. Amer. Ethnol. Soc., III, 51–57.—*Secretary S. I.*]

[1] Smithsonian Contributions, I, 222.

CHAPTER VIII.

CONCLUDING REMARKS.

It seems proper to present here some general conclusions to which the facts detailed in the preceding pages lead the mind of the inquirer, though many of them have already been expressed.

The American race is now, and probably always has been, divided into numerous distinct tribes or nations, occupying different portions of the country, and each having to some extent its own peculiar habits, customs, religion, and even language. Many of the tribes were of a roving disposition, with no fixed place of abode; while others were more permanent, only leaving their villages for the purpose of war or the chase. Since these nations have been known to us, and their history recorded, we are cognizant of numerous and important changes in the location of different tribes, and even nations. We know of tribes that have become extinct, and of others that have gradually united with their neighbors, adopting their habits, religion, and language.

We may, therefore, without assuming any far-fetched theories, suppose that a nation or tribe of red men formerly occupied the country now known as Wisconsin, whose superstitions, ceremonies, and beliefs, required the erection of mounds of earth of the various forms represented on the plates accompanying this work; and that these tribes may have emigrated, or been driven off by others having no veneration for their ancient monuments. These subsequent tribes may or may not be the same that until very recently occupied that country. They extended their cultivation over the mounds with as little feeling of respect as is manifested by men of the race who are now fast destroying them. It is quite certain that these later tribes continued the practice of mound-building so far as to erect a circular or conical tumulus over their dead. This practice appears to be a remnant of ancient customs that connects the mound-builders with the present tribes.

The extent of the ancient works in the West indicates a condition of society somewhat different from the purely savage or hunter state: for to accomplish the labor required for the completion of such large structures, it would be necessary to accumulate the means of subsistence; and this could be done only by an agricultural people, or at least agriculture must have been among the pursuits of a people capable of constructing those works. Now we know that nearly all the Indian tribes cultivate the soil to some extent; and is it not reasonable to suppose that the amount of attention devoted to that pursuit may have been greater at former times than at present? A tribe or nation may gradually change its habits in rela-

12

tion to one or another class of pursuits, and yet remain essentially the same people. Again, the Indians are to a certain extent migratory; and hence we may look for the posterity of the mound-builders of Wisconsin in remote portions of the country.

Some tribes of the Dacotah or Sioux family, especially the Mandans and Aricaras (Ricaras, or Riccarees), are much more stationary and fixed in their habits than other tribes of Indians. "They cultivate corn, not only for their own use, but also enough to make it a very prominent article of trade."[1]

Dr. Morton says: "the *Osages, Minetaris, Mandans, Assinaboins,* and many cognate tribes, are more or less connected with the great Sioux nation;"[2] and that the *Osages, Omahas, Konsas, Missouris,* and *Ouapans,* all speak a language so nearly allied that they can severally converse with each other without an interpreter.[3]

It is quite probable that a more thorough knowledge of the habits, religious ceremonies, and superstitious beliefs of this great family, or group of families of Indians, would throw much light upon the obscure subject of the mounds, and perhaps unravel the mystery of their origin and uses.

The ancient works in Wisconsin are mostly at the very places selected by the present Indians for their abodes; thus indicating that the habits, wants, modes of subsistence, &c., of their builders, were essentially the same.

If the present tribes have no traditions running back as far as the times of Allouez and Marquette, or even to the more recent time of Jonathan Carver, it is not strange that none should exist in regard to the mounds, which must be of much earlier date.

It is by considerations of this nature that we are led to the conclusion that the mound-builders of Wisconsin were none others than the ancestors of the present tribes of Indians.

There is some evidence of a greater prevalence than at present of prairie or cultivated land in this State, at no very remote age. The largest trees are probably not more than five hundred years old; and large tracts of land are now covered with forests of young trees, where there are no traces of an antecedent growth. Every year the high winds prostrate great numbers of trees; and frequent storms pass through the forest, throwing down nearly every thing before them. Trees are left with a portion of the roots still in the ground, so as to keep them alive for several years after their prostration. These "wind-falls" are of frequent occurrence in the depths of the forests, and occasion much difficulty in making the public surveys. The straight lines of the sections frequently encounter them, as may be seen by the accompanying map. (Fig. 61.)

The amount of earth adhering to the roots of a tree when prostrated by the wind, is, under favorable circumstances, very considerable, and upon their decay forms an oblong mound of greater or less magnitude, and a slight depression is left where the tree stood. These little hillocks are often, by the inexperienced, mistaken for Indian graves. From the paucity of these little "tree-mounds" we infer that no

---

[1] T. A. Culbertson's Journal, in 5th Annual Report of the Smithsonian Institution, p. 118.

[2] Crania Americana, pp. 199, 200.

[3] The Winnebagos are a branch of the Sioux stock.   Gallatin's Synopsis, p. 120.

very great antiquity can be assigned to the dense forests of Wisconsin; for during a long period of time, with no material change of climate, we would expect to find

FIG. 61.

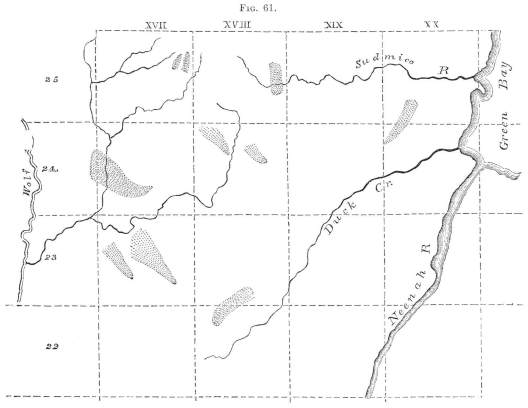

Map showing "Wind-falls," reported by the Surveyors of the Public Lands.　Six miles to one inch.

great numbers of these little monuments of ancient storms scattered every where over the ground.

Whether the greater extent of treeless country in former times was owing to natural or artificial causes, it is now difficult to determine; but the great extent of ancient works within the depths of the present forests, would seem to indicate that the country was at least kept free from trees by the agency of man.

Many of these tree-mounds were observed on and about the ancient works.

Another curious circumstance that may be noticed by inspection of the figures of mounds accompanying this work, is the gradual transition, as it were, or change of one form into another. Examples can be found of all forms, from a true circle, through the oval and elongated oval, to the oblong mounds and long ridges. Again, there is a succession of mounds, from the simple ridge of considerable size at one end, and gradually diminishing to a point at the other, through the intermediate forms, having one, two, three, or four projections, to the "turtle form." In this way, also, we may trace a gradual development (so to speak) of nearly all the more complicated forms.

It is not pretended to assert that this was the order in which the mounds were erected; or that the aborigines gradually acquired the art by successive essays or lessons. Indeed, we are led to believe that the more complicated forms are the most ancient.

The relative ages of the different works in Wisconsin, so far as they can be ascertained from the facts now before us, are probably about as follows:

First and oldest. The animal forms, and the great works at Aztalan.

Second. The conical mounds built for sepulchral purposes, which come down to a very recent period.

Third. The indications of garden-beds planted in regular geometrical figures or straight lines.

Fourth. The plantations of the present tribes, who plant without system or regularity.

Thus the taste for regular forms and arrangements, and the habits of construction with earthy materials, seem to have been gradually lost, until all traces of them disappear in our modern degenerate red men.

The animal-shaped mounds, and accompanying oblongs and ridges, constituting the first of the above series, are composed of whitish clay, or of the subsoil of the country.[1]

The mounds of the second series, or burial-mounds, are usually composed of black mould or loam, promiscuously intermixed with the lighter-colored subsoil.

The animal-shaped mounds appear to be peculiar to Wisconsin; for the few obscure instances noticed in Ohio, by Messrs. Squier and Davis, can hardly be deemed an exception to this remark. They indicate a difference in the character of the people occupying these regions, but not greater than often exists between the neighboring tribes or nations.

---

[1] It has been observed that the diluvial or drift clays, whether red, yellow, or blue in their original beds, assume a whitish color when exposed to the sun and dried.

ALPHABETICAL INDEX.

PUBLISHED BY THE SMITHSONIAN INSTITUTION,

WASHINGTON, D. C.

MAY, 1855.

ERRATA.

Page 66, line 10, *for* " eleven hundred," *read* " eleven thousand."
" 72, " 22, *for* " Mors Creek," *read* " Maus' Creek."
" 72, " 34, *for* " Moss Creek," *read* " Maus' Creek."
" 73, " 15, *for* " 730 chains," *read* " 7.30 chains."
" 77, " 17, *for* " page 368," *read* " page 66."
" 82, " 45, *for* " page 173," *read* " page 28."
" 88, " 32, *for* " page 79," *read* " page 81."

II.

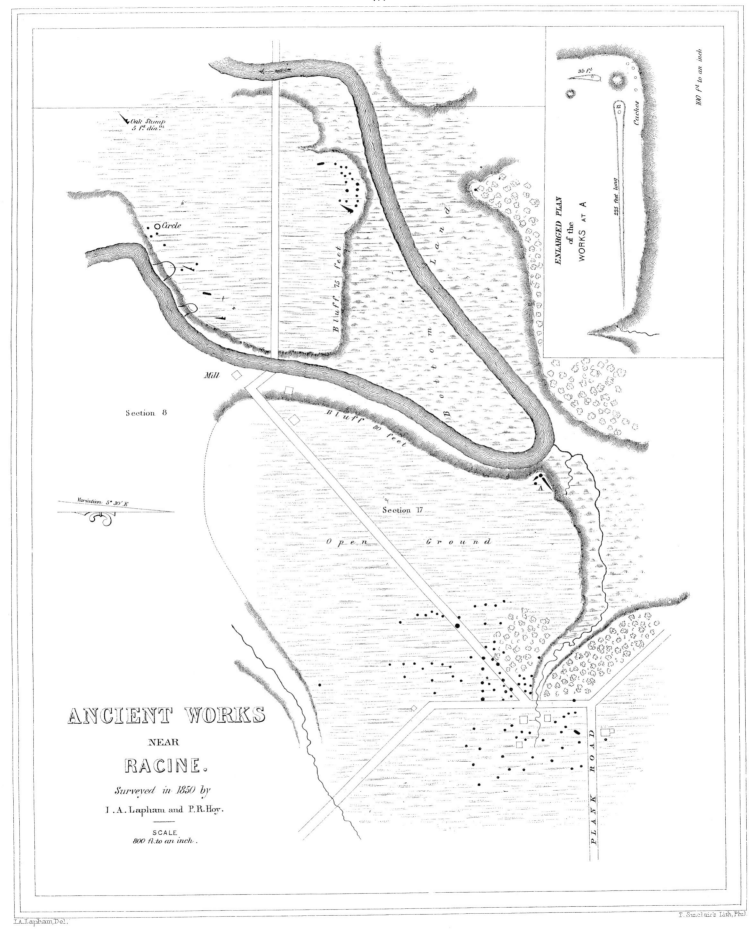

ENLARGED PLAN
of the
WORKS AT A

100 f.t to an inch

Oak Stump
5 f.t dia.m

Circle

Bluff 75 feet

Bottom Land

Mill

Section 8

Bluff 80 feet

Variation 5° 30′ E

Section 17

Open Ground

A

ANCIENT WORKS
NEAR
RACINE.
Surveyed in 1850 by
I. A. Lapham and P. R. Hoy.

SCALE
800 ft. to an inch.

PLANK ROAD

I.A.Lapham, Del.

T. Sinclair's Lith. Phil

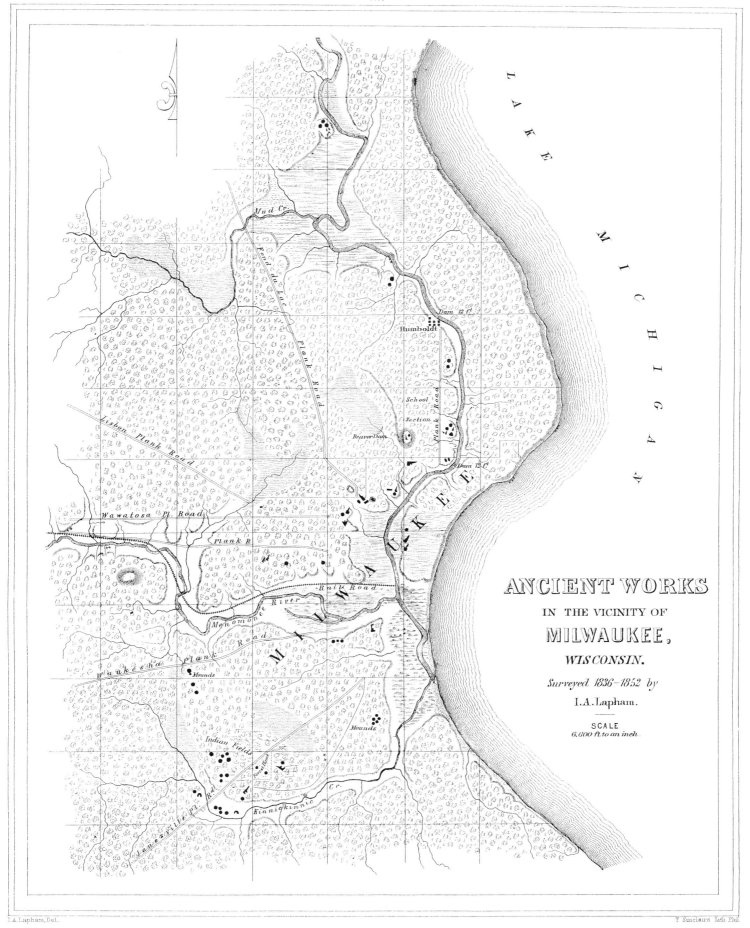

ANCIENT WORKS
IN THE VICINITY OF
MILWAUKEE,
WISCONSIN.

Surveyed 1836–1852 by
I.A.Lapham.

SCALE
6,600 ft. to an inch.

LAKE MICHIGAN

MILWAUKEE

Mud Cr.

Fond du la la

Plank Road

Lisbon Plank Road

Wawatosa Pl. Road

Plank R.

Railk Road

Menomonee River

Waukesha Plank Road

Humboldt

Dam 12 ft

School Section

Beaver Dam

Dam 12 C.

Mounds

Mounds

Indian Fields

Kinnickinnic Cr.

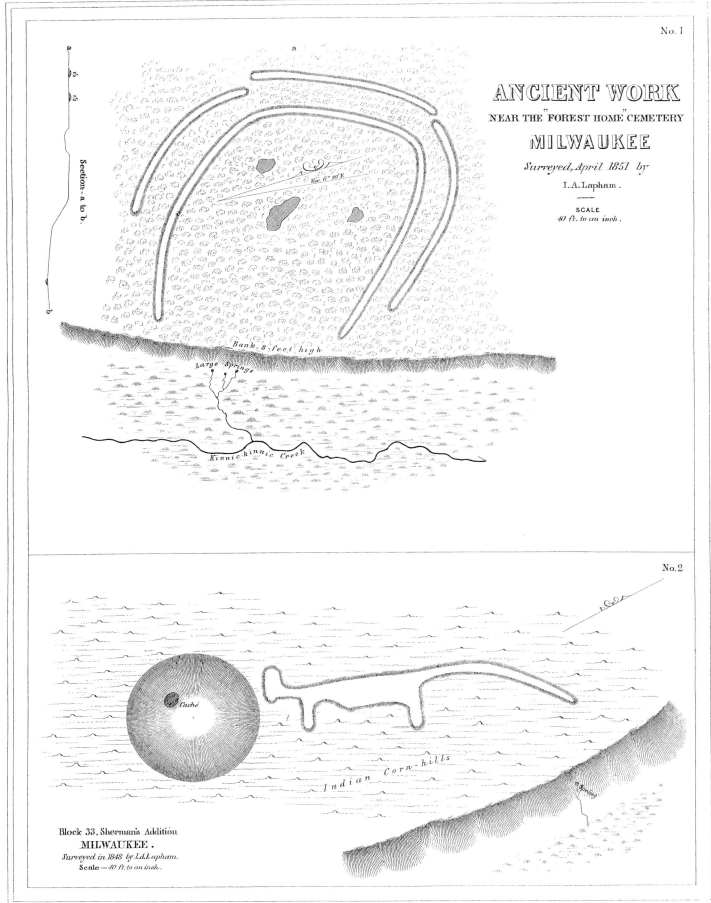

No. 1

ANCIENT WORK
NEAR THE "FOREST HOME" CEMETERY
MILWAUKEE
Surveyed, April 1851 by
I. A. Lapham.

SCALE
40 ft. to an inch.

Section - a to b.

Var. 6° 30' E

Bank 8 feet high

Large Springs

Kinnic-kinnic Creek

No. 2

Caché

Indian Corn-hills

Spring

Block 33, Sherman's Addition
MILWAUKEE.
Surveyed in 1848 by I.A.Lapham.
Scale — 40 ft. to an inch.

I.A.Lapham. Del.

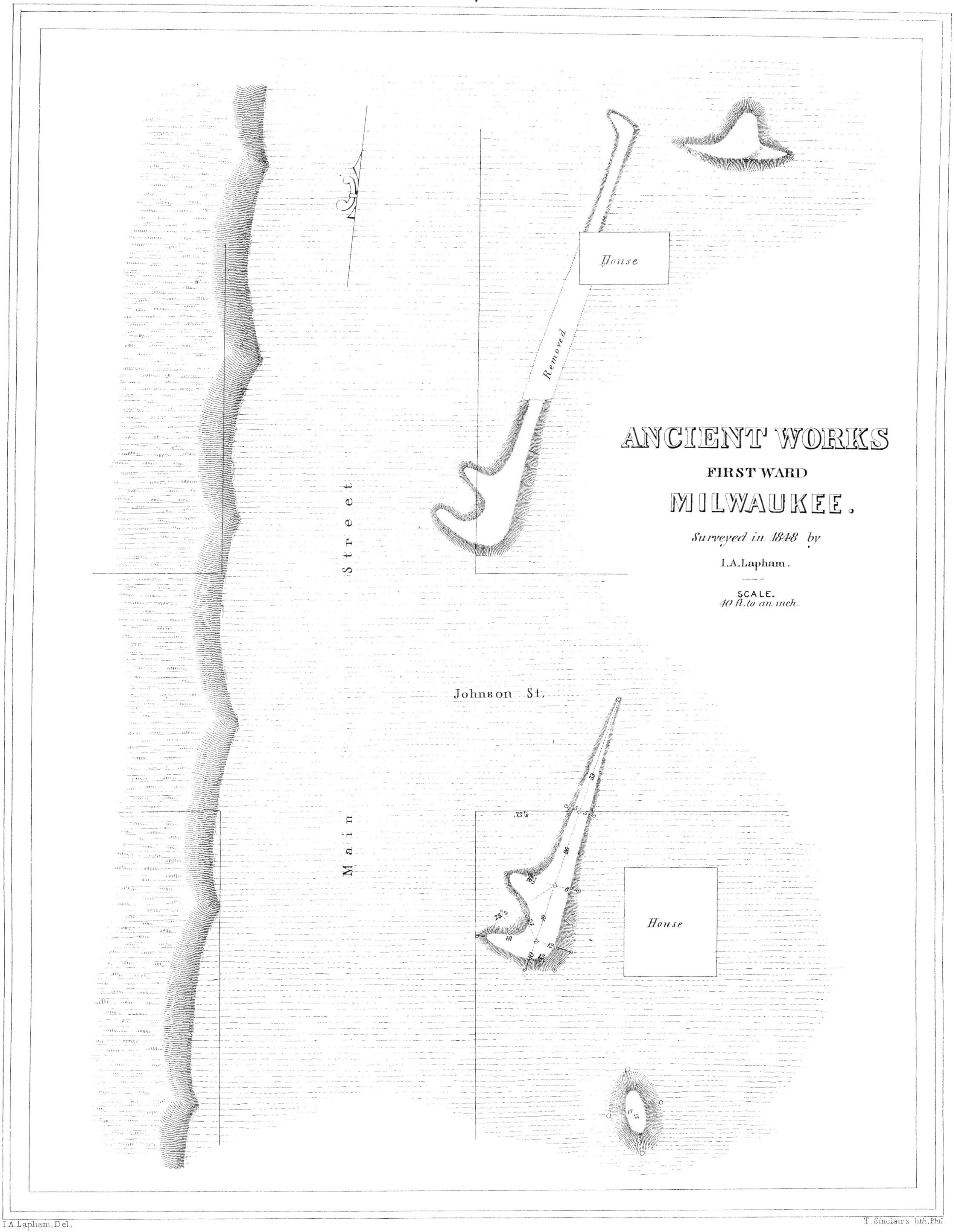

ANCIENT WORKS
FIRST WARD
MILWAUKEE.
Surveyed in 1848 by
I.A.Lapham.

SCALE.
40 ft. to an inch.

House

Removd

House

Johnson St.

Street

Main

I.A.Lapham, Del.

T. Sinclair's lith.Phil

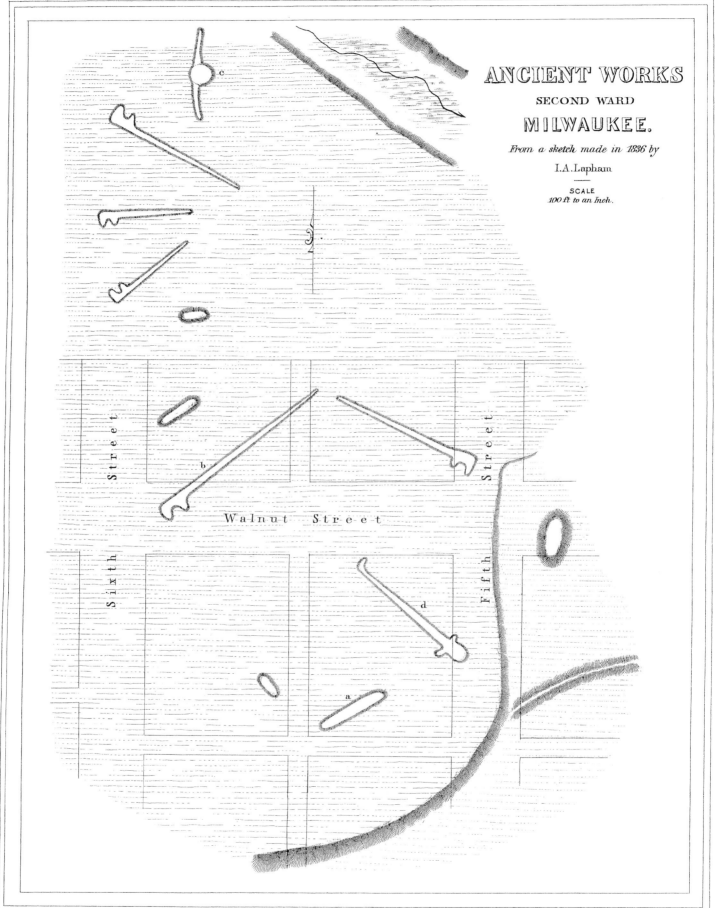

ANCIENT WORKS
SECOND WARD
MILWAUKEE.

From a sketch made in 1836 by
I. A. Lapham

SCALE
100 ft. to an Inch.

Sixth Street

Fifth Street

Walnut Street

I. A. Lapham, Del,

T. Sinclair's lith, Phil.

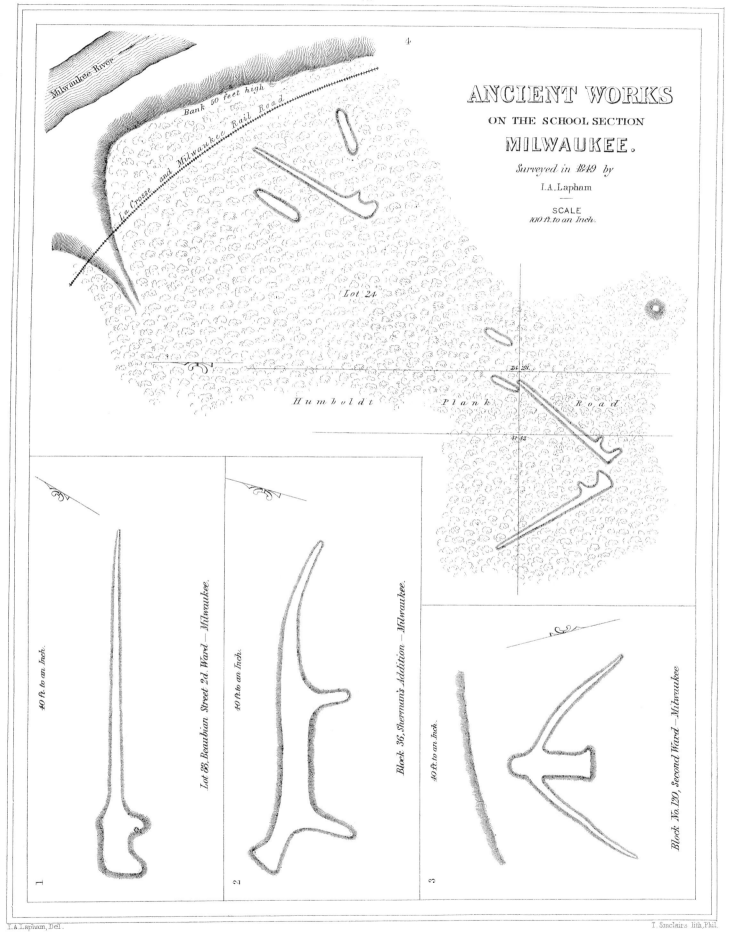

ANCIENT WORKS
ON THE SCHOOL SECTION
MILWAUKEE.

Surveyed in 1849 by
I.A.Lapham

SCALE
100 ft. to an Inch.

Milwaukee River.

Bank 50 feet high

La Crosse and Milwaukee Rail Road

Lot 24

Humboldt Plank Road

34 28

47 42

40 ft. to an Inch.

Lot 83, Beaubian Street 2d. Ward — Milwaukee.

40 ft. to an Inch.

Block 36, Sherman's Addition — Milwaukee.

40 ft. to an Inch.

Block No. 120, Second Ward — Milwaukee

1

2

3

4

I.A Lapham, Del.

T. Sinclair's lith, Phil.

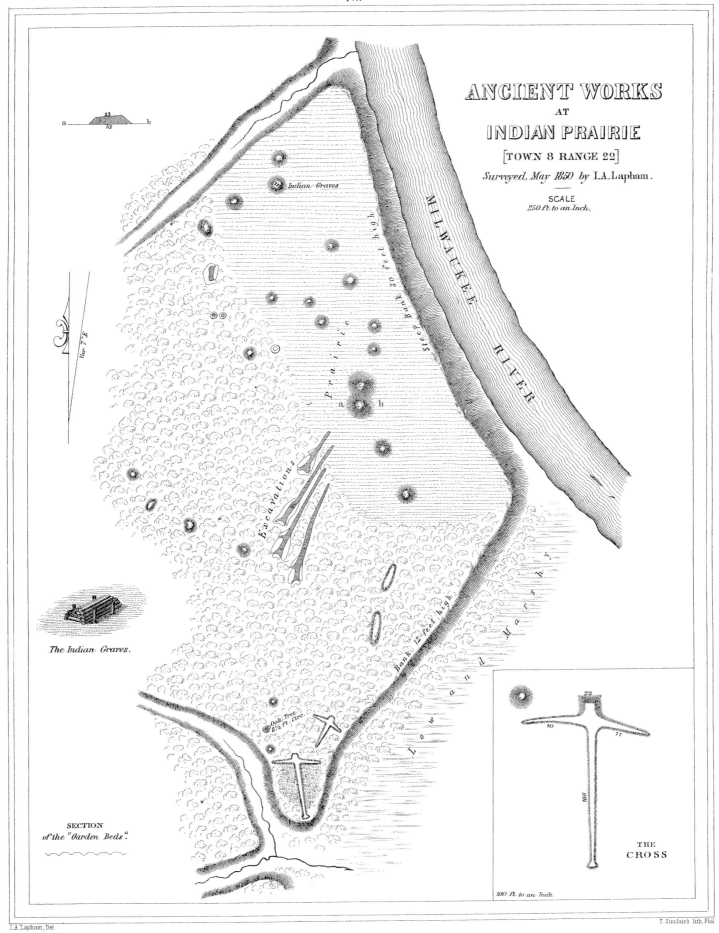

ANCIENT WORKS
AT
INDIAN PRAIRIE
[TOWN 8 RANGE 22]
Surveyed, May 1850 by I.A.Lapham.

SCALE
250 ft. to an Inch.

Indian Graves

MILWAUKEE

Steep Bank 30 feet high

RIVER

Prairie

Excavations

a b

The Indian Graves.

Bank 12 feet high

M a r s h y

Oak Tree
8½ Ft. Circ.

L o w   a n d

SECTION
of the "Garden Beds".

22

70   71

765

THE
CROSS

100 Ft. to an Inch.

I.A Lapham, Del

T. Sinclair's lith, Phil

IX.

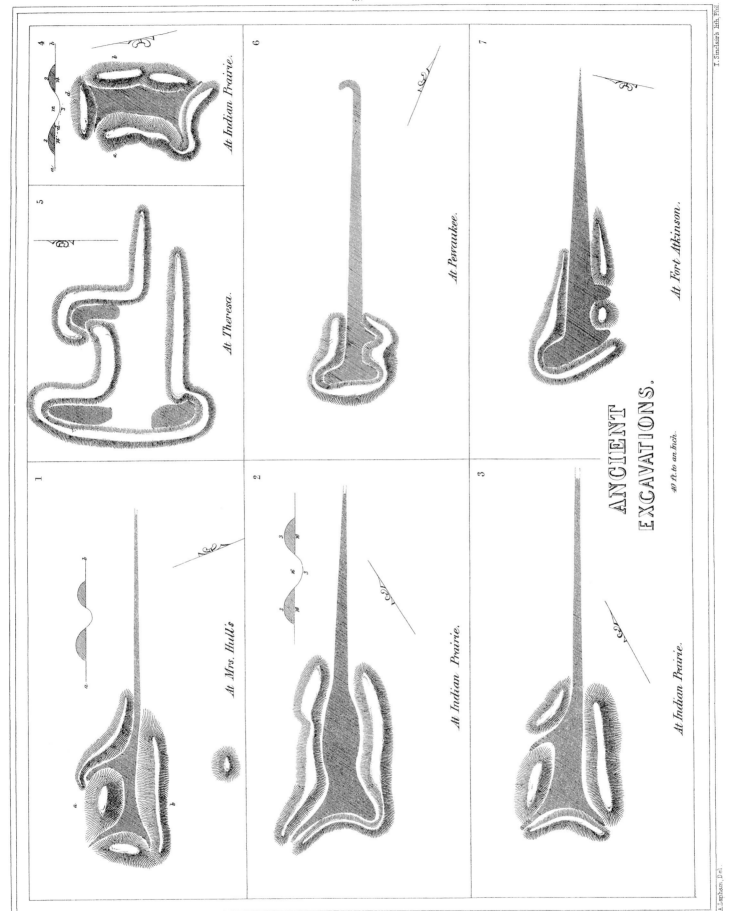

ANCIENT EXCAVATIONS.

40 ft. to an Inch.

At Indian Prairie.

At Theresa.

At Pewaukee.

At Fort Atkinson.

At Mrs. Hull's.

At Indian Prairie.

At Indian Prairie.

X

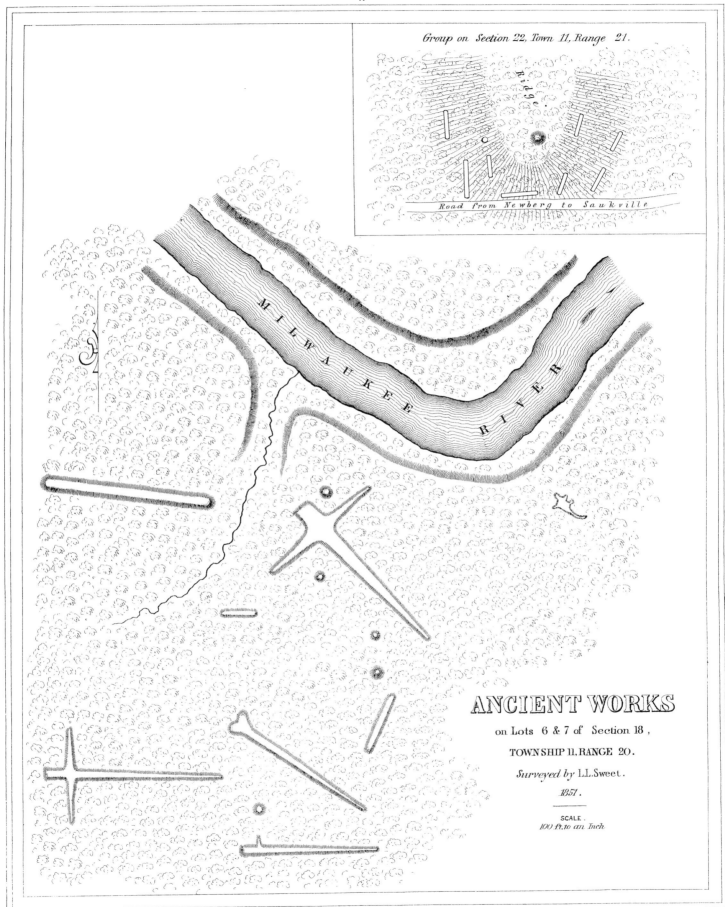

Group on Section 22, Town 11, Range 21.

Ridge.

Road from Newberg to Saukville

MILWAUKEE RIVER

ANCIENT WORKS
on Lots 6 & 7 of Section 18,
TOWNSHIP 11, RANGE 20.

Surveyed by L.L.Sweet.
1851.

SCALE.
100 ft. to an Inch.

A.Lapham, Del.

T. Sinclairs lith, Phil.

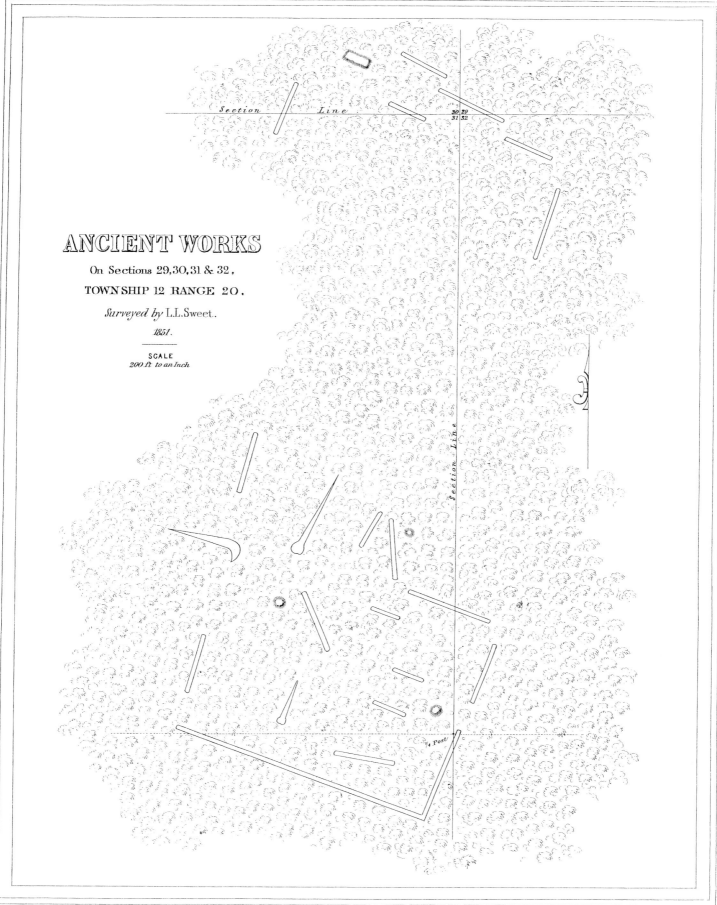

ANCIENT WORKS

On Sections 29, 30, 31 & 32,

TOWNSHIP 12 RANGE 20.

Surveyed by L.L.Sweet.

1851.

SCALE
200 ft to an Inch

I.A.Lapham, Del.

T. Sinclairs Lith.Phil

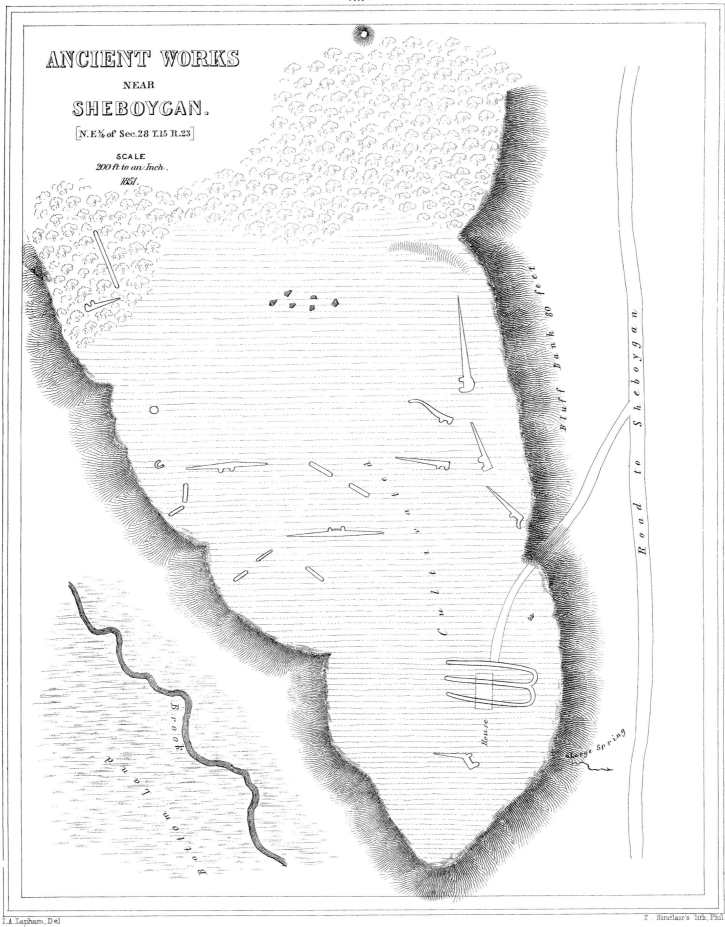

ANCIENT WORKS

NEAR

SHEBOYGAN.

[N.E.¼ of Sec. 28 T.15 R.23]

SCALE
200 ft to an Inch.
1851.

Bluff Bank 80 feet

Road to Sheboygan

Cultivated

Brook Bottom Land

House

Large Spring

I.A.Lapham, Del.

T. Sinclair's lith, Phil.

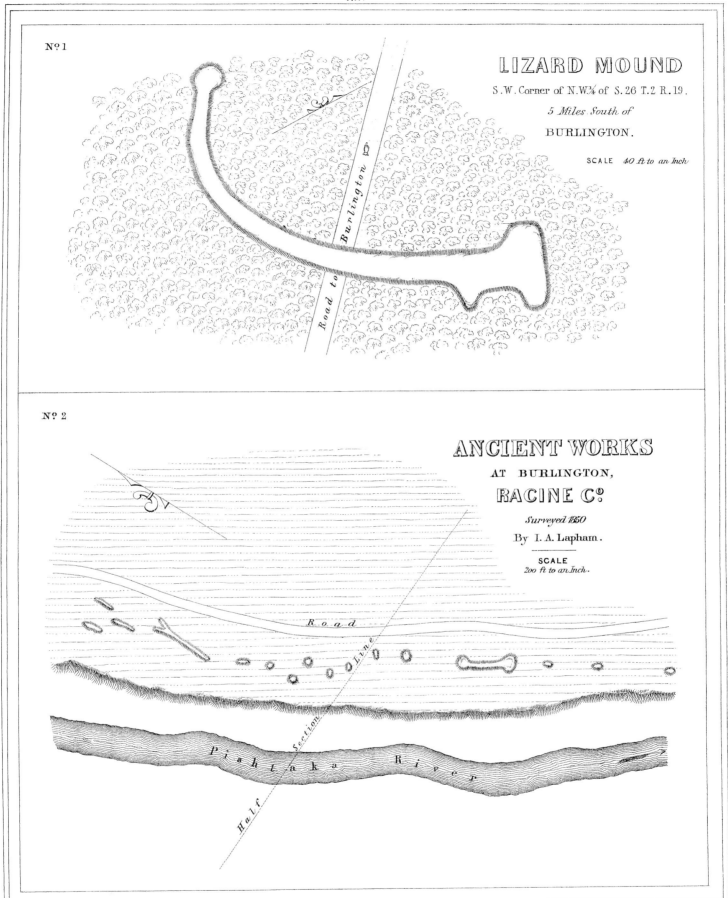

Nº 1

LIZARD MOUND

S.W. Corner of N.W.¾ of S. 26 T.2 R.19.

5 Miles South of

BURLINGTON.

SCALE 40 ft to an Inch

Road to Burlington

Nº 2

ANCIENT WORKS

AT BURLINGTON,

RACINE Cº.

Surveyed 1850

By I. A. Lapham.

SCALE
200 ft to an Inch.

Road

Half Section Line

Pishtaka River

I.A. Lapham, Del.

T. Sinclair's Lith. Phil.

GROUP OF

OBLONG MOUNDS

SOUTH OF

CRAWFORDSVILLE.

Surveyed in 1850
by
I. A. Lapham.

N.º 2

cultivated field

SCALE — *100 ft to an Inch*

N.º 1

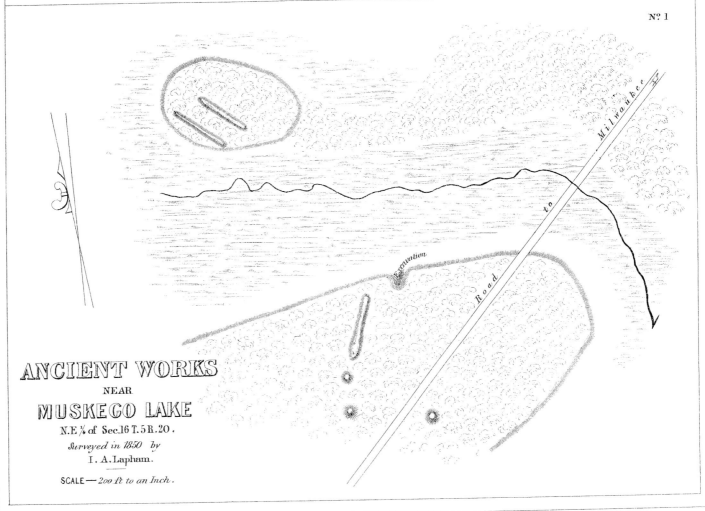

ANCIENT WORKS

NEAR

MUSKEGO LAKE

N.E ¼ of Sec.16 T.5 R.20.

Surveyed in 1850 by
I. A. Lapham.

SCALE — *200 ft to an Inch*.

I.A.Lapham, Del.   T. Sinclair's lith. Phil.

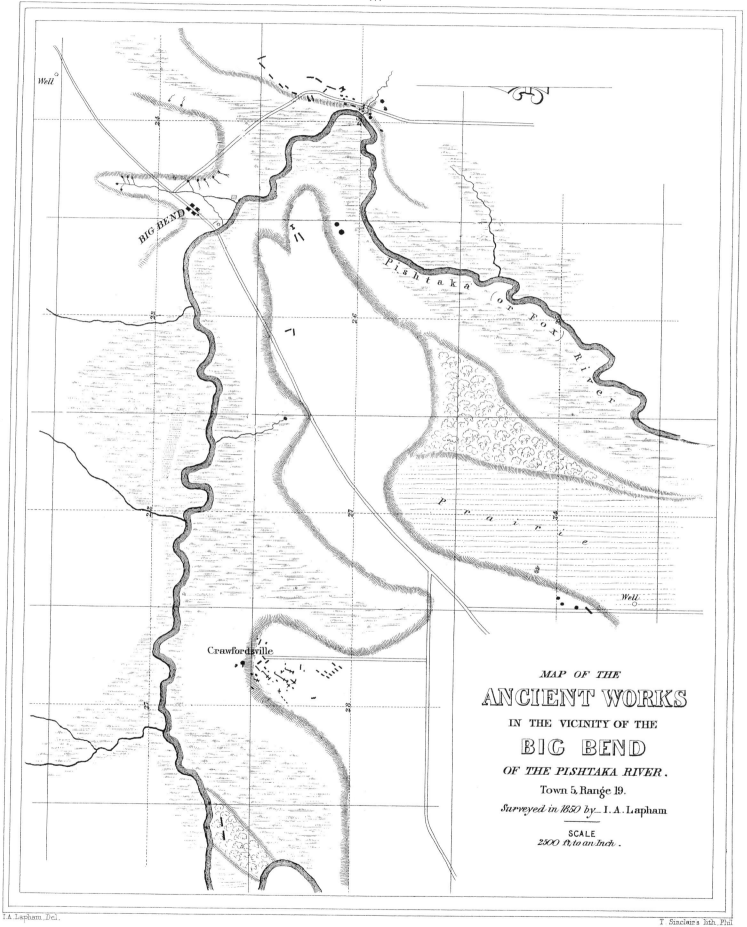

Well

BIG BEND

Pishtaka (or Fox) River

Prairie

Crawfordsville

Well

MAP OF THE

ANCIENT WORKS

IN THE VICINITY OF THE

BIG BEND

OF THE PISHTAKA RIVER.

Town 5, Range 19.

Surveyed in 1850 by I. A. Lapham

SCALE
2500 ft. to an Inch.

I. A. Lapham, Del.

T. Sinclair's lith., Phil

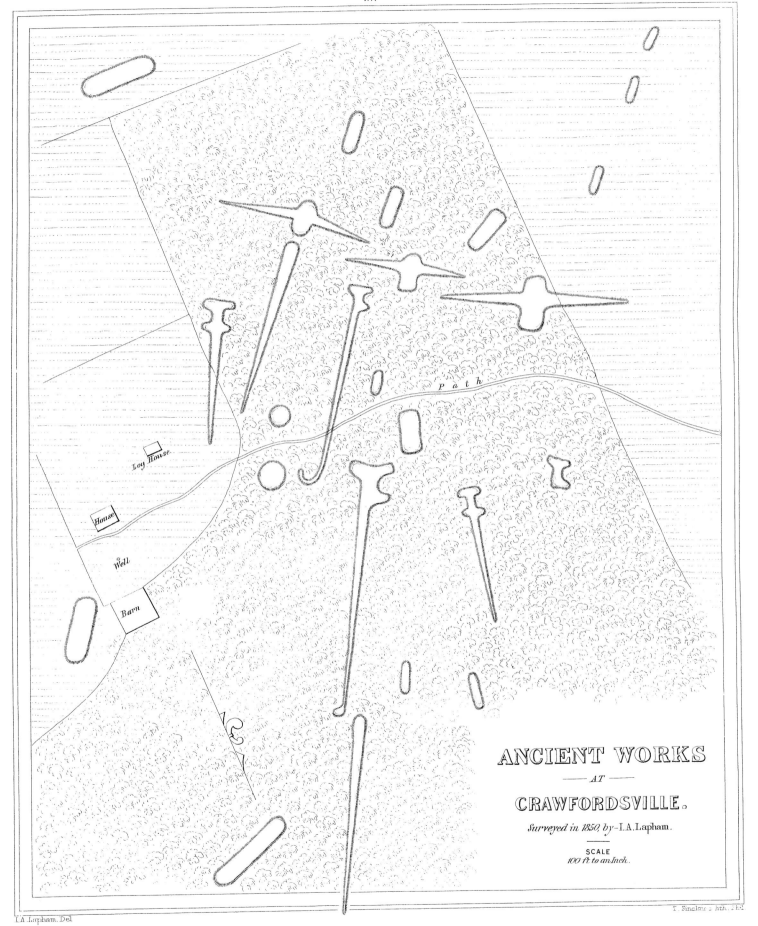

ANCIENT WORKS
— AT —
CRAWFORDSVILLE.

Surveyed in 1850, by I.A.Lapham.

SCALE
100 ft to an Inch.

I.A.Lapham. Del

Path

Log House

House

Well

Barn

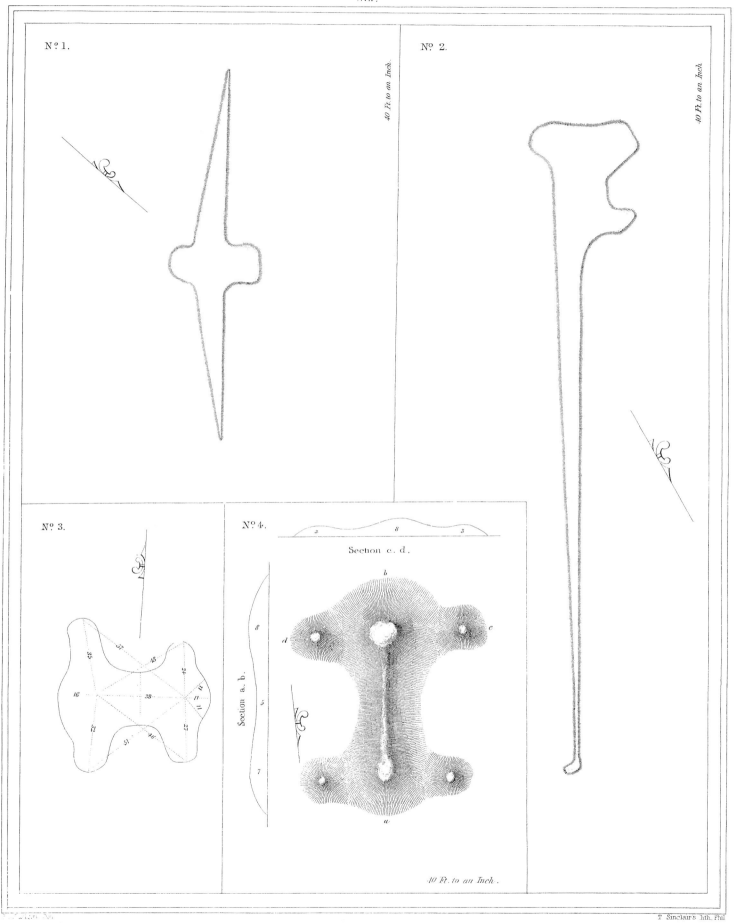

Nº 1.

Nº 2.

40 Ft. to an Inch.

40 Ft. to an Inch.

Nº 3.

Nº 4.

Section c. d.

Section a. b.

40 Ft. to an Inch.

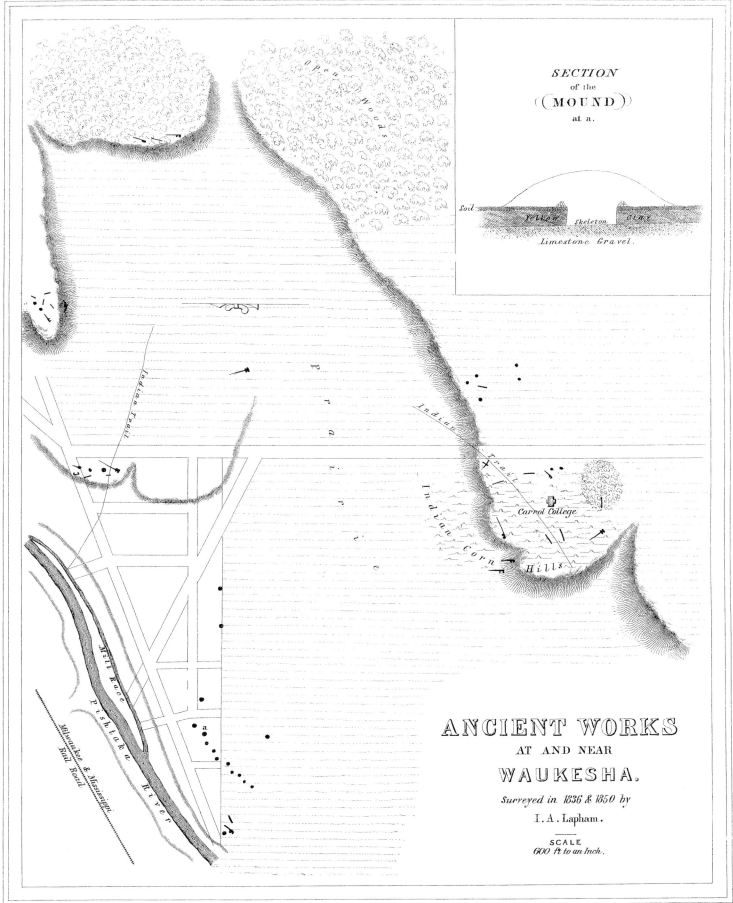

SECTION
of the
((MOUND))
at a.

Soil
Yellow Skeleton Clay
Limestone Gravel.

Open Woods

Indian Trail

Prairie

Indian Trail

Indian Corn Hills

Carrol College

Mill Race

Pishtaka River

Milwaukee & Mississippi Rail Road

ANCIENT WORKS
AT AND NEAR
WAUKESHA.

Surveyed in 1836 & 1850 by
I. A. Lapham.

SCALE
600 ft to an Inch.

I.A. Lapham, Del.

T. Sinclair's lith

XIX.

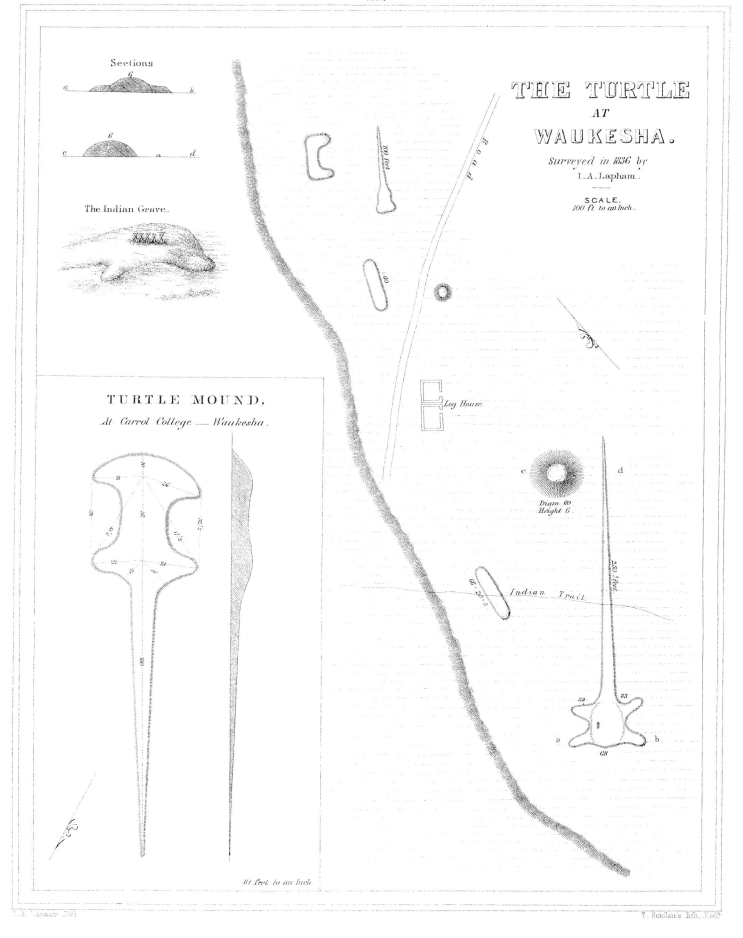

Sections

The Indian Grave.

TURTLE MOUND,

At Carrol College — Waukesha.

THE TURTLE
AT
WAUKESHA.

Surveyed in 1836 by
I. A. Lapham.

SCALE.
100 ft to an Inch.

Log House

Diam 60
Height 6.

Indian Trail

40 feet to an Inch

1

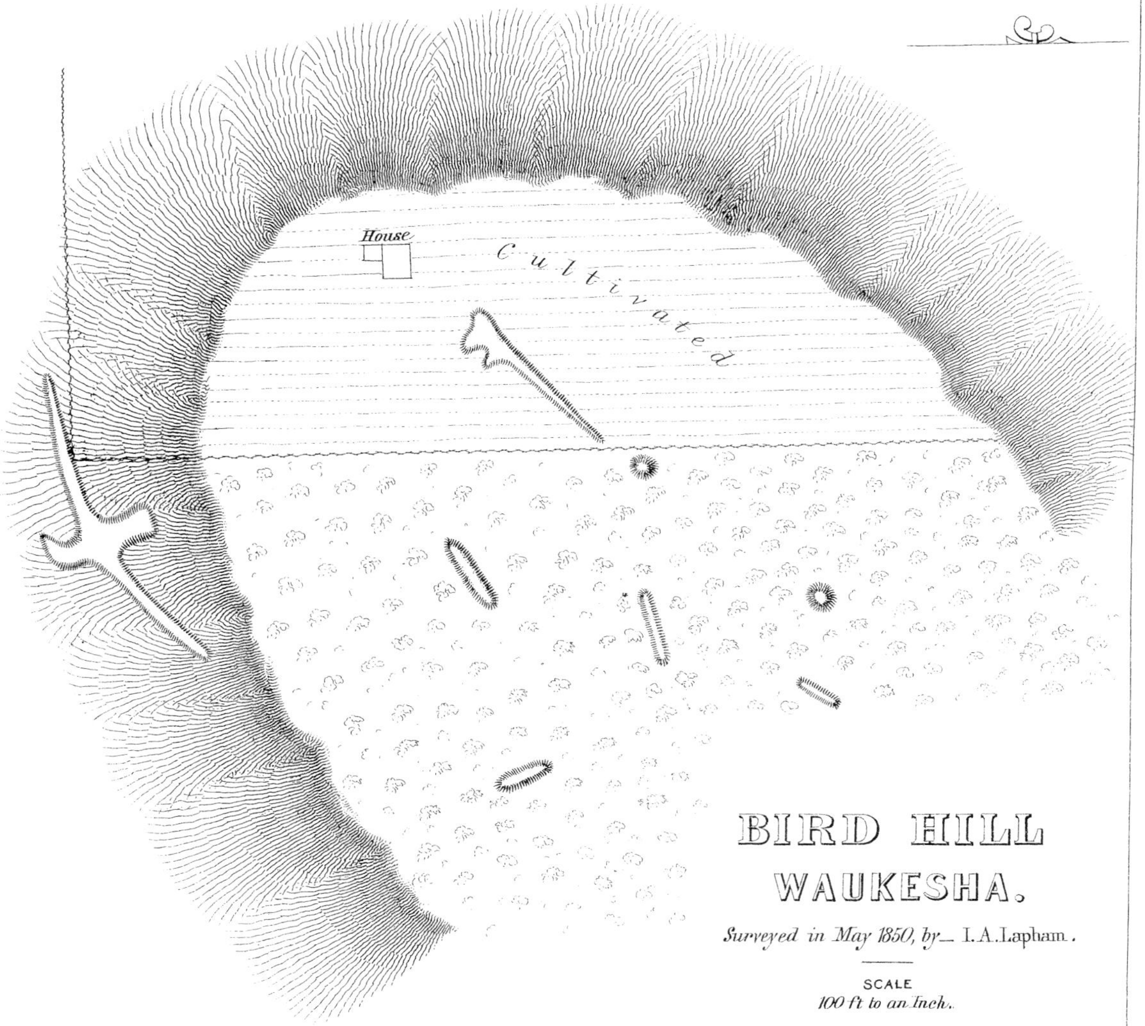

House

Cultivated

BIRD HILL
WAUKESHA,

Surveyed in May 1850, by I. A. Lapham.

SCALE
100 ft to an Inch.

2

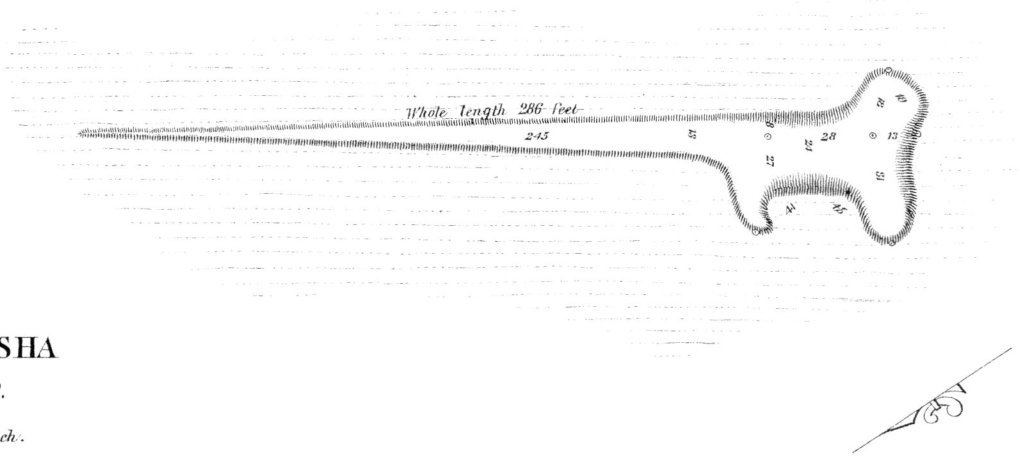

Whole length 286 feet.

AT
WAUKESHA

May 1850.

50 ft to an Inch.

I.A.Lapham, Del.   T. Sinclair's lith, Phila

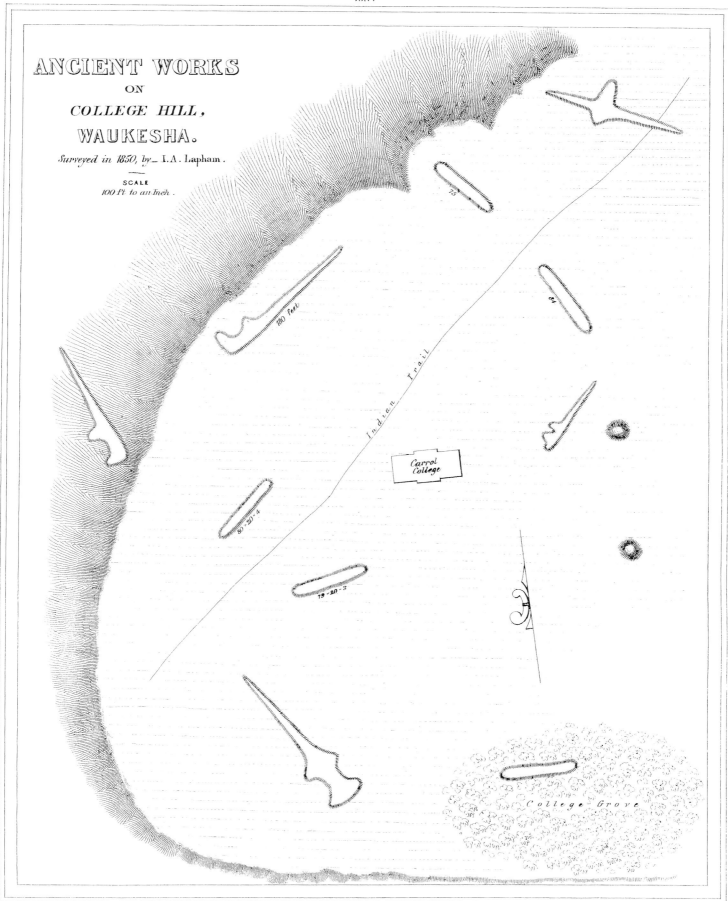

ANCIENT WORKS
ON
COLLEGE HILL,
WAUKESHA.

Surveyed in 1850, by— I.A. Lapham.

SCALE
100 Ft to an Inch.

Carrol
College

Indian Trail

180 feet

80 · 20 · 4

75 · 20 · 5

College Grove

I.A. Lapham Del.   T. Sinclair's lith. Phil.

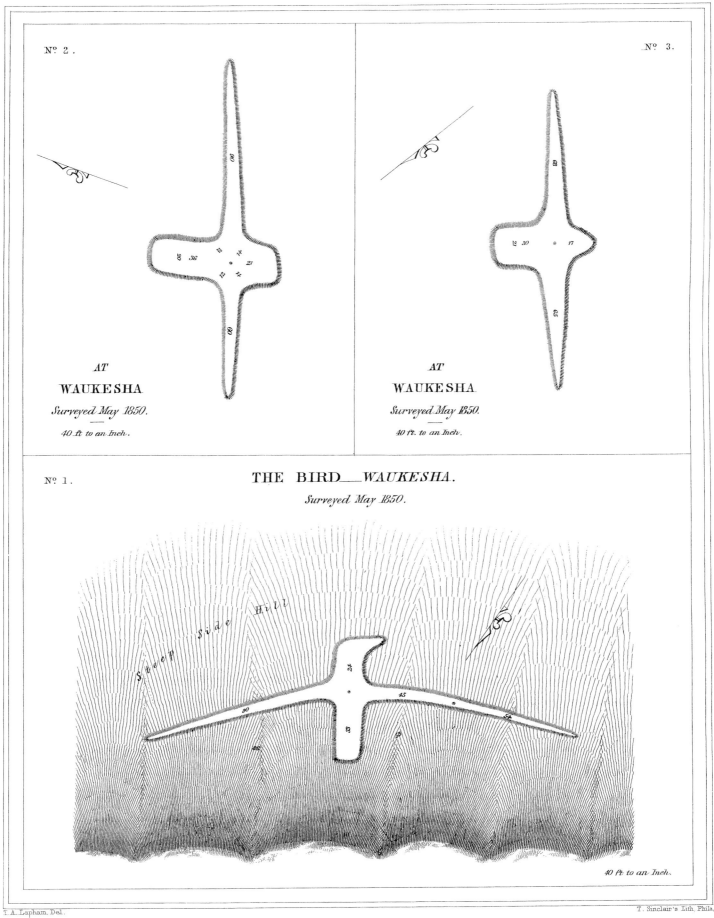

Nº 2.

Nº 3.

AT
WAUKESHA
Surveyed May 1850.
—
40 ft to an Inch.

AT
WAUKESHA
Surveyed May 1850.
—
40 ft. to an Inch.

Nº 1.

THE BIRD___WAUKESHA.
Surveyed May 1850.

Steep side Hill

40 ft. to an Inch.

T. A. Lapham, Del.

T. Sinclair's Lith, Phila.

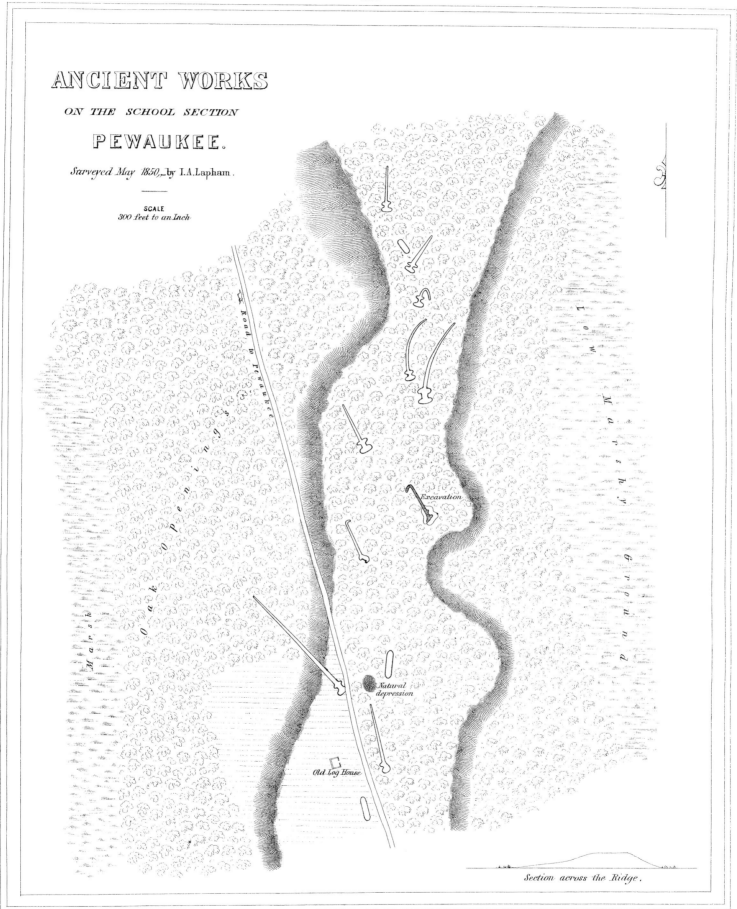

ANCIENT WORKS

ON THE SCHOOL SECTION

PEWAUKEE.

Surveyed May 1850, by I.A.Lapham.

SCALE
300 feet to an Inch

Section across the Ridge.

I A Lapham, Del.   I. Sinclair's lith.Phila

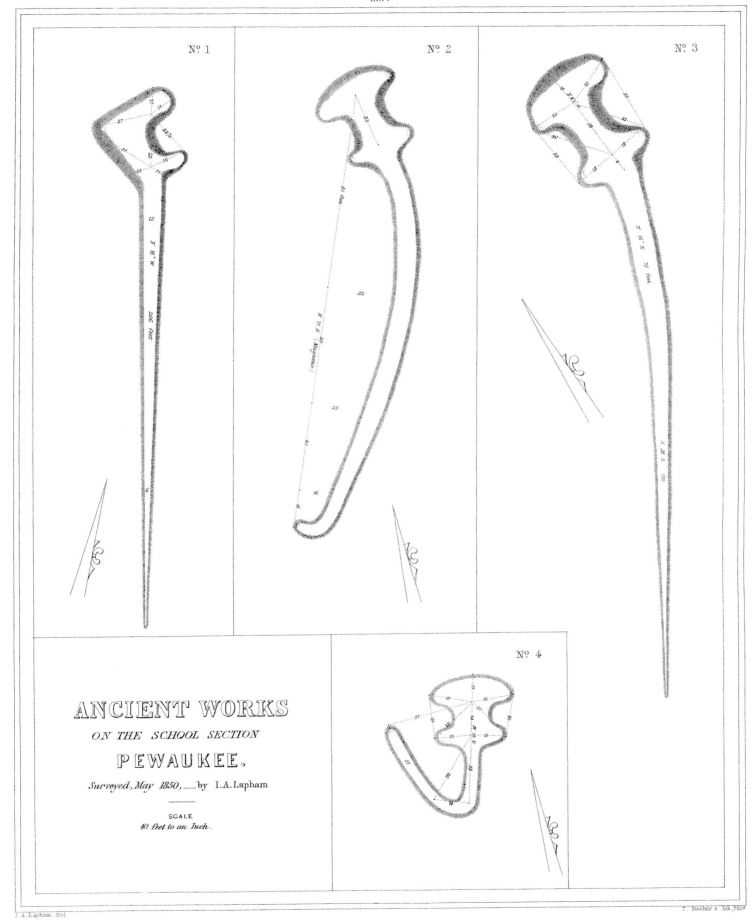

No. 1   No. 2   No. 3

No. 4

ANCIENT WORKS
ON THE SCHOOL SECTION
PEWAUKEE.

Surveyed, May 1850, ___ by I.A.Lapham

SCALE
10 Feet to an Inch.

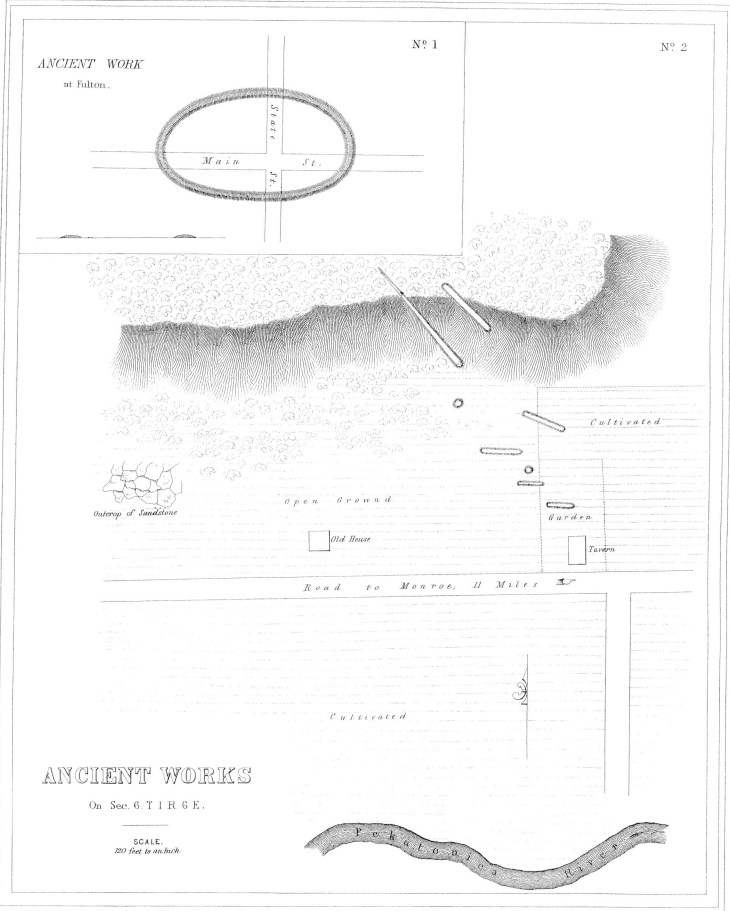

ANCIENT WORK
at Fulton.

Nº 1

Nº 2

State St.

Main St.

Outcrop of Sandstone

Open Ground

Cultivated

Garden

Old House

Tavern

Road to Monroe, 11 Miles

Cultivated

ANCIENT WORKS

On Sec. 6. T 1 R 6 E.

SCALE.
120 feet to an Inch.

Pekatonica River

I.A. Lapham, Del.

T. Sinclair's lith. Philª

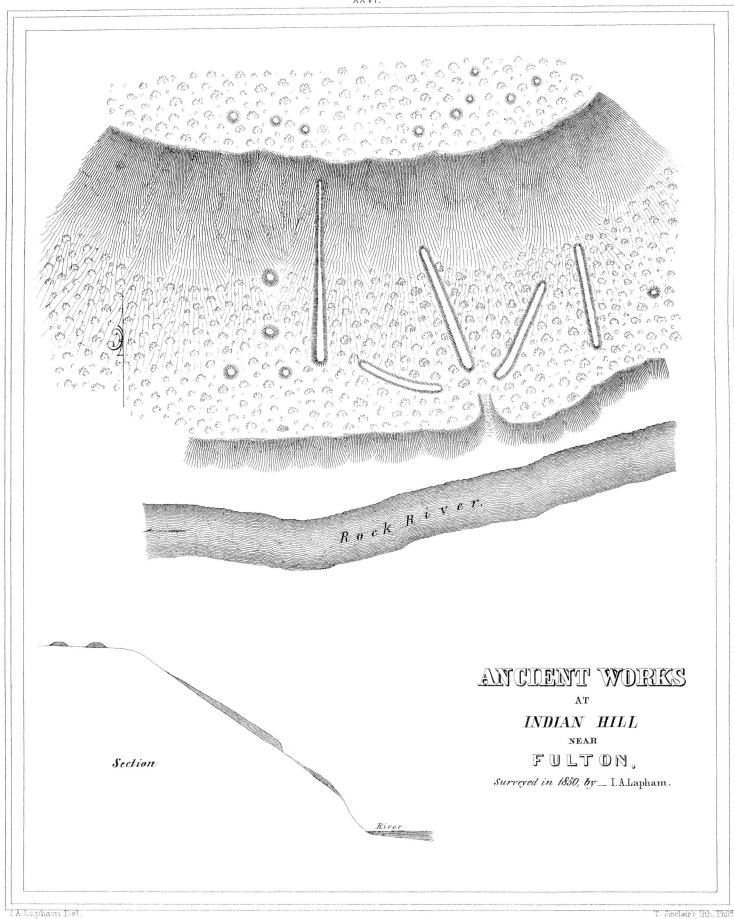

ANCIENT WORKS
AT
INDIAN HILL
NEAR
FULTON,
Surveyed in 1850, by I.A.Lapham.

Section

River

Rock River.

I.A.Lapham Del.

T. Sinclair's lith. Phila.

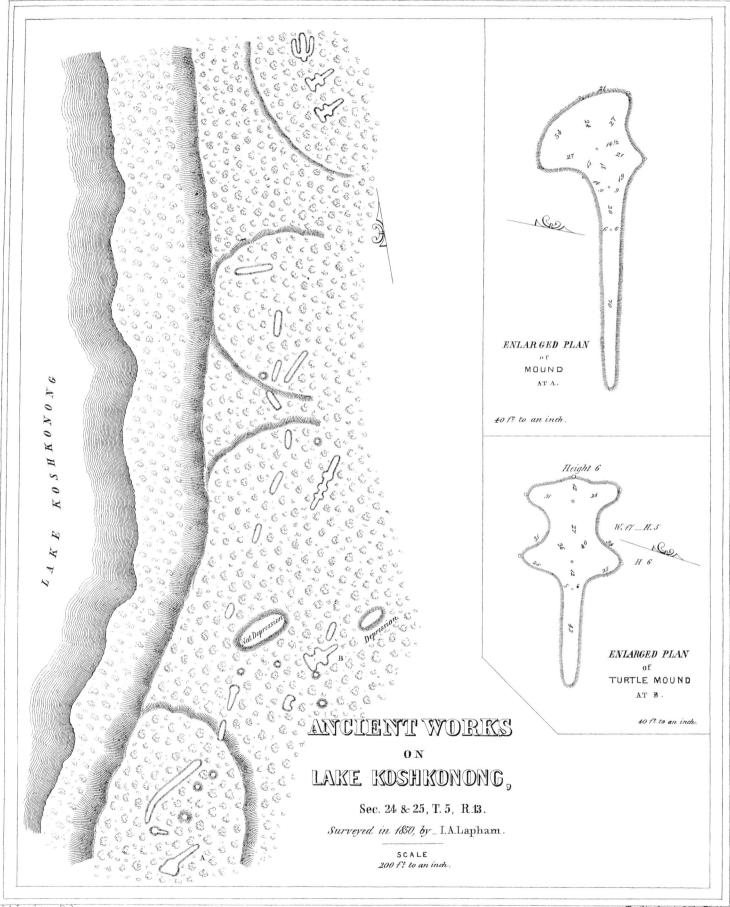

LAKE KOSHKONONG

Nat.Depression

Depression

B

A

ENLARGED PLAN
of
MOUND
AT A.

40 ft. to an inch.

Height 6

W. 17 — H. 5

H 6

ENLARGED PLAN
of
TURTLE MOUND
AT B.

40 ft. to an inch.

ANCIENT WORKS
ON
LAKE KOSHKONONG,
Sec. 24 & 25, T. 5, R. 13.
Surveyed in 1850, by I.A.Lapham.

SCALE
200 ft. to an inch.

I.A.Lapham Del.

T. Sinclair's lith. Phil?

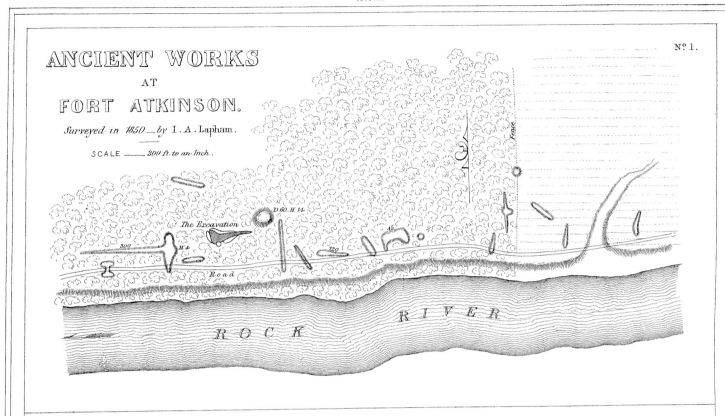

No. 1.

ANCIENT WORKS
AT
FORT ATKINSON.

Surveyed in 1850 — by I. A. Lapham.

SCALE —— 300 ft. to an Inch.

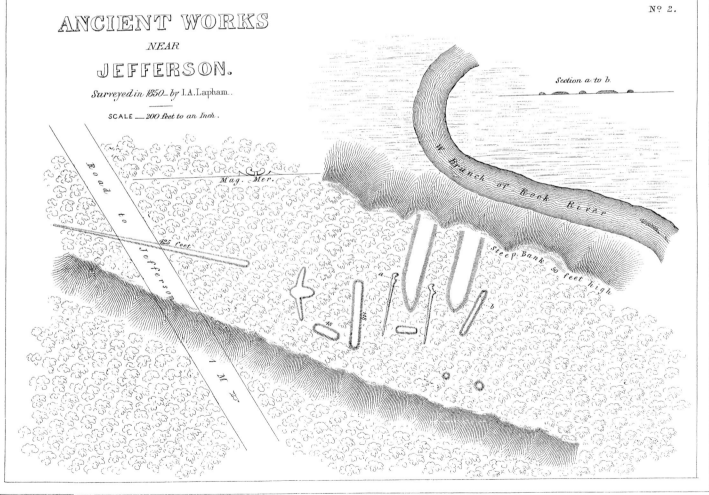

No. 2.

ANCIENT WORKS
NEAR
JEFFERSON.

Surveyed in 1850 — by I. A. Lapham.

SCALE —— 200 feet to an Inch.

I.A. Lapham, Del.

T. Sinclair's lith. Phila

XXIX.

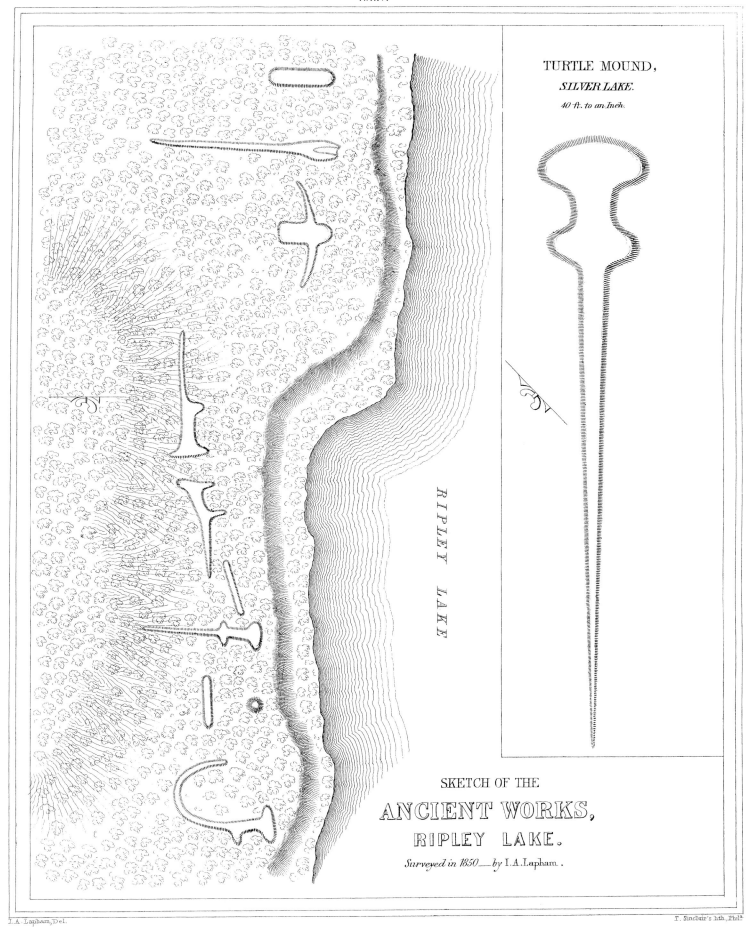

TURTLE MOUND,
SILVER LAKE.
40 ft. to an Inch.

RIPLEY LAKE

SKETCH OF THE
ANCIENT WORKS,
RIPLEY LAKE.
Surveyed in 1850 — by I.A.Lapham.

I.A.Lapham,Del.

T. Sinclair's lith. Phila

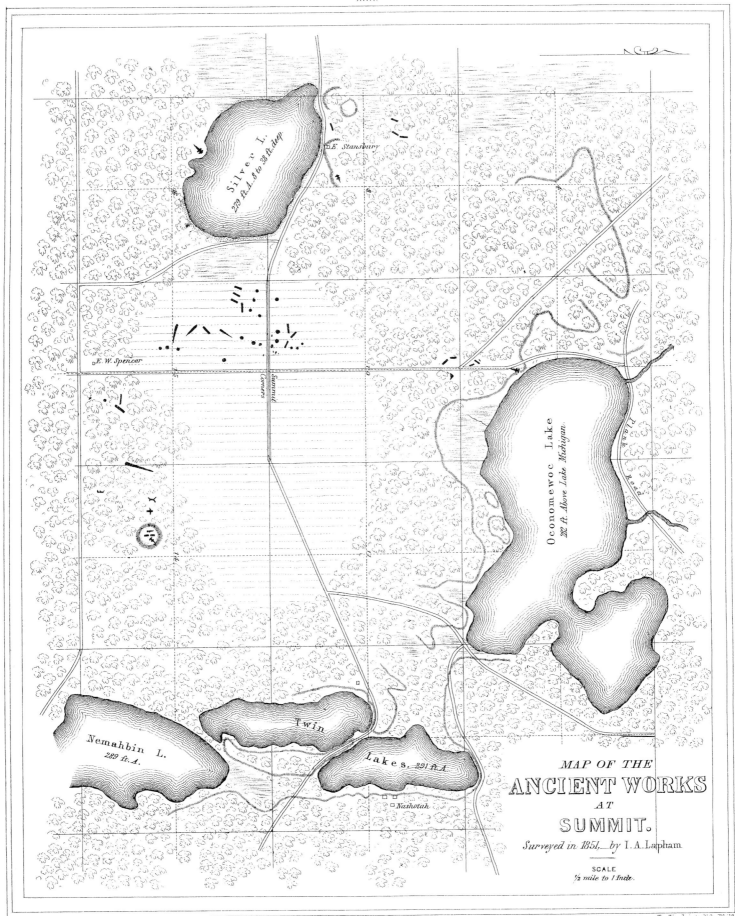

MAP OF THE
ANCIENT WORKS
AT
SUMMIT.

Surveyed in 1851, by I. A. Lapham.

SCALE
½ mile to 1 inch.

I. A. Lapham, Del.

T. Sinclair's lith. Phila

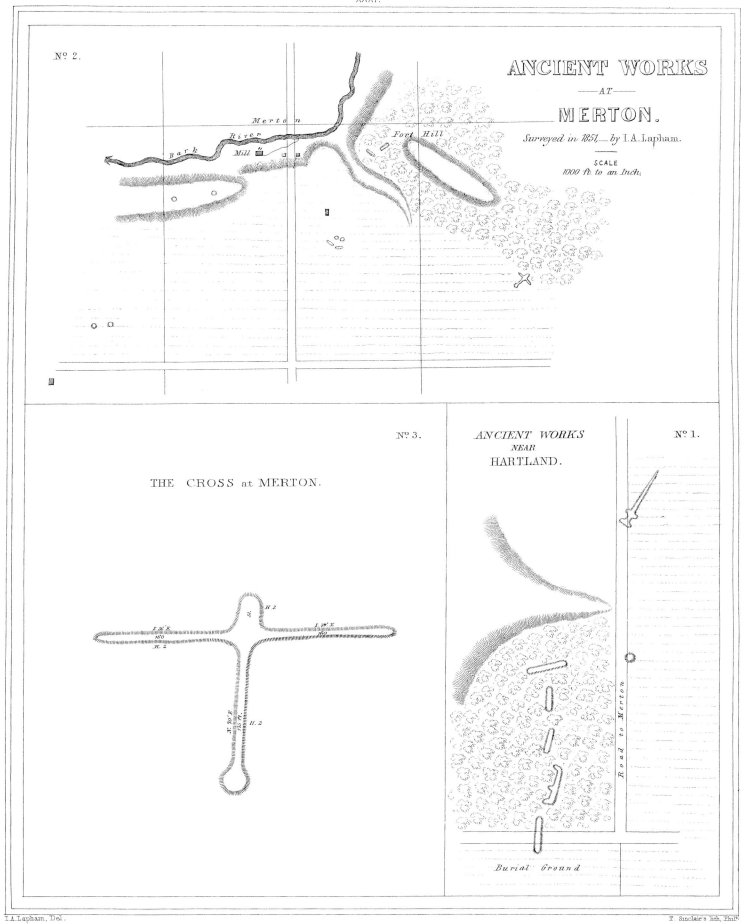

Nº 2.

ANCIENT WORKS
—AT—
MERTON.

Surveyed in 1851, by I.A.Lapham.

SCALE
1000 ft. to an Inch.

Merton

Bark River

Mill

Fort Hill

Nº 3.

THE CROSS at MERTON.

ANCIENT WORKS
NEAR
HARTLAND.

Nº 1.

Road to Merton

Burial Ground

I.A.Lapham, Del.

T. Sinclair's lith, Phil.

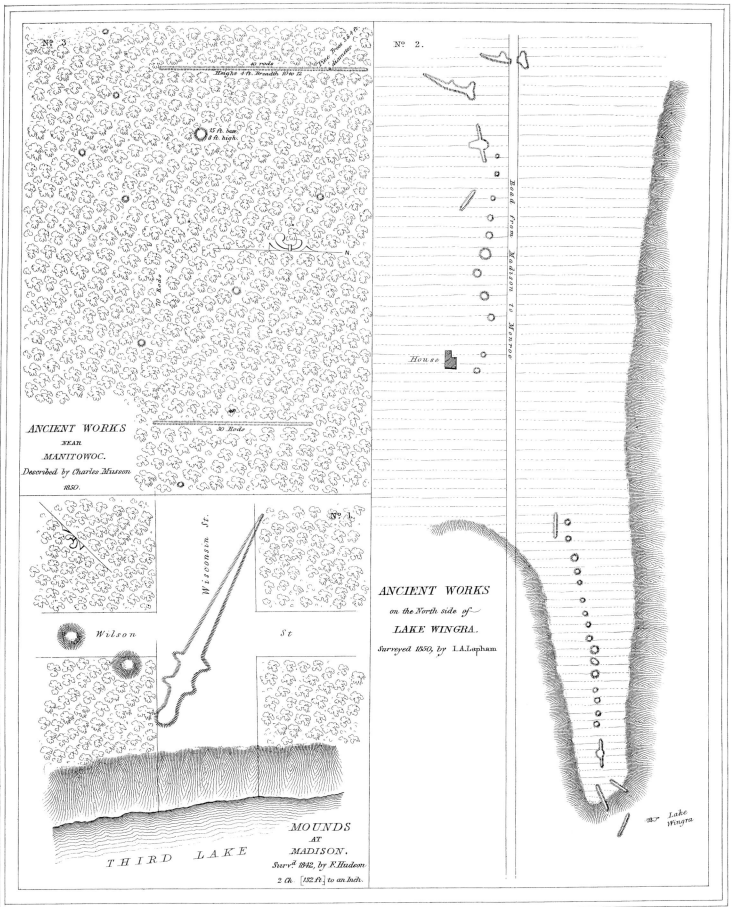

No. 3

40 rods
Pine Trees 3 & 4 ft. diameter
Haght 4 ft. Breadth 10 to 12

15 ft. base
8 ft. high.

70 Rods

N.

30 Rods

ANCIENT WORKS
NEAR
MANITOWOC.
Described by Charles Musson
1850.

No. 2.

Road from Madison to Monroe

House

ANCIENT WORKS
on the North side of
LAKE WINGRA.
Surveyed 1850, by I.A.Lapham

Lake Wingra

Wisconsin St.

Wilson

St

No. 1.

MOUNDS
AT
MADISON.
Survᵈ 1842, by F.Hudson
2 Ch. [132 ft] to an Inch.

THIRD LAKE

I.A.Lapham, Del.

T. Sinclair's lith, Philᵃ

ANCIENT WORKS
AT
AZTALAN.

Surveyed in 1851 — by I. A. Lapham.

SCALE
200 ft. to an inch

SECTION OF MOUND
at a.
as seen from c.

Mound Street

South Street

Aztec Street

Street

Excavations

Section Line

Oak Tree 2 ft. diam.

Oak Tree 2 ft. diam.

Oak Tree 2 ft. diam.

Burr Oak 30 in. diam.

Oak Tree 2 ft. diam.

Oak Tree 18 in. diam.

Oak Tree 2 ft. in diam.

631 feet

1450 feet

700 feet

b
a
c
d
f
c

Steep Bank 15 ft. high

Embankment

Brook

WEST BRANCH OF ROCK RIVER

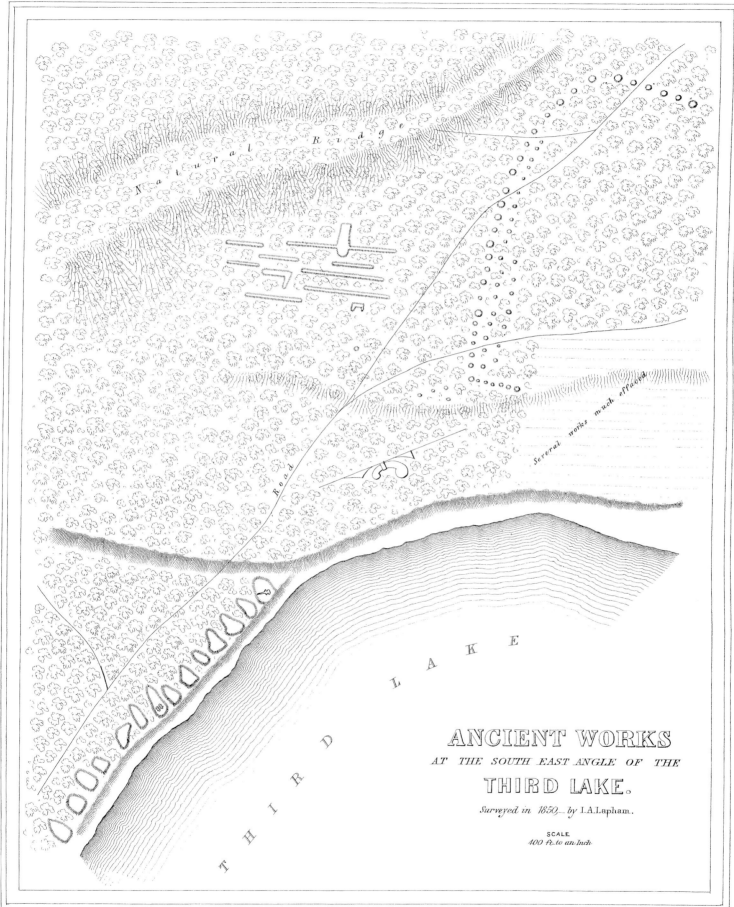

Natural Ridge

Road

Several works much effaced

THIRD LAKE

ANCIENT WORKS
AT THE SOUTH EAST ANGLE OF THE
THIRD LAKE.

Surveyed in 1850 by I.A.Lapham.

SCALE
400 ft. to an Inch

I A Lapham Del.   T. Sinclair's lith, Phil&

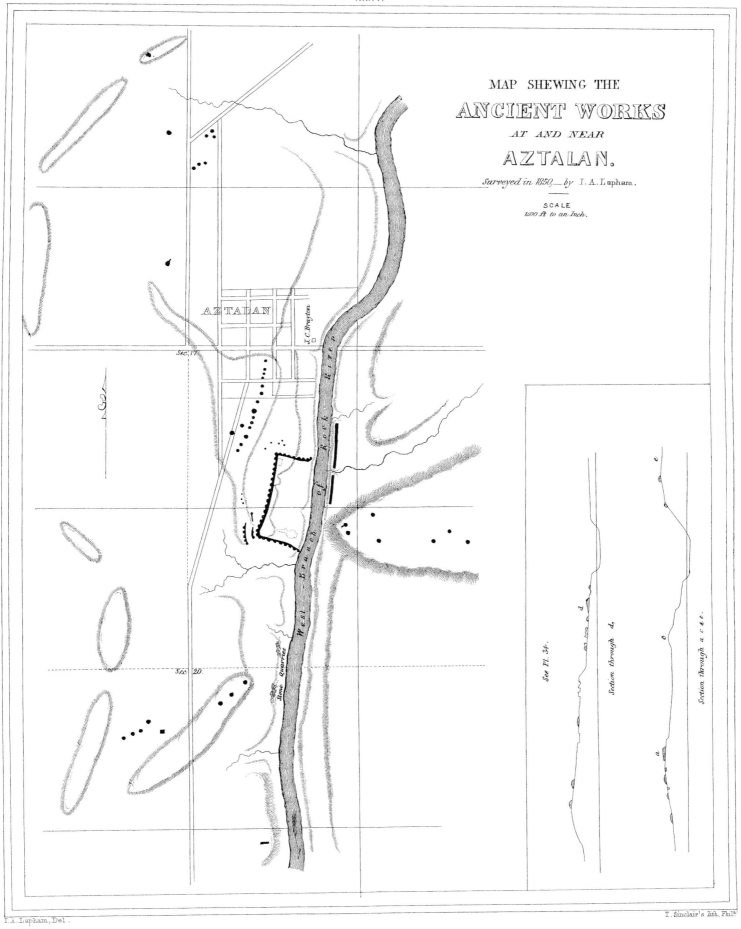

MAP SHEWING THE
ANCIENT WORKS
AT AND NEAR
AZTALAN.

Surveyed in 1850 — by I.A.Lapham.

SCALE
1500 ft. to an Inch.

AZTALAN

J.C.Brayton.

Sec. 17

Sec. 20

West Branch of Rock River

Stone Quarries

See Pl. 34.

Section through d.

Section through a. c & e.

I.A.Lapham, Del.

T. Sinclair's lith. Phila.

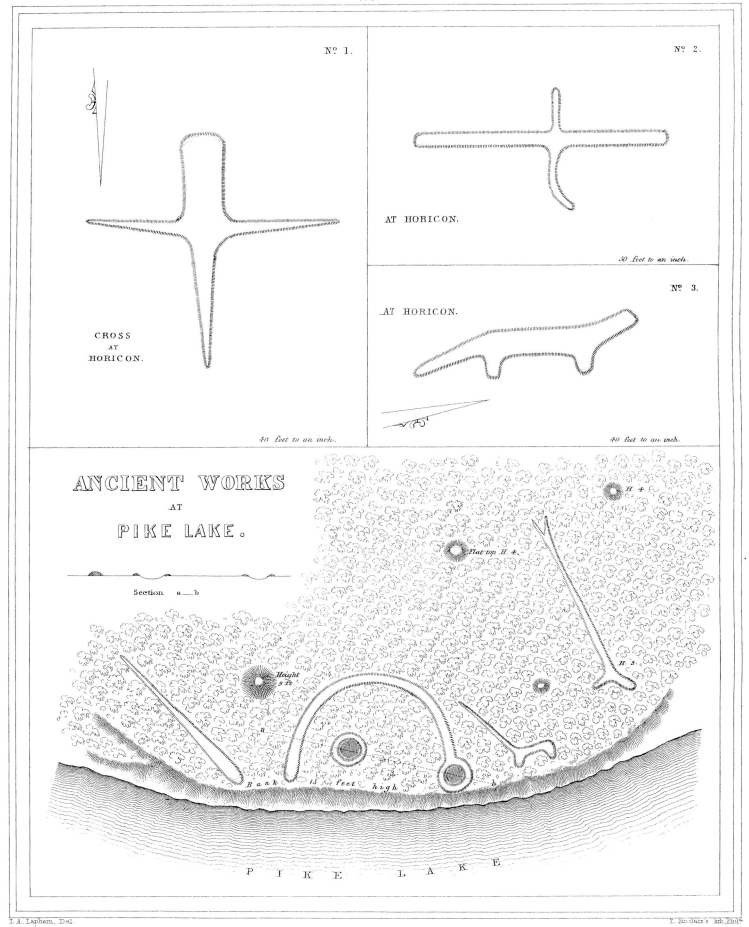

Nº 1.

CROSS
AT
HORICON.

40 feet to an inch.

Nº 2.

AT HORICON.

50 feet to an inch.

Nº 3.

AT HORICON.

40 feet to an inch.

ANCIENT WORKS
AT
PIKE LAKE.

Section a ____ b

Flat top H. 4.

H. 4.

H. 3.

Height
9 Ft.

Bank 15 feet high

a

b

PIKE LAKE

I. A. Lapham, Del.

T. Sinclair's lith. Phil.

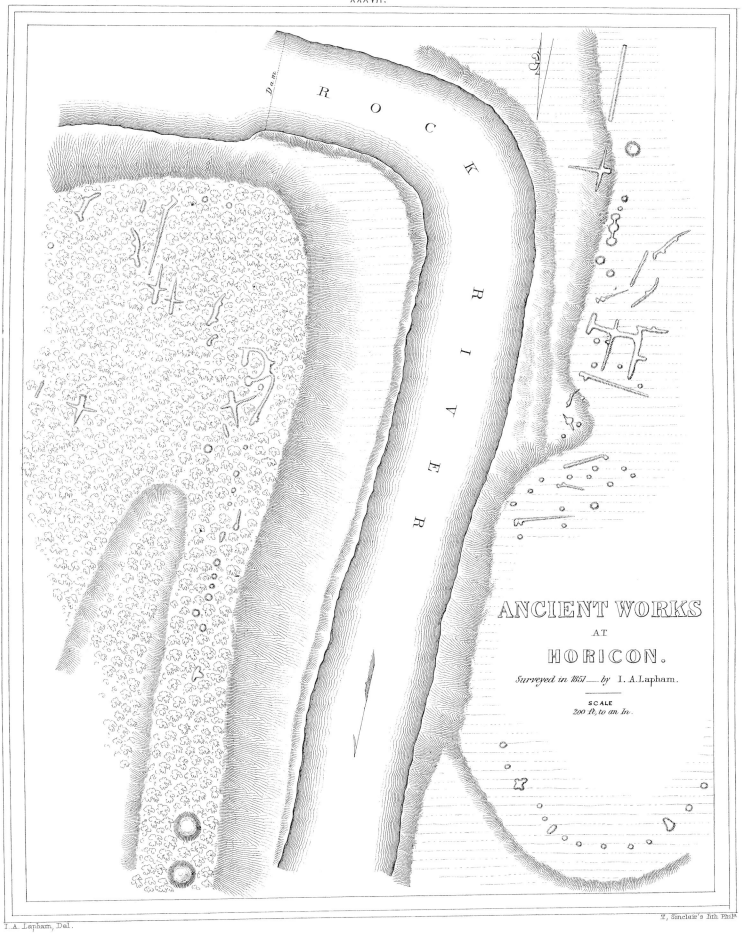

R O C K   R I V E R

Done

ANCIENT WORKS
AT
HORICON.

Surveyed in 1851 ___ by I. A. Lapham.

SCALE
200 ft, to an In.

I. A. Lapham, Del.

T, Sinclair's lith Phila

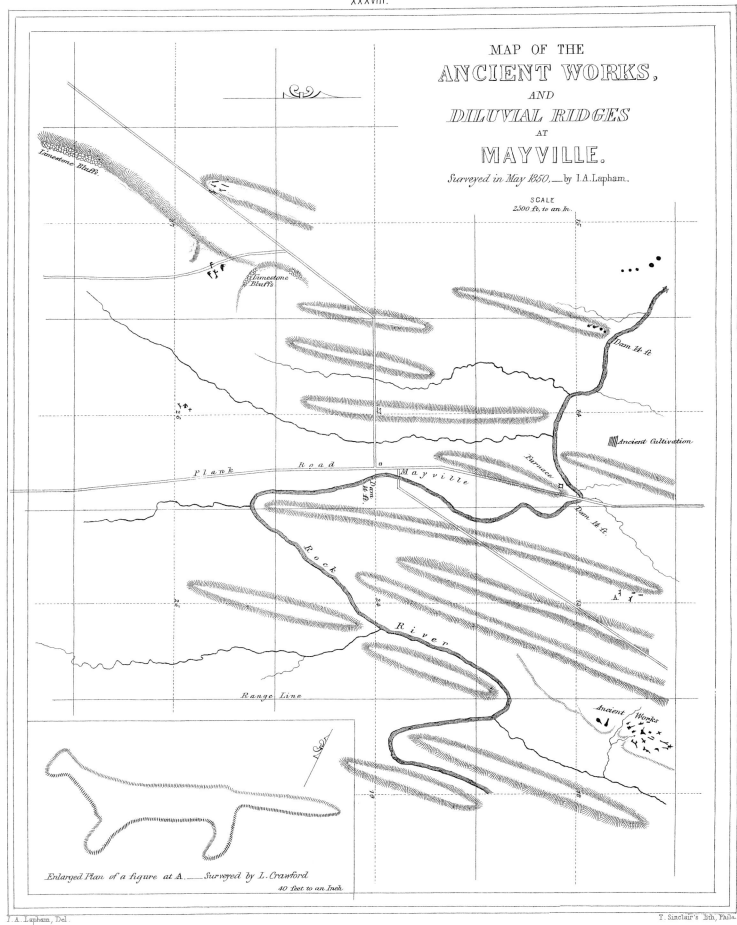

MAP OF THE
ANCIENT WORKS,
AND
DILUVIAL RIDGES
AT
MAYVILLE.

Surveyed in May 1850,—by I. A. Lapham.

SCALE
2500 ft, to an In.

Limestone Bluffs.

Limestone Bluffs

Dam 14 ft.

Ancient Cultivation

Furnace

Plank Road

Mayville

Dam 14 ft.

Dam 14 ft.

Rock

River

Range Line

Ancient Works

Enlarged Plan of a figure at A.——*Surveyed by L. Crawford*

40 feet to an Inch

J. A. Lapham, Del.

T. Sinclair's lith, Phila.

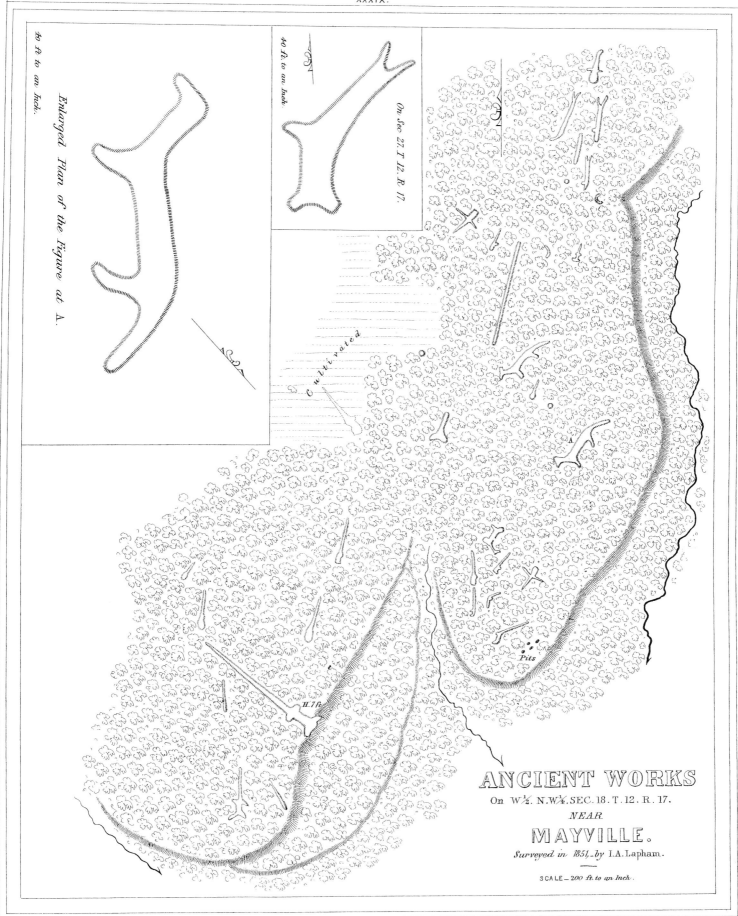

XXXIX.

Enlarged Plan of the Figure at A.
40 ft. to an Inch.

On Sec. 27. T. 12. R. 17.
40 ft. to an Inch.

Cultivated

Pits

H. 7 ft.

ANCIENT WORKS
On W.½. N.W.¼. SEC. 18. T. 12. R. 17.
NEAR
MAYVILLE.
Surveyed in 1851, by I. A. Lapham.

SCALE — 200 ft. to an Inch.

I. A. Lapham, Del.

T. Sinclair's lith. Phila

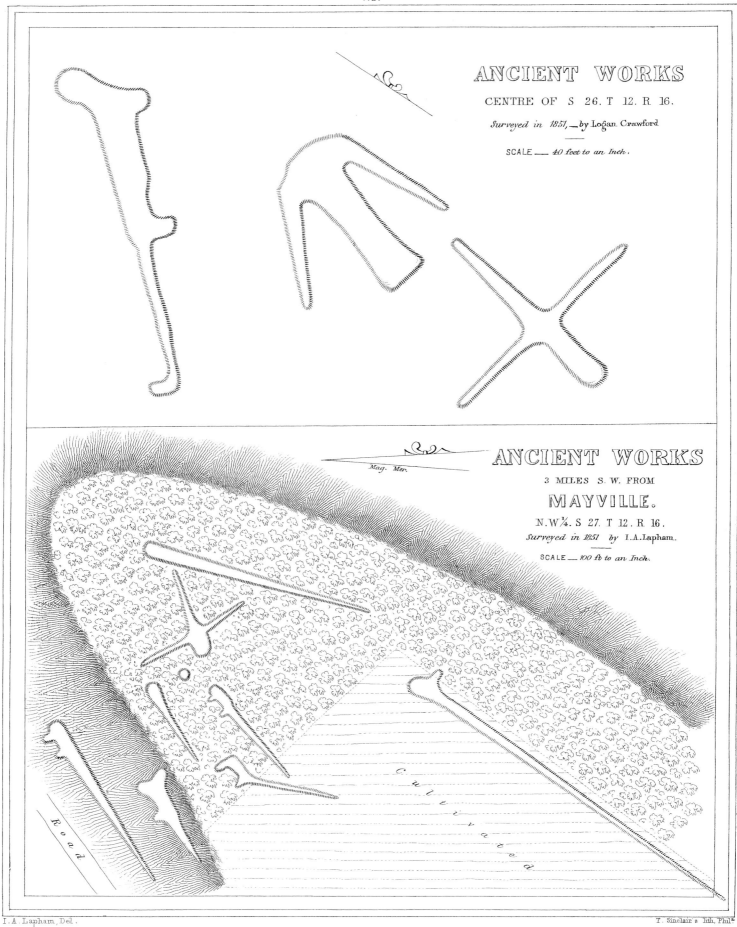

ANCIENT WORKS

CENTRE OF S 26. T 12. R 16.

Surveyed in 1851, — by Logan Crawford

SCALE ___ *40 feet to an Inch.*

ANCIENT WORKS

3 MILES S.W. FROM

MAYVILLE.

N.W.¼. S 27. T 12. R. 16.

Surveyed in 1851 by I.A.Lapham.

SCALE ___ *100 ft to an Inch.*

Mag. Mer.

Road

Cultivated

I. A. Lapham, Del.

T. Sinclair's lith. Phil.ª

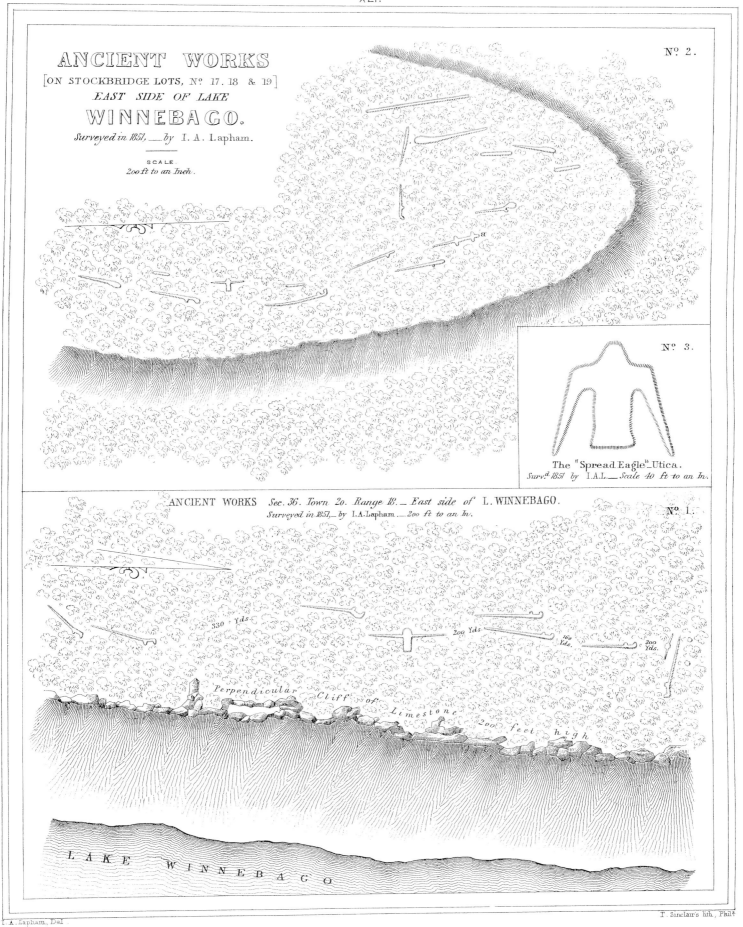

N.º 2.

ANCIENT WORKS

[ON STOCKBRIDGE LOTS, N.º 17. 18 & 19]
EAST SIDE OF LAKE
WINNEBAGO.

Surveyed in 1851, — by I. A. Lapham.

SCALE.
200 ft to an Inch.

N.º 3.

The "Spread Eagle" Utica.
Surv.ᵈ 1851 by I.A.L. — Scale 40 ft to an In.

ANCIENT WORKS   Sec. 36. Town 20. Range 18. — East side of L. WINNEBAGO.
Surveyed in 1851, — by I.A.Lapham. — 200 ft to an In.

N.º 1.

330 Yds.   200 Yds.   160 Yds.   300 Yds.

Perpendicular Cliff of Limestone 200 feet high

LAKE WINNEBAGO

I.A.Lapham, Del.   T. Sinclair's lith, Phil.ᵃ

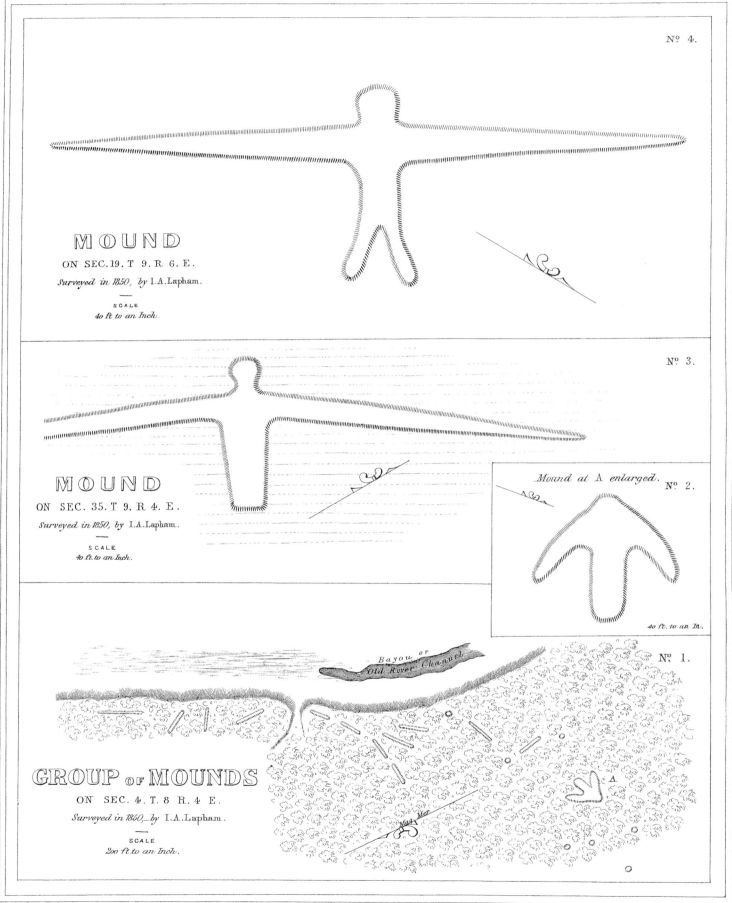

Nº 4.

MOUND

ON SEC. 19. T 9. R 6. E.

Surveyed in 1850, by I. A. Lapham.

SCALE
40 ft to an Inch.

Nº 3.

MOUND

ON SEC. 35. T 9. R 4. E.

Surveyed in 1850, by I. A. Lapham.

SCALE
40 ft. to an Inch.

Mound at A enlarged. Nº 2.

40 ft. to an In.

Bayou or Old River Channel

Nº 1.

GROUP OF MOUNDS

ON SEC. 4. T. 8 R. 4 E.

Surveyed in 1850, by I. A. Lapham.

SCALE
200 ft. to an Inch.

I. A. Lapham Del.

T. Sinclair's lith. Phila.

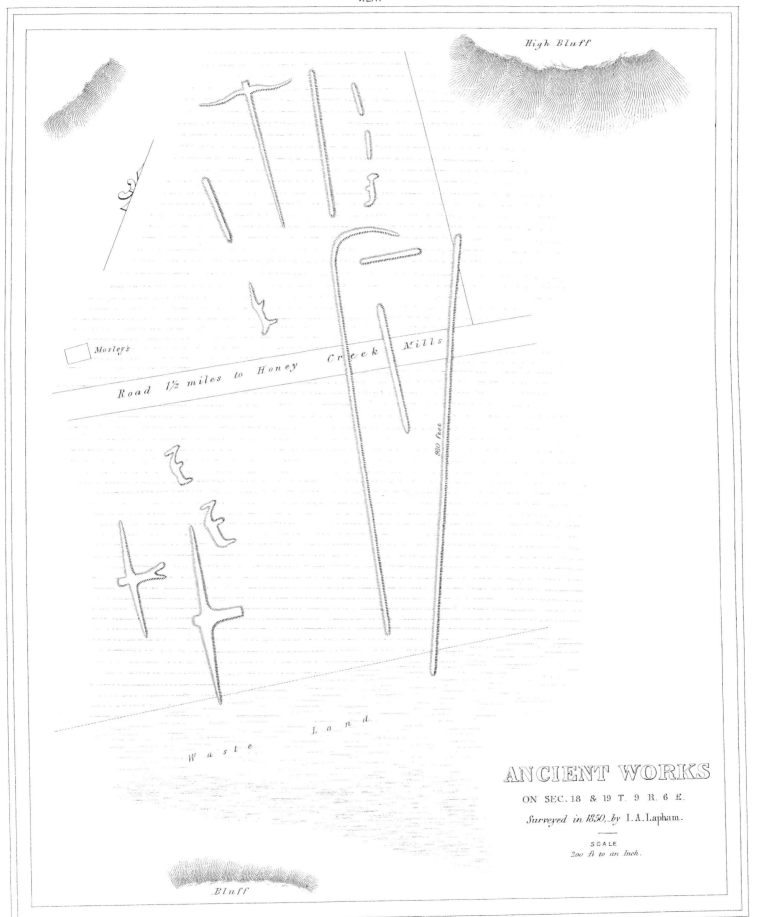

High Bluff

Mosley's

Road 1½ miles to Honey Creek Hills

350 feet

Land

Waste

Bluff

ANCIENT WORKS

ON SEC. 18 & 19 T. 9 R. 6 E.

Surveyed in 1850, by I. A. Lapham.

SCALE
200 ft to an Inch.

I. A. Lapham, Del.

T. Sinclair's Lith. Phila.

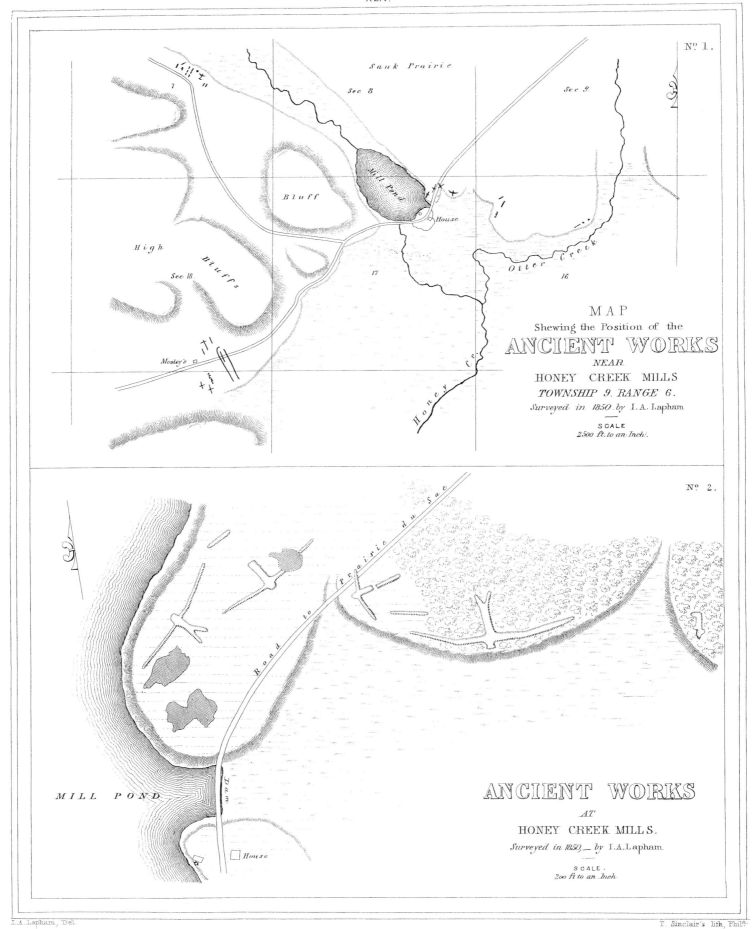

Nº 1.

Sauk Prairie

Sec 8

Sec 9.

Mill Pond

Bluff

House

High

Bluffs

Sec 18

Otter Creek

17

16

Mosley's

Honey Cr.

MAP

Shewing the Position of the

ANCIENT WORKS

NEAR

HONEY CREEK MILLS

TOWNSHIP 9. RANGE 6.

Surveyed in 1850 by I. A. Lapham.

SCALE

2500 ft. to an Inch.

Nº 2.

Road to Prairie du Sac

MILL POND

Dam

House

ANCIENT WORKS

AT

HONEY CREEK MILLS.

Surveyed in 1850, by I. A. Lapham.

SCALE.

200 ft to an Inch

I. A. Lapham, Del.

T. Sinclair's lith, Philᵃ

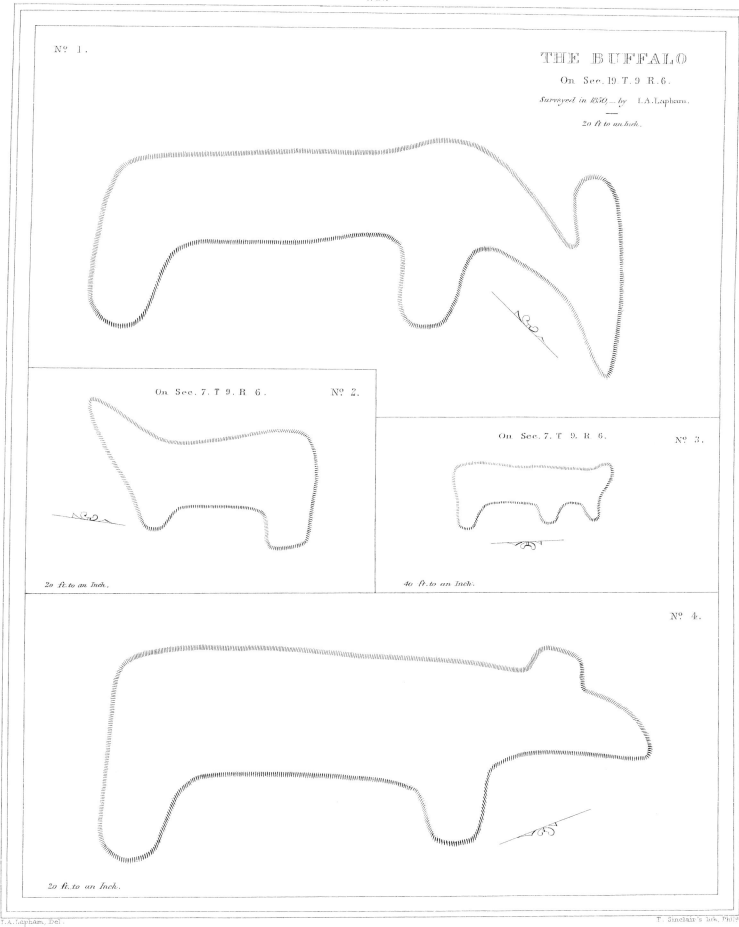

Nº 1.

THE BUFFALO

On Sec. 19 T. 9 R. 6.

Surveyed in 1850, — by I. A. Lapham.

20 ft to an Inch.

On Sec. 7. T 9. R. 6.   Nº 2.

20 ft. to an Inch.

On Sec. 7. T 9. R. 6.   Nº 3.

40 ft. to an Inch.

Nº 4.

20 ft. to an Inch.

I. A. Lapham, Del.   T. Sinclair's lith, Phil?

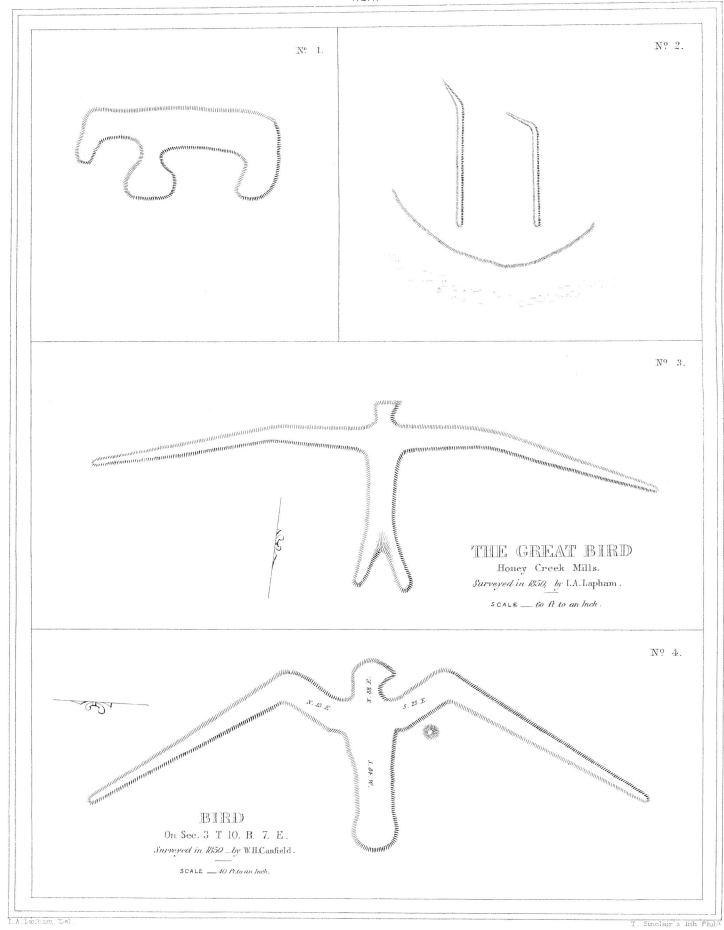

Nº 1.

Nº 2.

Nº 3.

THE GREAT BIRD
Honey Creek Mills.
Surveyed in 1850, by I.A. Lapham.

SCALE ___ 60 ft to an Inch.

Nº 4.

N. 15 E.   N. 88 E.   S. 23 E.

S. 84 W.

BIRD
On Sec. 3 T 10. R. 7. E.
Surveyed in 1850 ___ by W.H. Canfield.

SCALE ___ 40 Ft to an Inch.

I.A. Lapham Del.   T. Sinclair's Lith Phila.

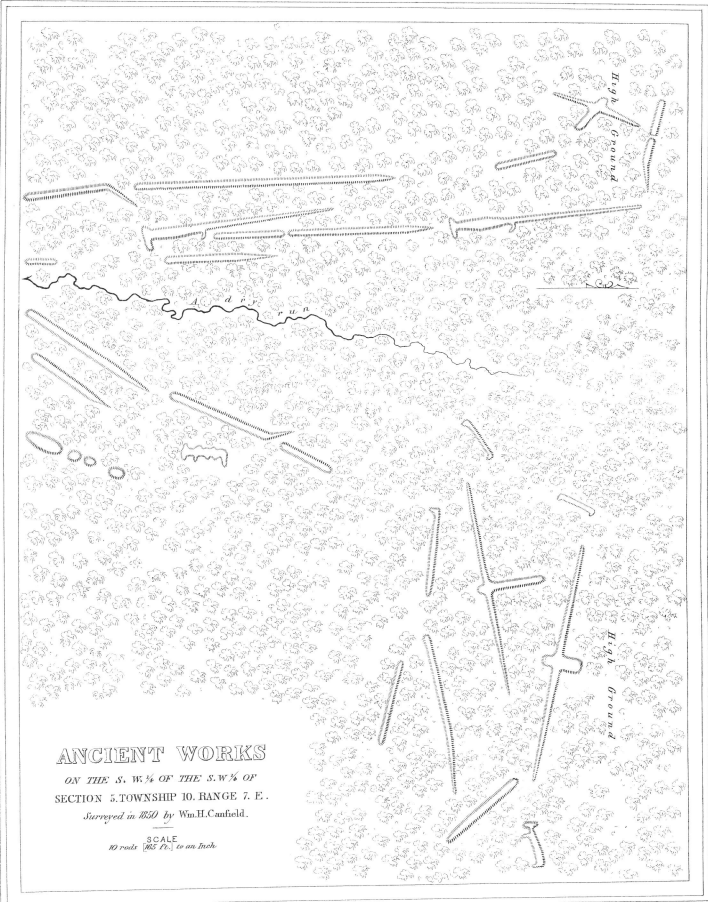

High Ground

A dry run

High Ground

ANCIENT WORKS

ON THE S. W. ¼ OF THE S.W ¼ OF

SECTION 5. TOWNSHIP 10. RANGE 7. E.

Surveyed in 1850 by Wm. H. Canfield.

SCALE
10 rods [165 ft.] *to an Inch*

I. A. Lapham, Del.

T. Sinclair's lith, Phila

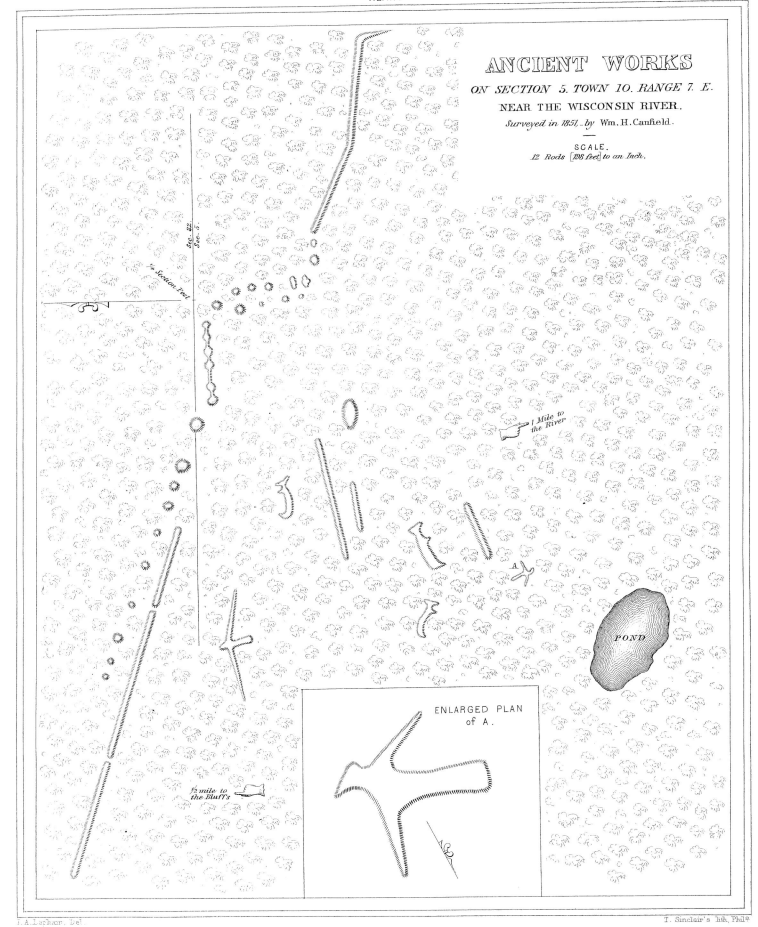

ANCIENT WORKS
ON SECTION 5. TOWN 10. RANGE 7. E.
NEAR THE WISCONSIN RIVER.
Surveyed in 1851, by Wm. H. Canfield.

SCALE.
12 Rods [198 feet] to an Inch.

Sec. 32
Sec. 5.

¼ Section Post

1 Mile to
the River

POND

A.

ENLARGED PLAN
of A.

½ mile to
the Bluffs

J. A. Lapham, Del.

T. Sinclair's lith, Phila.

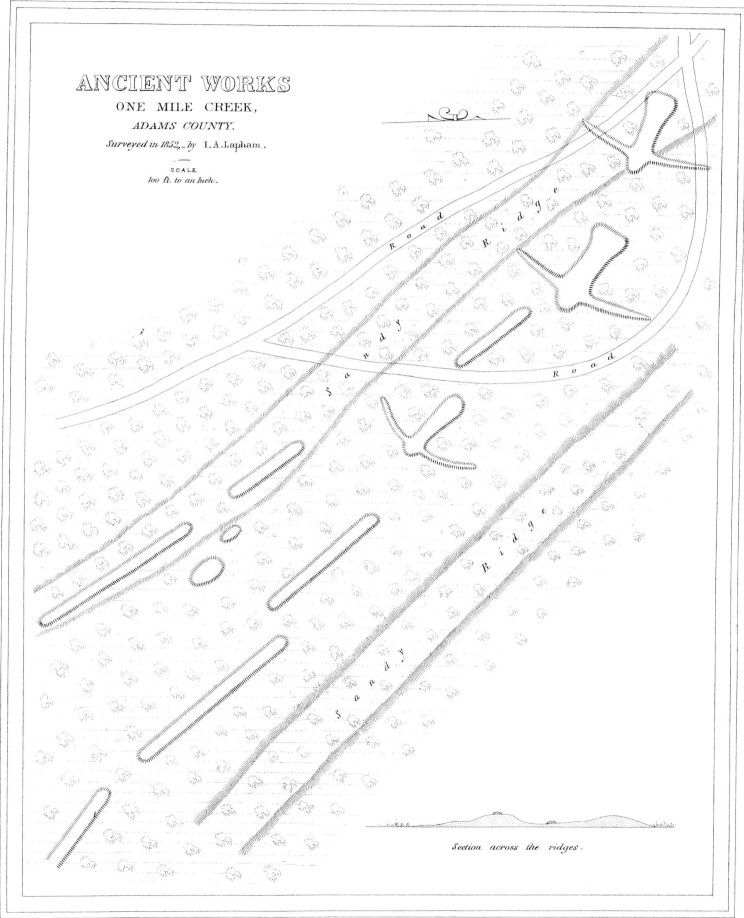

ANCIENT WORKS
ONE MILE CREEK,
ADAMS COUNTY.

Surveyed in 1852, by I. A. Lapham.

SCALE
100 ft. to an Inch.

Section across the ridges.

I. A. Lapham, Del.

T. Sinclair's lith, Philᵃ

L.

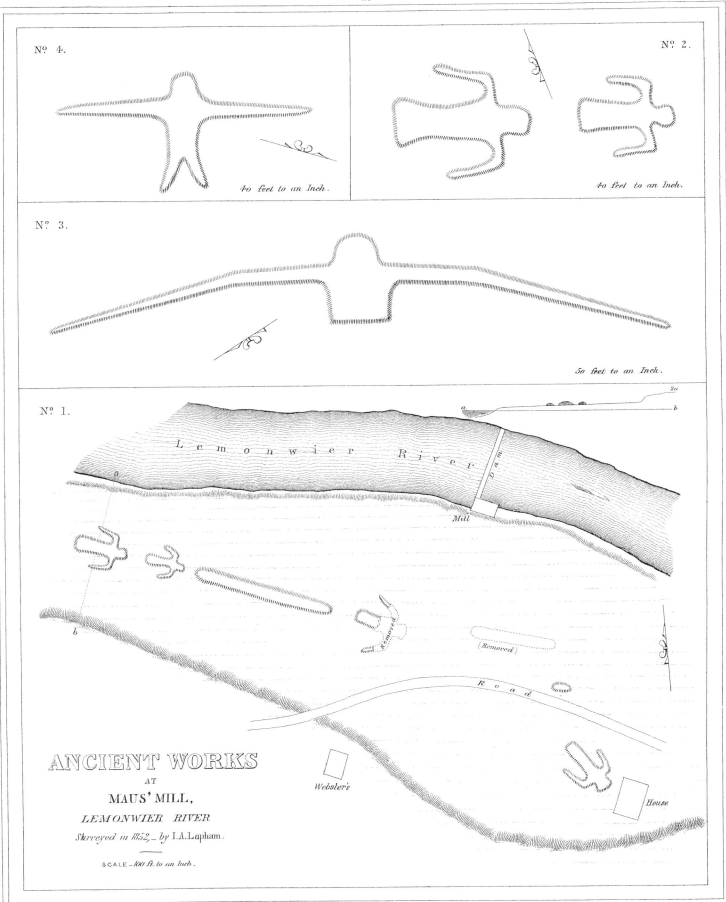

Nº 4.

40 feet to an Inch.

Nº 2.

40 feet to an Inch.

Nº 3.

50 feet to an Inch.

Nº 1.

Lemonwier River

Dam

Mill

Removed

(Removed)

Road

Webster's

House

ANCIENT WORKS
AT
MAUS' MILL,
LEMONWIER RIVER
Surveyed in 1852, by I.A.Lapham.

SCALE—100 ft. to an Inch.

I.A.Lapham Del.

T. Sinclair's lith. Philᵃ

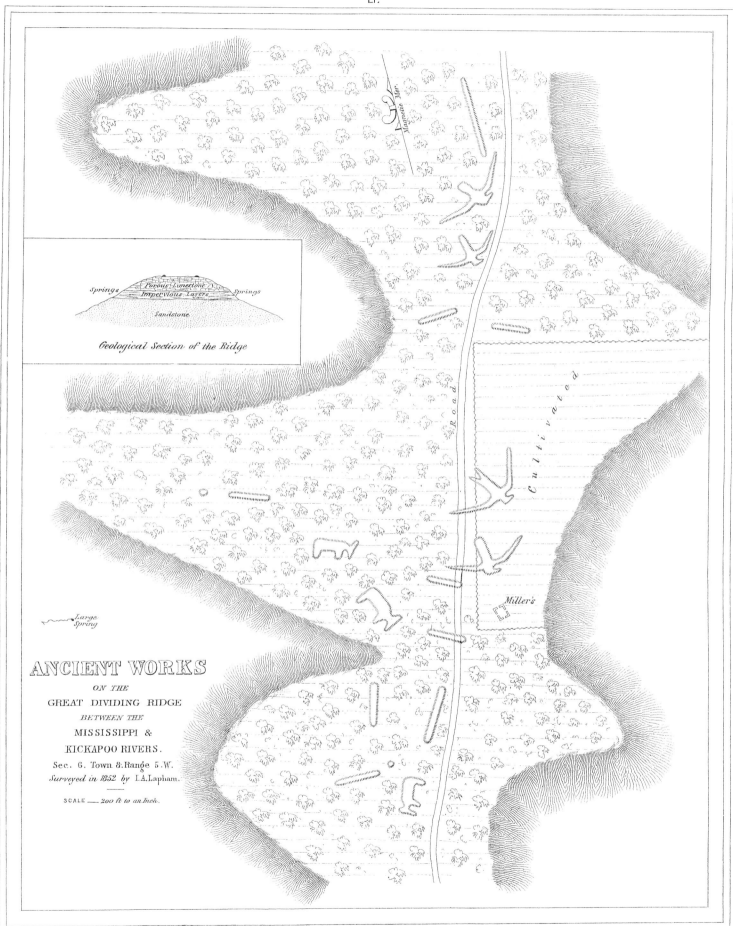

Magnetic Mer.

Springs   Porous Limestone   Springs
Impervious Layers
Sandstone

Geological Section of the Ridge

Road

Cultivated

Miller's

Large
Spring

ANCIENT WORKS

ON THE
GREAT DIVIDING RIDGE
BETWEEN THE
MISSISSIPPI &
KICKAPOO RIVERS.

Sec. 6. Town 8. Range 5 .W.
Surveyed in 1852 by I. A. Lapham.

SCALE —— 200 ft to an Inch.

I. A. Lapham Del.   T. Sinclair's lith. Phila.

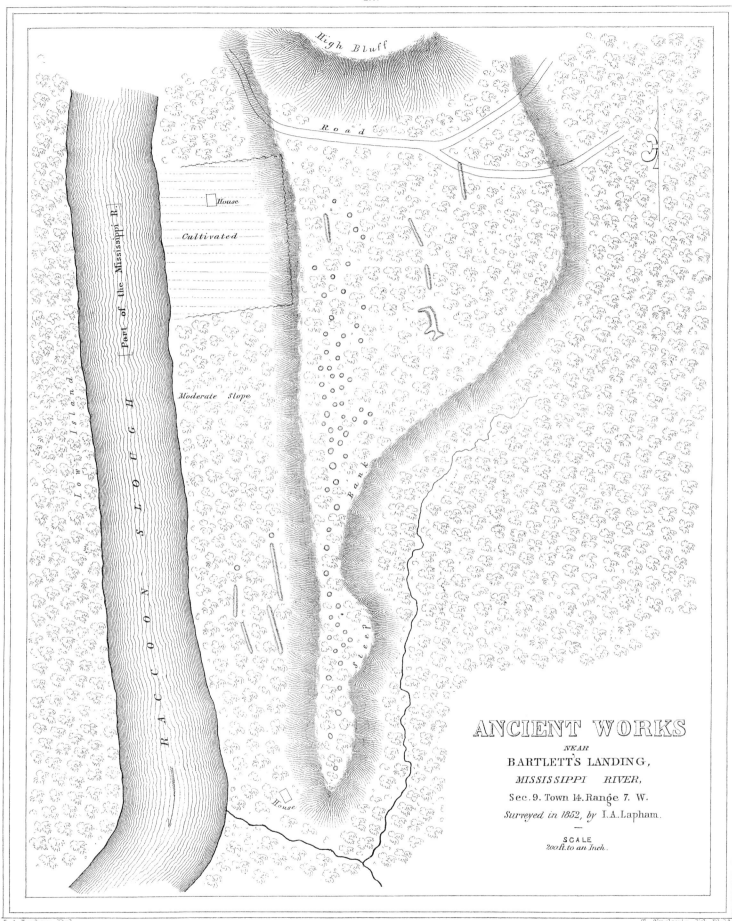

High Bluff

Road

House

Cultivated

Moderate Slope

Iowa Island

Part of the Mississippi R.

RACCOON SLOUGH

Bank

Steep

House

ANCIENT WORKS
NEAR
BARTLETT'S LANDING,
MISSISSIPPI RIVER,
Sec. 9. Town 14. Range 7. W.
Surveyed in 1852, by I. A. Lapham.
—
SCALE
200 ft. to an Inch.

I. A. Lapham, Del.

T. Sinclair's lith. Phila.

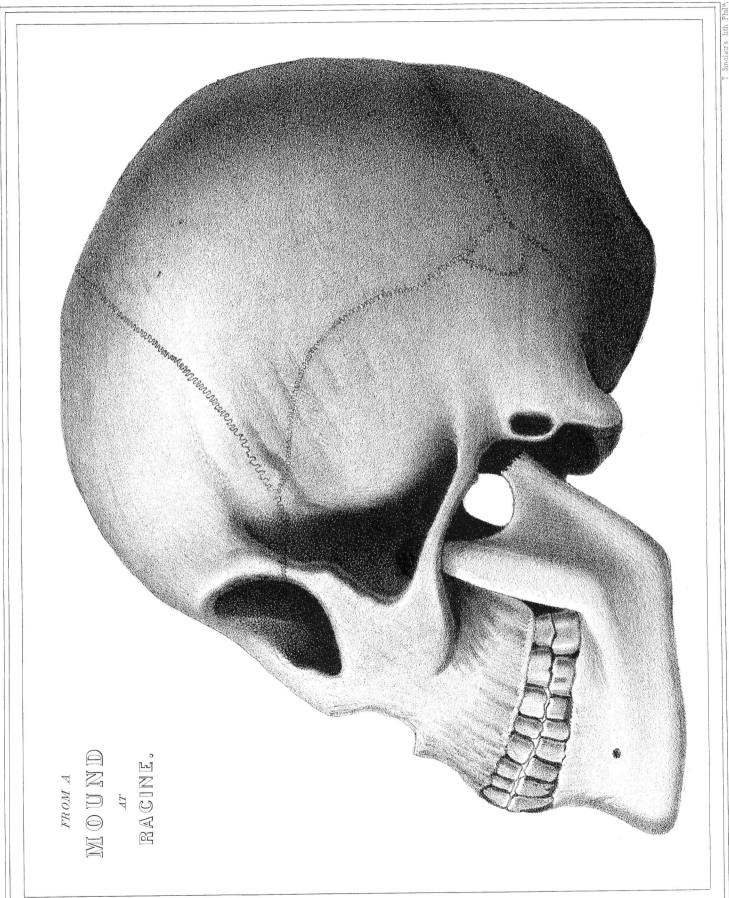

LIII.

T. Sinclair's lith. Phila.

FROM A
MOUND
AT
RACINE.

I. A. Lapham Del.

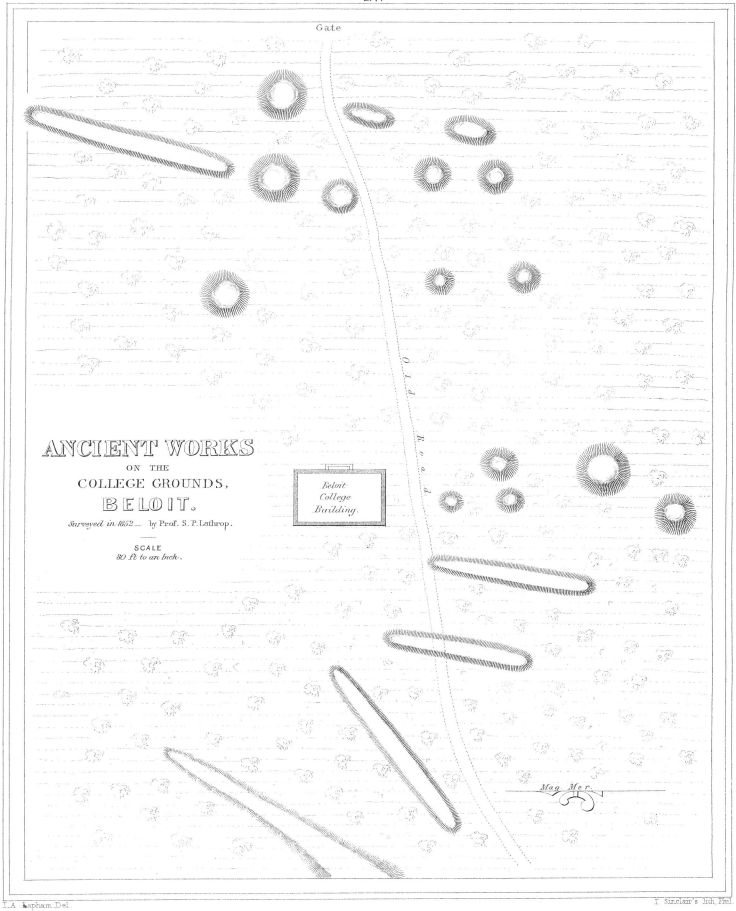

Gate

Old Road

Beloit
College
Building.

ANCIENT WORKS
ON THE
COLLEGE GROUNDS,
BELOIT.
Surveyed in 1852 by Prof. S. P. Lathrop.

SCALE
80 ft to an Inch.

Mag. Mer.

I.A.Lapham.Del.

T. Sinclair's lith.Phil.

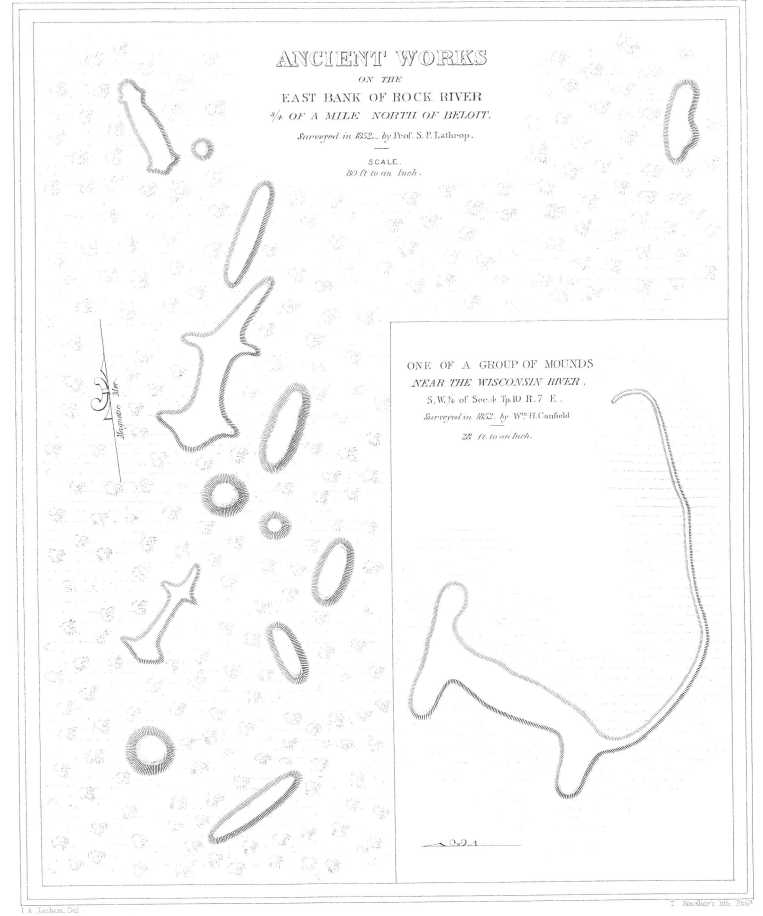

ANCIENT WORKS

ON THE

EAST BANK OF ROCK RIVER

¾ OF A MILE NORTH OF BELOIT.

Surveyed in 1852.— by Prof. S. P. Lathrop.

SCALE.

80 ft to an Inch.

Magnetic Mer.

ONE OF A GROUP OF MOUNDS

NEAR THE WISCONSIN RIVER.

S. W. ¼ of Sec.4 Tp.10 R.7 E.

Surveyed in 1852. by Wm. H. Canfield.

28 ft. to an Inch.

I. A. Lapham, Del.

T. Sinclair's lith. Phila.